TEACHING
PSALMS

Volume 2

*A Christian Introduction
to each Psalm*

From text to message

CHRISTOPHER ASH

TEACHING PSALMS

Volume 2

*A Christian Introduction
to each Psalm*

From text to message

CHRISTOPHER ASH

SERIES EDITORS: DAVID JACKMAN & JON GEMMELL

PT RESOURCES

CHRISTIAN
FOCUS

Copyright © Proclamation Trust Media 2018
ISBN: 978-1-5271-0005-3
ebook ISBN: 978-1-5271-0772-4
10 9 8 7 6 5 4 3

Published in 2018,
reprinted in 2019 and 2023

by

Christian Focus Publications Ltd,
Geanies House, Fearn, Ross-shire,
IV20 1TW, Scotland, Great Britain

with

Proclamation Trust Resources,
Willcox House, 140-148 Borough High Street,
London, SE1 1LB, England, Great Britain.
www.proctrust.org.uk

www.christianfocus.com
Cover design by Moose77.com

Printed and bound by
Bell and Bain, Glasgow

Contents

To Carolyn, my dear wife and daily prayer-partner

ತಿ♥ ತಿ♥ ತಿ♥

Almighty God, you alone can order the unruly wills and passions of sinful men: grant that your people may love what you command and desire what you promise so that among the many and varied changes of this world our hearts may be firmly fixed where true joys are to be found through Jesus Christ our Lord. Amen.[1]

---

1. Collect for fourth Sunday after Easter, taken from *An English Prayer Book* (The Church Society, 1994).

Author's Preface

I have grown to love the Psalms. It was not always so. At my (very old-fashioned) school we chanted the Psalms and Canticles in daily Chapel services. We didn't chant them well; you wouldn't expect that from 650 schoolboys in the late 1960s and early 1970s. Sometimes we showed what heroic rebels we were by refusing to sing them; but by and large we conformed. Not being sufficiently musical, I did not understand the pointing marks in the chapel Psalter; I didn't know whether the note should go up or down; and I was unsure when it should go wherever it was meant to go. I was completely at sea in understanding the old English of Coverdale's wonderful sixteenth Century translation. It conveyed a kind of atmosphere; I remember that. But no clarity of meaning. I was not yet converted; and even when I was (in my final year in school), I was not edified. The problem was not one of musical incompetence (though I *was* incompetent); it was that nobody taught me to sing the Psalms from the heart with feeling and meaning.

If you love the Psalms, or want to love the Psalms, or think perhaps you ought to love the Psalms (but don't really), these volumes are for you. I hope they will help you pray the Psalms. If you have the privilege of preaching, teaching, or leading Bible studies on the Psalms, I hope they will be of particular help to you. But you cannot teach them until you yourself learn to pray them. I want to help you to do that. It is not as easy as Christians sometimes think. But it is important, and it is possible.

Although I love the Psalms, my love is tinged with frustration at the prevalence of Christless handling of them; or readings to which Christ is a somewhat arbitrary 'add on', tacked on the end to make it feel 'Christian'. I want first to persuade you that the Psalms are filled with Christ, that Christ does not have to be 'glued on' to the Psalms to make them 'Christian', but that Christ emerges from the warp and woof of the Psalms themselves. Then I want to equip you to read them Christianly, to pray them in Christ, and to love them in Christ.

I am also frustrated by the near absence of the Psalms from much of our corporate prayer life, and the superficiality and selectivity in the Psalms that we do make reference to. A former student wrote to me that in his experience, 'we do not get any teaching from the Psalms, but only a good feeling, especially when one is downcast.'[1] There is a way of using the Psalms that is like pic'n'mix in a sweet shop; it skims the Psalms for nuggets that appeal, little gems to be printed on the devotional calendar. This has the same nutritional value for our souls that sugary sweets have for our bodies. It is deeply unsatisfactory.

---

1. from Christopher Thwala, used with permission.

What is more, even when the Psalms *are* taught, it is generally only a small subset of the Psalms. I suspect that an analysis of Psalms sermons would reveal that the large majority come from a mini-psalter within the Psalter, a selection of the favourites. This would include Psalms 1, 2, 8, 23, and so on. But perhaps a hundred or more would scarcely be taught, if at all. J. Clinton McCann comments that, since the Psalms have such an honoured place in Christian history, 'it is all the more strange and striking that the church in relatively recent years has virtually lost the Psalter' and that, even when Psalms are included in metrical versions, 'the selection of Psalms seldom does justice to the rich variety of the Psalter.'[2] I want to broaden my own range, and yours.

Volume One is a handbook to introduce the task, the problems, the method, and some of the main themes. Volume Two gives a brief Christian introduction to each Psalm; it is not a substitute for a good commentary, but it offers what few commentaries attempt.

The Psalms are an ongoing project for me, both experientially (as I begin to learn to pray) and didactically (as I seek to teach others to pray them). God willing, I shall write a fuller commentary at a later date. For I feel I have scarcely begun. Luther wrote, 'There is no book of the Bible to which I have devoted as much labour as to the Psalter.'[3] And yet, 'I must openly admit that I do not know whether I have the accurate interpretation of the Psalms or not.'[4] Indeed, he observes with characteristic acuity,

---

2. McCann 1993b: 13f.

3. Quoted in Brock 2007:169.

4. Brock 2007:169.

'The Spirit reserves much for Himself, so that we may always remain His pupils. There is much that He reveals only to lure us on, much that He gives only to stir us up… I know that a person would be guilty of the most shameless boldness if he dared claim that he had understood even one book of the Scriptures in all its parts. In fact, who would even dare to assert that anyone has completely understood one single Psalm? Our life is one of beginning and of growth, not one of consummation.'[5]

If that was true of Luther, it is certainly true of me! But I hope, in the mercy of God, that even these introductory volumes may be of help.

---

5. Brock 2007:169.

Series Preface

We now understand that those called to preach and teach the word of God need to have a firm grasp on biblical theology; the way the whole Bible story unfolds and fits together culminating in the coming, death, resurrection, ascension and return of Jesus Christ. Our *Teaching* series, with its aim of equipping and encouraging those called to this great task, lets the discipline of biblical theology (alongside its co-disciplines) sit firmly at the centre of our work.

It is quite disappointing therefore that so little effort has been made to apply this important methodology to the Psalms. We have worked hard at New Testament narrative, epistles, Old Testament story and even Law, but we have given very little time to the 150 Hebrew poems that make up the Psalter. This omission is even more surprising because we often sing or pray the Psalms in church and often give a psalm to new or inexperienced preachers to cut their teeth on. Sometimes we use the Psalms as summer 'fillers', a series on some psalms that can stand as individual sermons, catering to those away at different times on holiday.

These two volumes therefore, are some of the most important we have published. Whilst some of our other eighteen volumes in the series are those a preacher might dip into when needing some help with a particular Bible passage, these brilliant contributions from Christopher need to be read more carefully. This means that we have taken a slightly different approach from the other volumes in the series. There is an argument to be made before we get to the detailed work on a psalm by psalm basis. Volume 1 is the basis of for this argument and needs to be read carefully. Volume 2 builds on this argument (and largely assumes it) as Christopher takes us through the Psalms one by one.

Readers should not suppose that this way of approaching the psalter is novel or radical. As others have shown, the desire to understand the Psalms in their whole Bible Christological context is as old as Christianity itself.[1] All through Christian history, preachers have returned again to the struggle to be faithful to the biblical theology of the Psalms. Writing in the nineteenth century, this understanding was neatly summarized by Free Church of Scotland minister, Andrew Bonar, 'The writers were prepared by God, through personal and public circumstances, for breathing forth appropriately the mind of Him [Christ] who used them.'[2]

Despite the fact that these books may feel a little different from others we have previously published in this series, our ultimate aim for them remains the same: we trust and

1. See, for example, Jerry Shepherd's doctoral thesis submitted to Westminster Theological Seminary in 1995, available online at http://bit.ly/2figu43

2. Bonar, Andrew, *Christ and his church in the Book of Psalms* (London, James Nisbet & Co, 1859), p. vi.

pray that men and women who are called to preach and teach the word of God will be encouraged and equipped to do so faithfully and clearly in a way that exalts the Saviour above all.

We are, as always, very thankful to our friends at Christian Focus for their partnership in this important project.

JONATHAN GEMMELL &
DAVID JACKMAN
Series Editors
London 2018

Note on 'The Lord'

I have usually used the phrase 'the covenant God' to translate the Hebrew word often read as *Yahweh* and printed 'the LORD' in English translations. This is to make clear the connection between this sacred Name of the God of the Bible and the covenant relationship between God, the King, and the King's people.

INTRODUCTION

The purpose of this volume is to give a Christian introduction to each psalm. I believe that reading the Psalms in the light of their fulfilment in Jesus Christ is not only heartwarming, but ultimately the right and true way to pray them. This has not been the dominant approach among commentators in recent decades. I therefore have work to do, both in persuading scholars and preachers, and also in helping all of us who are disciples of Jesus to learn how to pray the Psalms in an authentically Christian manner. I have outlined my overall approach in Part 1 of Volume One of *Teaching Psalms* ('How to pray the Psalms in Christ').

This second volume is an attempt to work through this approach with each of the 150 Psalms in turn. It is a work in progress. I shall no doubt change my mind about some of the details of my interpretation, and indeed I expect that others will help me change my mind. I hope that fulfilment in Christ can be seen to emerge naturally from the original context and meaning of the Psalms, rather than being artificially added on at the end of the interpretation.

I want to persuade you that, when we pray the Psalms in the light of the full canon of Christian Scripture, this kind of Christ-centred reading is persuasive, true, and edifying.

These brief guides are intended to do two things that few commentaries attempt (or, at least, not systematically).

1. To draw the lines that most naturally and persuasively connect each particular psalm in its original context to Jesus Christ, who is the fulfilment of all the Old Testament Scriptures.

2. To indicate the strongest lines of valid response to the psalm, that is, what it means for us to pray and sing them today as the church of Christ.

Good commentaries will help us with the meanings of words, the structural markers, and the cross-references within the Old Testament (and occasionally the New Testament too). But only rarely and somewhat sporadically do they draw the lines to Christ or indicate valid application.

This volume is also frustratingly brief, allowing only an average of around 500 words on each psalm; God willing, I hope to attempt a longer and more thorough commentary in due course. But for the moment this will have to do.

I suggest that this book is best used alongside Volume One; each psalm is cross-referenced both to places in Volume One where that psalm is mentioned and to the big themes in Volume One that relate to that psalm. If you are studying in greater depth, you will need a good technical commentary for the detail that I am not able to cover.

I have used the NIV (2011) as my base text, but not much hinges on the choice of translation. I have worked from the Hebrew and tried to make sure that my comments relate to that, rather than to any particular interpretative decisions that the NIV (or any other) translators may have taken.

SOME QUESTIONS ARISING FROM VOLUME ONE

Many conversations have arisen since the publication of Volume One, and I felt it appropriate to comment briefly on five significant areas of discussion.

A. Is Christ praying the Psalms the only way to read them?

In chapters 1–4 of Volume One I think I may inadvertently have overstated my case. I was so conscious that a Christ-led singing of the Psalms involves a sometimes traumatic paradigm shift for many Christians, that I may have given the impression that this is the only way to read or pray the Psalms. Chapter 5 nuances this and develops the important idea of different 'voices' in the Psalms. I should perhaps have anticipated Chapter 5 nearer the start of the book. Nevertheless, I think it is probably true to say that the *dominant* model for the Psalms ought to be the Lord Jesus Christ singing them, and leading His church in praying them. It is not the *only* model, but it does predominate. To this extent, it is psychologically beneficial really to work at getting a feel for this way of reading before nuancing it with other kinds of Psalm.

B. What does it mean to 'pray' the Psalms, since some Psalms are not addressed to God?

I have perhaps spoken too loosely about 'praying' the Psalms. It has been objected that, for example, Psalms 1 and 2 are not prayers or praises addressed to God; and this is true for a number of others (e.g. Ps. 37). So let me clarify what I mean. Strictly, I mean that the Psalms are for us to join in saying or singing together as the people of Christ. What it means for us to say or sing them will depend on the address and the content of the particular psalm we are saying. If it is a prayer, we pray it to God in Christ; if it is praises, we declare it to the world and simultaneously address it in worship to God in Christ. But if, for example, it contains instruction (such as Pss. 1, 2, 37), then what does it mean to speak the words together? Is this different from simply hearing them read or preached to us, as we do with many other parts of Scripture? I think there is a difference; when we join in speaking the words of instruction, we are implicitly acknowledging our agreement and our commitment not only to hear but to heed these words; to speak the instruction of a psalm is to 'sign up' to live a life in accord with what the psalm proclaims. For example, when I join with the church of Christ in declaring 'Blessed are all who take refuge in him' (the King), I affirm that I believe this blessing and I commit myself to live as one who trusts himself to be blessed in Jesus Christ my King.

C. How can we say that the voice of the Teacher in the Psalms is the voice of Christ our Teacher?

In Volume One (p. 49) I noted that Matthew 13:35 takes the voice of the Teacher in Psalm 78:2 to be – ultimately

– the voice of Christ. I have taken this to be, at the very
least, a hint that wherever we hear the voice of a divinely
authoritative Teacher in the Psalms we are to hear the
voice of Christ (or of a psalmist speaking by the Spirit of
the Christ to come). But is it safe to generalize in this way
from one New Testament quotation? I think it is, and my
reason for so thinking is theological. Jesus Christ is the
Word of God, God the Son by whom God has spoken
His final word (Heb. 1:1-4). As the Lord Jesus Himself
taught, ultimately 'you have one Instructor, the Messiah'
(Matt. 23:10). Behind the voice of every prophet is the
voice of Christ the Word of God. So, for example, when
Psalm 37 says, 'Do not fret because of those who are evil'
these are words that Jesus of Nazareth heard, and needed
to hear, in His earthly life; but they then become words
that He speaks to His church.

D. Is there a place for believers to
pour out their hearts to God?

A strong quotation from Dietrich Bonhoeffer warns us
that 'Praying certainly does not mean simply pouring out
one's heart' (quoted in Volume One, p. 52). This can be
misunderstood and I want to clarify what I mean by it (and
what I think Bonhoeffer meant by it). This is most certainly
not to deny that believers ought to pour out their hearts to
God in prayer, lament, or praise; certainly we ought to do
this in the presence of God. Bonhoeffer's point is that true
prayer needs more than this. The disordered outpourings
of the natural human heart may be authentic, but they are
not acceptable prayers before God. Only in the name of
Jesus Christ is prayer heard by God the Father. What the
Psalms do is to *shape* the outpourings of our disordered

hearts so that they are *reordered* by the desires, yearnings, tears, and joys of the Lord Jesus, by whose Spirit they were spoken. I do not simply pour out my overflowing heart; the Psalms teach and train me *how* to pour out my heart according to the will of God and the heart of Jesus.

E. Why does the 'old' way of reading the Psalms simply as 'my personal devotion' so often seem to 'work'?

I think this is a very important question. Those who have been Christians for many years know in precious personal experience that the Psalms, read as their personal devotion, 'work'; they authentically express true Christian prayers and praises. And they do. The question is: why do they? And the answer is that, in such praying, the unspoken but vital implicit assumption is that the one praying is a man or woman united with Jesus Christ by faith. What I am seeking to do is to make the Christ-centredness – always implicit in such praying – explicit, to bring it out into the open that we may see more clearly the beauty and wonder of the Christ in whom all these spiritual blessings may be ours. At the same time, all sorts of difficulties with the Psalms (noted in Volume One, pp. 31-38) are seen to have a solution, when the words are understood to be, first and foremost, the words of Christ our King.

A Christian Introduction to each Psalm

BOOK 1

Themes to watch for in Book 1
As well as the foundational affirmations of Psalms 1 and 2 (see below), look out for:

1) The recurrent theme of the sufferings of the king and his prayer for subsequent vindication.

2) The relationship between the one man, the king, singing the psalm, and the king's people, whose destiny is inextricably tied up with what happens to the king. Sometimes these people – ultimately Christ's church – are explicit in a psalm; sometimes they (we) are only there in the background. Nevertheless they (we) are always there.

A Note on Psalms 1 and 2

Psalms 1 and 2 are the 'front door' to the Psalter. Each ends with a reference to the 'way' of the wicked that leads to 'destruction' (1:6; 2:12). Psalm 1 begins with a declaration of blessing and Psalm 2 ends with another promise of blessing. The word for 'meditates' in Psalm 1:2 is the same as the word for 'plot' in Psalm 2:1. They are almost the only psalms in Book 1 without the 'of David' superscription. This suggests that what Psalm 1 says about the Law should be read in the light of what Psalm 2 says about the King. Deuteronomy 7:18-20 makes the same connection between the righteous King and the Law. As we begin the Psalms, we are looking for a Psalm 1 man who will be the Psalm 2 King, the King who is Righteous, the Righteous Man who is King.

Psalm 1

[Vol. 1: 39-45, 100, 106, 108, 181-189, 200-204, 224]

Psalm 1 declares a **blessing** (1-3, 6a) and warns of a **judgement** (4, 5, 6b). The blessing is on the one described in verses 1-3. The covenant God watches over the one who loves Him, and who therefore delights in God's law with all his heart. This 'blessed one', delights in his heart and meditates with his lips (2); meditation (in Hebrew) is a vocal and declarative act[1]; this man delights, and speaks his delight. The recipient of this blessing is, in principle, generic (NIV 'the one who...' whoever he, she or they may be); but in reality, he is singular (ESV 'the man who...'), for there is only one who truly fits this description, the man Christ Jesus. He, uniquely and supremely, is the man of Psalm 1.

What is more, Jesus is the only one who can declare the words of Psalm 1 with complete integrity. When we say, 'Blessed is the one who...' we commit ourselves to walk this way of blessing, for it would be folly not to, if it is true. When we do not walk this way, we demonstrate that we do not fully believe what the psalm says, for we show that we think blessing is also to be found in walking other paths.

---

1. LeFebvre in Johnston and Firth 2005:217-220.

We think that some wickedness in us will be advantageous, when the Psalm declares the exact opposite. Only one man has ever spoken Psalm 1, fully believed it to be true, and lived it out.

When Christian people share in saying Psalm 1, we join with this Righteous Man in affirming the blessings that rest on him, and are to be found in him alone. 'Blessed is the one who…' Blessed is Jesus our Righteous one! And we pledge ourselves afresh to live as men and women in whom the Spirit of this Righteous Man dwells, as men and women who live under the blessings of Psalm 1.

This will save us responding in a moralistic way ('I must stir myself up to try to be more like the good person and less like the wicked'); it will arouse in us wonder for our king here described, and gratitude for every spiritual blessing that we have in Him; and then, flowing out of that, it will stir in us a Spirit-given desire to walk His righteous way and not the way of the wicked. Our preaching and praying of the Psalm will then be pure gospel in Christ.

Psalm 2
[Vol. 1: 39-45, 99-100, 106, 108, 181-189, 200-204, 224]

Psalm 2 begins with a **desire** for 'freedom' (vv. 1-3) from the unwelcome constraint of God's rule exercised by God's Ruler. All of us by nature (v. 1, nations… peoples…) conspire and plot (the word 'plot' is the same as 'meditate' in Psalm 1:2); the more power we have, seemingly the more we plot (v. 2, kings… rulers…). We do not have much in common, and are constantly fighting one another; but we unite against God and His Christ. For we believe in ourselves and our right to rule our own lives.

The desire of verses 1-3 is answered by the **declaration** of verses 4-9. God declares that the good rule of Psalm 1 will be exercised by his good Ruler, the king on Zion[2]. This king will be unlike the rebellious kings of verses 1-3. In verses 7-9 the king speaks to declare what the covenant God has said to him. God promises him a relationship (my son, v. 7) and invites him to pray to rule the world (Ask me… vv. 8, 9), with a promise that this prayer will be fully answered.

There is therefore a **decision** (vv. 10-12). The 'kings' and 'rulers' of verse 2 are addressed in verses 10-12. If they are wise they will submit to this king, serve the covenant God, celebrate His 'rule', kiss His son, the king, with the kneeling kiss of homage (as in our 'kissing the hand') and escape the destruction that will otherwise be theirs, the same destruction that is the destiny of the wicked in Psalm 1:6.

Those who take refuge under this king's rule will inherit the blessing (v. 12) of the righteous man in Psalm 1:1, because the rule of this Ruler is the good Law of the covenant God. Only the righteous man of Psalm 1 can be the world-ruler of Psalm 2.

The promise of Psalm 2 is foreshadowed in David and his line; it echoed down through Old Testament history and must often have appeared absurd, as David's heirs fell short of the righteousness of Psalm 1 and the reign of Psalm 2. And then the man came who lived the righteousness of Psalm 1 and inherits the promises of Psalm 2. The rest of the world united to plot against Jesus the Messiah (Acts 4:25, 26, echoed in Rev. 11:18). But God declares him to be His Son, at His baptism (Matt. 3:17, Mark 1:11, Luke 3:22) and at His Transfiguration (Matt. 17:5, Mark 9:7, Luke 9:35),

---

2. Vol. 1, chapter 13 on 'Zion in the Psalms'.

as declared also in Acts 13:33 and Hebrews 1:5 and 5:5. This man will inherit the nations (v. 8 echoed in Heb. 1:2 'heir of all things') and rule them with an iron scepter (v. 9 echoed in Rev. 12:5 and 19:15).

When we sing Psalm 2 we affirm that we too believe in the universal kingship of Jesus the Messiah. One day the kingdom of the world will become the kingdom of our Lord and of His Messiah (Rev. 11:15). What is more, we affirm that, if we continue to trust in him to the end and are thereby 'victorious', we too will share with him in ruling the nations (Rev. 2:26,27, echoing Ps. 2:8, 9 and applying it to the Christian believer). And we declare that we too heed the warning that rebellion is futile and leads to inescapable destruction.

Keep Psalms 1 and 2 in mind when reading the Psalms
Psalms 1 and 2 have set before us a good rule and a good Ruler. The good rule is the Law of God and blessing comes to the man who loves both God and His Law (Ps. 1). But if the good rule of God's Law is to be effective in the world it needs a good Ruler, the Psalm 2 King who is the Psalm 1 Law-lover of God. These twin entrance markers will stay with us as we walk through the Psalter.

Psalm 3
[Vol. 1: 43, 66-76, 98, 230-231]

After the triumphant confidence of Psalm 2, we are plunged straight into a number of psalms in which the king is under tremendous pressure. The superscription to Psalm 3 tells us it comes from the terrible days of 2 Samuel 15-19, when King David was usurped by his son Absalom. The king is promised worldwide triumph; but his experience is a stolen kingdom.

We begin (vv. 1, 2) with the king's pressures. David was heavily outnumbered (cf. 2 Sam. 15:13); the enemies under Absalom are the concrete expression of the general rebellion of Psalm 2:2. There is a crescendo of pressure with the three uses of 'many', rising from the static 'how many *are* my foes,' through the active 'rise up against me' and climaxing in what they say in verse 2: 'God will not deliver him' (cf. what Shimei said to David in 2 Sam. 16:7, 8). This is the most serious attack, poisoning the very roots of the king's confidence in God's covenant with him.

David continues by holding on to the king's promise (vv. 3, 4). He affirms that the covenant God is 'a shield around' him, his 'glory' (the one who gives him dignity and influence), the one who 'lifts (his) head high', unlike the covered head of disgrace in 2 Sam. 15:30. This is not wishful-thinking, for the covenant God answers 'from his holy mountain,' a precise echo of Psalm 2:6. As the anointed king, he claims the promise of Psalm 2.

In verses 5-6 David speaks of the king's rest. He appropriates subjectively in trust the objective truth of the covenant promise. He sleeps, confident of protection at night, as happened precisely to David in 2 Samuel 17:1, 16, when God saved him from disaster at night. David's plight is unchanged; still he is heavily outnumbered (6); and yet he trusts.

David prays in verse 7 for the king's rescue, echoing words used when the Ark of the Covenant symbolized the presence of the covenant God in battle (Num. 10:35 'Arise, LORD!'). He prays that his now-toothless enemies will be unable to say the words they hurled at him in verse 2.

In all this we see a foreshadowing of the pressures on Jesus the King, against whom everyone conspired (e.g. Mark 3:6), and whom they were confident God would not rescue (Matt. 27:42,43). King Jesus likewise trusted the promise of His Father that he would be the Zion King over all the earth (cf. the symbolic description of Rev. 14:1 'standing on Mount Zion'). Jesus also rested and trusted; He slept in a boat in a wild storm (Mark 4:38); night after night he appropriated subjectively the rest that was based on the objectivity of God's promise to Him. Jesus prayed for final rescue, was confident of final deliverance, and experienced final victory, in bodily resurrection.

This psalm cannot immediately be your prayer or mine. The military language precludes that, to say nothing of the original context. We come in at the end. The Psalm concludes, 'From the LORD comes deliverance'; that is, the covenant God does give victory to the Psalm 2 King, in contradiction to the slur of verse 2. When we pray 'May your blessing be on *your people*' we pray that the deliverance of the King will overflow with blessings to the King's people. We too experience the overflow of His pressures (vv. 1, 2), claim in Christ the surety of the King's promise (vv. 3, 4), enjoy in some measure the subjective assurance of the King's rest (vv. 5, 6), pray with confidence for the rescue of all the King's people, our certainty resting on the victory given to our King. They said God wouldn't rescue King David, but he did. They said God wouldn't rescue Jesus, but he did. They say God will not rescue Jesus's people, but he will, because he rescued Jesus our King.

Psalm 4

[Vol. 1: 100]

King David begins this psalm under pressure and ends with peace in the midst of pressure.

David begins (vv. 1, 2) by praying and lamenting. He calls to his 'righteous God', the God of his righteousness, the God who will vindicate him as the righteous man (sc. of Psalm 1). He longs for 'relief' (that is, space or room, the opposite of being squeezed). The pressure comes from 'you people' (v. 2, lit. 'sons of man', an expression which means significant or influential people; in Ps. 49:2 and Ps. 62:9 it is translated 'high' or 'highborn'; hence ESV footnote 'men of rank'). These people turn David's 'glory' (i.e. kingly reputation, cf. Ps. 3:3) into 'shame' (2a); they malign him, bear false witness against him. They will not honour God's King because they love delusion and falsehood (2b).

In verses 3-5 David affirms, warns, and exhorts these people. He affirms (3) that the covenant God has set apart 'his faithful servant' (the godly one, the *chasîd*, the recipient of faithful love, *chesed*, and one who shows that faithful love to others) for himself. Or, in other words, he is the man whose prayers are heard (3b). In verse 1 David *calls* and asks to be *heard*; in verse 3 he affirms that the LORD *hears* when he *calls*. That is, David affirms Psalm 2. He prays in Psalm 2 to rule the world, and his prayer will be heard ('Ask me, and I will...'). He warns these powerful people (4) that, while they 'tremble' (that is, tremble with anger) they should not turn their anger into sin (a warning echoed in Eph. 4:26), and while they search their angry hearts, they will do well to remain silent on their beds. Instead, in verse 5 David exhorts them to sacrifice the sacrifices of the righteous (the person of Ps. 1:6) and trust in the covenant God.

David prays (6, 7) for joy in the midst of doubt. These verses are bracketed by the word 'many'. 'Many' doubters ask if God will bring prosperity (6a), because they are surrounded by these powerful people whose grain and new wine 'abound' (lit. 'are much/many'). Much godless prosperity, many doubters. So David[3] prays for the blessing of Aaron (Num. 6:25, 26), the light of God's face to shine on him and his people ('on us'), that his heart may be filled with joy; their hearts are full of trembling anger and must be stilled (5), his with joyful trust in God's covenant.

David concludes (8) by lying down to sleep (as in Ps. 3:5) in peace, because the God he trusts makes him dwell in safety. It is appropriate that this should be used as an evening psalm.

In praying this psalm, David again foreshadows his greater Son, Jesus, who was squeezed by powerful people maligning His 'glory', exposing Him to a shameful death on the Cross. And yet Jesus knows He is the set-apart faithful servant, the man whose prayers God always hears (John 11:41, 42). We hear Jesus exhort us to know this (3), and not to sin (4), but to follow His example of trust (5). In Christ we too are 'set apart' for God in Christ His faithful servant. We hear Jesus answering doubt (6a) with prayer for joy in the presence of God, even when the godless prosper (6b, 7), and we echo His prayer. In Christ we too lie down and sleep, confident that in Christ we have all the safety we need (8).

Psalm 5

[Vol. 1: 106, 108, 181]

As so often in this Book 1 of the Psalms, the king prays under pressure. The righteous are contrasted with the wicked, as in Psalm 1; again this is seen frequently throughout Book 1.

---

3. The quotation may extend to the end of the verse (as in ESV/NRSV), in which case the prayer for the Aaronic blessing is spoken by the doubters. Either way, David clearly echoes it.

In verses 1-3 David the human king prays and laments urgently to God his King (2). Morning by morning he lays his requests before God and waits expectantly for an answer.

The reason he can wait with confidence is given in verses 4-7 ('For…'). It comes in two parts. First (4-6) because God hates wickedness and evil people; second (7), David has access into God's house because of the abundance of God's covenant love ('your great love'). He prays and knows he will be heard because he is in covenant with God as the promised king. In verse 8 he prays to be led in a straight way, 'the way of the righteous' in Psalm 1:6. He prays to be the Psalm 2 covenant king who will also be the Psalm 1 righteous man.

By contrast (9, 10) his enemies cannot be trusted and David prays for their banishment. Instead (11, 12), he exhorts all who – like him – take refuge in the covenant God to be joyful and glad because they come under the protection and blessing promised in Psalm 1 to the righteous. Those who heed the king's exhortation and join him under the protective blessing of God may know gladness in the midst of a deceitful and malicious world.

The reason I cannot make this my personal psalm is that by nature I am among the wicked. In Romans 3:13a, Paul cites verse 9b amongst his proof texts that all human beings are wicked by nature. The first thing this Psalm does, therefore, is to convict us afresh of our sin (Rom. 3:20); it should make us tremble with fear.

But our response does not end with fear. The Psalm 1 man who is the Psalm 2 King, great David's perfect and greater Son, can truly invite us under the protective covenant arms of God His Father so that we, like Him, take refuge in God and are glad (11). In Christ the assurance of this Psalm is ours, a wonderful assurance that our prayer for protection from malicious wickedness will be answered.

Psalm 6

[Vol. 1: 46]

In an intensely individual prayer, the king pleads for grace. In verse 1 David cries out not to be 'rebuked' by God's 'anger' and 'wrath'. Although there is no explicit confession of sin, this explains why Psalm 6 is one of the traditional penitential Psalms often sung on Ash Wednesday (along with Pss. 32, 38, 51, 102, 130, and 143). What lies behind this is David's conviction that, while there may be no direct connection between individual sin and individual suffering (cf. John 9:1-3), all suffering is the result of sin. There is one true God alone; all life and health comes from Him; all suffering and ultimately death comes from a troubled or disordered relation to Him. David prays because he knows he is identified with a sinful people; the shadow of wrath falls on him because of them.

In verses 2-7, two points are to be noted. First, David stresses how *'troubled'* he is by the intensity and totality of his suffering (2, 3), which affects his *'bones'* (his physicality) and his *'soul'* (his inner person), and causes a flood of grief (6, 7). David's greater Son knew what it was to have a 'troubled' soul (John 12:27). Second, the king pleads on the basis of the *'steadfast'* covenant *'love'* (*chesed*) of the covenant God (notice how often 'the LORD' is addressed). If he were to die and stay dead (5), the promise of that covenant love would be contradicted. God has promised (Ps. 2) that the king will live and govern the world in praise of God.

At the end of verse 7 (*'my foes'*), the start of verse 8 (*'you workers of evil'* ESV), and verse 10 (*'all my enemies'*) it becomes clear that the king is surrounded by hostility. In the midst of such opposition, see how the king's threefold grief of verse 6 is answered by the threefold confidence of verses 8b and 9. The covenant God has heard the weeping of verse 6, and the plea and prayer of verses 1 and 2. Because the king is in covenant with God, he knows that God will hear and heed his prayer (cf. John 11:41, 42). When the LORD 'turns' (4), his enemies will 'turn' back (10), and his 'troubled' bones and soul (2, 3) will be exchanged for greatly 'troubled' enemies (10a).

As we join in this Psalm of David we enter into the intensity of King Jesus's troubled soul as He identifies as the Representative Head of a sinful people. We too share in the overflow of His sufferings and experience something of His griefs. And we too share in the assurance that, because our King's prayers are heard, so our prayers will be heard in His name.

Psalm 7
[Vol. 1: 106, 108]

Justice is the major theme of this Psalm (v. 6 'decree *justice*'; v. 8 'Let the LORD *judge… Vindicate* me… *righteousness… integrity*'; v. 9 'the *righteous*… the *righteous* God'; v. 11 'God is a *righteous* judge'; v. 17 'his *righteousness*').

In verses 1-5 the innocent king uses vivid metaphors from hunting (1, 2, 5) and the courtroom (3-5) to make us feel the desperate, life-threatening seriousness of the injustice he faces. We do not know who 'Cush, a Benjaminite' was or what he did. Benjamin was King Saul's tribe, so perhaps that lay behind the unfair hostility towards David. David seems to be accused of robbery (4), or perhaps it is that his foes are robbing him of his security and life. Whatever the detail, David is unfairly accused and in danger of losing his life through false witness.

In verses 6-13 David entrusts himself to the covenant God, confident that he is righteous and will act in judgement. He calls on Him to 'Arise', the cry when the Ark of the Covenant symbolized the covenant God going in to battle for his people (Num. 10:35, 36). He calls on the righteous 'anger' of God to overcome the unrighteous 'rage' of his enemies (6). He calls for the cosmic courtroom (7) in which the covenant God will judge 'the peoples' – not just his particular enemies here, but all the enemies of God's King and therefore of God's righteous rule on earth. David prays, not only that he will himself be 'vindicated' (8), but that all who are 'righteous' and 'upright in heart' through belonging to him will be made 'secure' (9, 10). He trusts that God judges, not only in the final judgement, but 'every day' (11), bringing on humankind something of the consequences of our sins (cf. Rom. 1:18-32).

Because there is a God who judges justly, the king trusts that evil is bound to fail (14-16); it is self-defeating. Evil is a process (14), like conception and gestation, but it gives birth to 'disillusionment' (nothingness, emptiness) (cf. James 1:15). Evil plots traps for others but ends up trapped in its own trap (15). Its violence rebounds upon its own head (16) (cf. Prov. 26:27; Gal. 6:7,8).

And so the king gives thanks to the covenant God in heaven for his 'righteousness' (17), celebrating that he can safely 'take refuge' in this God who judges justly (1). King Jesus did exactly this. When faced with death through false witnesses (Matt. 26:59-61), He was confident that His Father God in heaven, who was in covenant with Him, was the one who judges justly; and so He entrusted Himself to Him (1 Pet. 2:23).

Injustice matters deeply. If we care about injustice, then a God of justice is good news. Except that, by nature, we are all on the wrong side of the judgement. Only by taking refuge, with Jesus our King, in the covenant God, only by being covered by Jesus's righteousness, only by being changed by the Holy Spirit so that we too begin to exhibit 'integrity' and 'righteousness' can this Psalm become our joyful prayer.

Psalm 8

[Vol. 1: 44, 148, 156-7]

After the 'front door' pillars of Psalm 1 (the righteous man) and Psalm 2 (the anointed king), Psalms 3-7 have been very personal songs of the king's struggles and sufferings. On the face of it, Psalm 8 comes out of nowhere and seems to have no connection to Psalms 1-7; it speaks – in the first explicit praise of the Psalter – of the dignity of human beings over God's creation. But there is in that a profound connection with what precedes.

Modern translations (e.g. NIV, NRSV) struggle with singulars and plurals (see the extensive footnotes): should the singular words (in Hebrew) for a man or a human being be translated as generic, 'mankind', 'human beings', 'them' or 'mortals'? The answer is yes, and no, as we shall see.

The opening and closing refrain (1a, 9) set the theme, which is the majestic name, or revelation, of God on earth. This is what the Psalm is about, the covenant God (the LORD) demonstrating His rule (our Lord, or our Governor) over all the earth. How does He do this? In a very surprising way! When the feeblest human being takes His name on their lips in praise (2), they enter into a dignity that is stronger than all human autonomous pride (the foe and the avenger). On the face of it a human being is small (by comparison with the moon and stars, v. 3) and frail. In verse 4a 'mankind' is literally 'a human being' a Hebrew word that emphasises frail mortality, used in Pss. 9:20; 90:3; and 103:15 of mortals in our weakness. And yet God reveals and demonstrates His Lordship over all living beings on earth (7, 8) through a man – originally Adam, with Eve (Gen. 1:26-28), and then through that man's descendants, humankind. This rule extends over domestic animals (7a), wild animals (7b), flying beings (8a), fish (8b) and 'all that swim the paths of the seas' (8c), which suggests even the sea monsters, and supremely Leviathan, that symbol of dangerous evil (of whom more in Ps. 104).

We need to tie this to the promise of worldwide rule given to the anointed king in David's line in Ps. 2:8,9. David in his sufferings looks to the God who gave this promise as the one who will lift his head high in victory (e.g. Ps. 3:3). The drama of one man promised a kingdom (in which we have been immersed in Pss. 3-7) points to the much bigger drama of one man promised government over all the earth, the second Adam. Jesus said that when the children acclaimed him as 'Son of David' they fulfilled this Psalm (Matt. 21:16, quoting Ps. 8:3). They began to grasp that in the man they acclaimed was the key to the revelation of God's 'name' in the government of all the earth. For he is Jesus, the righteous man of Psalm 1 and the worldwide King of Psalm 2. This is precisely how the New Testament reads this Psalm.

In 1 Cor. 15:20-28 we learn that the risen Christ is the second Adam under whose feet everything is placed (Ps. 8:6 quoted in v. 27). This is His 'kingdom'; and so the second Adam and the final Son of David merge. The words 'everything under his feet' are echoed also in Ephesians 1:22. The risen Christ is seated 'far above all rule and authority, power and dominion... And God placed all things under his feet...' The writer to the Hebrews teaches (Heb. 2:5-9) from Psalm 8 that we do not yet see everything subject to the good rule of humankind; but we do see Jesus, the man who spearheads the fulfilment of Psalm 8 and of Gen. 1:26-28, and who is the guarantor that one day His people will share with Him in the government of the world (1 Cor. 6:2).

When we declare in this psalm the majesty of the Lordship of the covenant God we declare that the risen Jesus is the Second Adam, the King who rules the world. In this declaration we acknowledge the unique dignity of all human beings made in the image of God; but above all we rejoice that, in Christ, we enter that dignity and prepare to exercise that wonderful rule.

Psalms 9 and 10

[Vol. 1: 189]

Psalms 9 and 10 are separate in the Hebrew, but one psalm in the Septuagint. There are technical reasons for thinking that they are best read as one longer psalm, but not much hinges on this, and opinions differ. I will take them together. The Psalms form, together, a broken acrostic, with the alphabetical consonants of the Hebrew alphabet beginning alternate verses but with some omissions and exceptions. The Psalms weave their themes alongside one another. We should note four major features.

First, the wicked 'nations' and 'enemies' (i.e. the ungodly outsiders to the people of God) feature much (9:3, 5, 6, 13,

15, 16, 17, 19, 20; 10:2-11, 13, 15, 16). In 10:2-11 there is a sustained portrait of this functionally atheistic mindset, which is proud (10:2-6), complacent (see the sayings of 10:6, 11, and 13), and desperately destructive, for persecution is writ large in these Psalms (10:7-11). Here is a mindset that is autonomous, confident that it can create for itself a 'name' that endures. Job 21 similarly acknowledges that often in human history it looks as though the wicked are right in their arrogant complacency.

Second, the reality and pain of affliction is described repeatedly and with searing force. People described with two synonymous Hebrew words, often translated 'afflicted', 'helpless', 'weak', 'the oppressed', together with other descriptions of them as 'fatherless' or 'innocent' appear throughout (9:9, 12, 18; 10:2, 8, 9, 10, 12, 14, 17, 18). They appear to be on the wrong side of history, and it hurts.

Third, there is an oscillation of singular and plural. The individual who sings the Psalm is David the King (9:1-6; 13-14). This explains his mention of 'Zion' (9:11, 14), echoing the covenant of Ps. 2:6. It is on the implied basis of this covenant that David prays. Sometimes we are in the midst of his individual sufferings. And yet – just as David's particular enemies are the representatives of 'the nations' – what happens to him will affect what happens to all the afflicted who belong to him and entrust themselves to him; much of Psalm 9 and all of Psalm 10 focuses on the wider group (9:7-12; 15-20; 10:1-18). The comment of O. Palmer Robertson is especially pertinent here: 'As it fares with the messianic king, so it fares with each member of the messianic kingdom'.[4] The drama of wickedness persecuting the afflicted king will

---

4. O. Palmer Robertson, *The Flow of the Psalms*, p. 63 (his italics).

demonstrate whether or not the covenant God, who appears sometimes to be absent, is really the active judge who will vindicate his king. The confidence that David exhibits (especially at the end, 10:16-18) is not just an assurance of his own rescue; on the lips of the great and now Risen Son of David this is an assurance of the rescue of all who belong to him.

Fourth – as in many psalms – the oscillation of suffering and confidence, issuing in final assurance, opens for us a window into the human sufferings and confidence of Jesus, and sets for us a pattern of expectation for our own lives of faith, as we live in a hostile world as men and women in Christ. These psalms begin (9:1, 2) with praise of God's 'name' revealed in His 'deeds' of judgement. These psalms end (10:16-18) with confidence that the covenant God is king, that He hears the cry of the afflicted, defends them, and puts an end to terror. In between God is described as 'he who avenges blood' (9:12, echoing Gen. 4:10 and 9:5). There is a 'Most High' (9:2) judge who hears the cry of His afflicted king (cf. Heb. 5:7) and will hear the cry of all the afflicted who entrust themselves to this king. And yet we, like the Lord Jesus, will experience times of anguished prayer (e.g. 9:13-14, 19-20; 10:1; 10:12-13).

Psalm 11

[Vol. 1: 189]

Although this is an individual prayer (v. 1 '...say to *me*') it is prayed in the context of a struggle between two groups. On the one hand are 'the righteous' or 'the upright', which means the Righteous King of Psalms 1 and 2 and all who belong to him; these appear in verses 2, 3, 5, and 7. On

the other are 'the wicked', who appeared first in Psalm 1
and then again as the rebellious people who will not have
God's King rule over them in Psalm 2. These appear in
verses 2, 5, 6, and 7.[5] They were prominent in Psalms 9 and
10, appearing as 'the wicked' or 'the nations' and inflicting
great suffering on the righteous. They feature darkly also
in Psalms 12 and 14.

The Psalm begins (1-3) with the king answering a
persuasive suggestion. Some people ('you' plural, v. 1) were
saying he should run away and hide. 'Flee...' they say!
Why? Because the attacks of the wicked on the upright,
ambushing them from places of shadow (cf. Ps. 10:8, 9)
are so destructive of the moral order of the kingdom that
they destroy the very foundations of society. And there is
nothing the righteous can do to protect goodness and truth
('what can the righteous do?' – nothing!). The king will be
the number one target since he is the Righteous one who
upholds moral order. So he must flee. No, says David, I 'take
refuge' in the covenant God (1a); and that, paradoxically,
means I persevere in my role of costly kingship.

David was hunted by Saul at the start (cf. 1 Sam. 26:20,
like a hunted bird) and by Absalom later (cf. Ps. 3). Jesus
too was hunted and exhorted to flee (Luke 13:31,32 'Leave
this place and go somewhere else. Herod wants to kill
you'). And yet he persevered with his calling as king. His
followers likewise will sometimes feel there is nothing they

---

5. The conflict between the righteous and the wicked is particularly
   acute in Book 1 of the Psalms. In a book that is about a quarter of the
   Psalter, half the references to the wicked and to the righteous appear.
   O. Palmer Robertson comments, 'Quite clearly, the concentration on
   conflict between the righteous and the wicked in the Psalms is located
   in Book I' (O. Palmer Robertson *The Flow of the Psalms* p. 56).

can do to preserve justice and truth, and they might as well hide in a Christian ghetto. No, we must follow our king and take refuge in God while persevering with the public work of the kingdom.

The confidence David expresses (4-7) includes a telling contrast of who *sees* what or whom. The wicked think God won't *see* them (10:11 'God will never notice; he covers his face and never *sees*.'); but He does and He will (4). And He acts on what He sees, with a passionate hatred of evil (5), culminating in a destructive judgement like that on Sodom and Gomorrah in Genesis 19 (6). God *sees* everyone. And then (7), the upright will one day *see* God's face and experience all the blessing implied in that wonderful phrase from the Aaronic blessing (Num. 6:24-26). Jesus believed and acted on that promise as He pressed on with His kingship; we too may share that confidence even when the moral foundations of society are destroyed all around us.

Psalm 12

The atmosphere of threat continues from Psalms 9, 10 and 11. Again the 'poor' and 'needy', the 'afflicted' (v. 5) are in danger. But, where Psalm 11 was individual (David is telling why *he* will not run away from his kingship), here the Psalm is corporate (v. 7 'protect *us*'). The king leads his people in prayer.

The scope of the Psalm is all humanity; it is bracketed (1, 8) by references to 'the human race' (lit. 'the sons of Adam').

The theme of the Psalm is words ('...lies ...lips ...tongue ...tongues ...lips ...says... the words').

We begin (1-4) with a terrible lament about the destructive power of lies. Verse 1 begins with an urgent cry:

'Help!' (lit. 'Save!'). As he looks around, the king cannot
see a faithful or loyal person (1). 'The faithful one' (*chasîd*)
means the recipient of God's covenant love (*chesed*) and one
who shows it to others in truthful, reliable, honest dealings.
Instead, in the three-line portrait of verse 2, all the king
hears is those whose speech is empty (lies, 2a), this style
of speech is smooth (flattery, 2b), words that say what
people want to hear, calculated to manipulate people, and
the source of their speech is deception in the heart (2c, lit.
a double heart, i.e. double standards). The mindset that
speaks like this is arrogant (3, 4) and comes from the self-
confidence of autonomous human beings who think words
are an instrument to gain power over people. Their final
question exposes their hearts: 'who is lord over us?' The
arrogance of godless secularism is terrible to hear.

Oh, sure, these are only words. But the result is that
the poor and needy are plundered and groan (5a). In a
post-truth generation, justice disintegrates in a society and
the weakest go to the wall. This is the default condition
of humankind. David and his people lament it and feel its
misery. Jesus the King knew what it was to be surrounded
and attacked by clever wordsmiths (e.g. Luke 11:54) whose
inspiration came from the father of lies (John 8:44).
His people experience those same attacks; perhaps the
flattering words are the most dangerous, for they seduce us
(e.g. Rom. 16:18).

And then the covenant God speaks words. And what
words! He promises (5b, c) to 'arise' (cf. Num. 10:35) and
protect the poor and needy, the king and his people who
belong to Him. And, in shining contrast to the lips and
tongues of verses 2-4, God's words are pure, like a precious
metal refined and refined and refined, with no trace of

dross, deceit or flattery. And so His promise (5) can be trusted, as David does (7, 8), and Jesus does, and Jesus's people can do, even when 'what is vile is honoured by the human race' (cf. Rom. 1:32). As we sing this Psalm, we feel the pain and we rejoice in God's words.

Psalm 13
[Vol. 1: 207]

At the heart of this short gem of a psalm lies a strange paradox. There is probably no change in David's circumstances during the singing or writing of the psalm. And yet – simultaneously, it would seem – he says there is sorrow in his heart and joy in his heart (2, 6). How can this be?

This is an intensely personal psalm. And yet – because it is spoken by the king – it cannot be narrowly individual. For, as we have seen, what happens to the king impacts deeply the king's people.

The structure is clear and simple, with three couplets. In verses 1 and 2 the king laments. In five agonized lines his suffering feels as if it has no end: 'How long…? How long…? How long…? …day after day…How long…?' Because at its root lies the experience of alienation from God. This feels like a foretaste of eternal hell and seems to have no end.

David's sufferings are focused on God (1), himself (2a, b) and his enemy (2c). First, and most deeply, he feels that the covenant God has forgotten him and hidden His face from him, the opposite of the promise of, for example, Psalm 11:7 and the Aaronic blessing of Numbers 6:24-26. In some way, the king bears the shadow of his people's sin; for David this included his own sin, but for Jesus it was entirely the sin of His people.

Second, precisely because David feels alienated from God, he focuses on himself. He wrestles with his own thoughts and has sorrow in his own heart. There is a deep loneliness about his sufferings.

Third, there is an 'enemy' who threatens to triumph over him. This 'enemy' is singular here and in verse 4a, but plural in the 'foes' of verse 4b. Perhaps the 'foes' are the human embodiment of the powers of evil; maybe the (singular) enemy is death itself[6] or him who holds the power of death (cf. Heb. 2:14).

Then, in verses 3 and 4, the king prays. His 'eyes' grow dim, in desperate need of the light of life that comes from seeing the face of God (cf. 11:7). He is close to death. But what is significant is the grounds he offers for his prayer. 'I must not die', he says, 'because if I do my enemy will rejoice at defeating me' (4). This would be a poor argument from any random individual, for who is to suppose that God must preference my life over my enemy's joy? Maybe it would be better, in God's sight, for my enemy to rejoice! But David is the King of Psalm 2. God has made a covenant with him; if the heir of that covenant dies and stays dead, that covenant has failed. For this reason, God must and will answer the prayer of the covenant king.

And so, in verses 5 and 6, the king rejoices in trust. He trusts in God's 'unfailing love' (His *chesed*, covenant love) and rejoices in his 'salvation' (the same root as the cry of 'Help!' at the start of Psalm 12).

Jesus the King knew what it was to endure the threefold sorrow of separation from God His Father, of the loneliness of a troubled soul, and of the jubilation of a vicious enemy.

---

6. As Craigie suggests.

But, as the King in covenant with God, He too could pray verses 3 and 4 and know, in the midst of a sorrowful heart, the simultaneous and paradoxical experience of a joyful, trusting heart. His followers too may know, in Christ, what it is to be 'sorrowful, yet always rejoicing' (2 Cor. 6:10); this psalm helps us both to feel, and to express, this strange paradox of Christian experience.

Psalm 14 (*see also* Psalm 53)

Apart from verse 7, David speaks horizontally to people rather than vertically to God in prayer. King David, speaks as a prophet on God's behalf. He gives us God's assessment followed by God's assurance.

In verses 1-3 we hear God's assessment of 'all mankind' (2a, the same phrase that brackets Ps. 12), with no exceptions (note the repeated 'no one...no one...not even one'). It begins with 'There is no God' and continues with a closely parallel sentence, literally, 'There is no doer of good'. Human beings by nature are practical atheists. This is the voice of the wicked in Psalm 10:6, 11, 13. Whether or not there is a God (and there were no theoretical atheists in David's day), there is no danger that God makes any moral difference to my life. God is not watching, he will not intervene to judge me. And therefore my moral compass is infinitely flexible and I am not able to 'do good' in any unblemished sense: 'no God' means 'no good'. We are deeply corrupted inside by our turning away from God. The root problem is the direction of the heart: we will not 'seek God' (2b) but 'turn away' (3a). Paul quotes this in his proof that all human beings without exception are sinful and without excuse (Rom. 3:10-12).

But David does not give this assessment as an abstract argument of theology. It is of urgent practical importance that there be an answer. And so (4-6) he continues with divine assurance. We learned in verse 2 that turning away from God leaves us without 'understanding'. Now – using a synonym – David assures us that by nature we 'know nothing', that is to say, we do not know the unshakeable truth that God is with the righteous (the king and those who belong to him), as their refuge (5b, 6b). Our natural moral compass has self at the centre and therefore treats other people as if they are there for me; they exist to satisfy my appetites, which is why – if I can – I will eat/devour them as if I were eating bread (4b). I have no sense of need and will not truly pray (4c 'they never call on the LORD'). But I do not know the truth I need to know. There is a covenant God and I cannot devour His people without being overwhelmed with dread on some judgement day. When David refers to 'my people' (4b), he speaks both of God's people and, derivatively, of his own people, the people of God's king. We, who are that people if we belong to the king, take heartfelt assurance from verses 4-6. But only after we have been convicted of our sin by verses 1-3 and driven to find refuge in Christ.

In verse 7, David leads his people in urgent prayer that salvation will come to the downtrodden people of God 'out of Zion,' the place of the anointed King of Psalm 2; that is, that the promised Messiah, the Righteous Man of Psalm 1 who is the King of Psalm 2, will come as the rescuer. That was a time of great gladness (e.g. Mark 2:19); when he returns it will be a time of yet greater gladness.

Psalm 15
[Vol. 1: 182]

Dark wickedness has been prominent in Psalms 9-14. This is a dangerous world for the godly. Psalm 15 begins with a question (1) and ends with a promise (5b); the two are related and set the theme for the psalm.

The question (1), addressed to the covenant God (the LORD) is who can gain admission to His 'sacred tent' (the tabernacle, and later the temple); that is to say, who can live on His 'holy mountain', which is Zion, the place of the covenant with David (Ps. 2:6); this is where the covenant God dwells on earth. This matters for this 'place' is the only safe place in a dangerous world.

We might expect the answer to be couched in terms of religious observance (an elite of zealotry), ethnicity (a racial elite), education (an intellectual elite), or religious experience (a mystical elite). But it is expressed entirely in terms of character.

The one who can dwell with God is precisely the Righteous Man of Psalm 1. Verses 2-5a give a picture of this man. His general character is described in the three lines of verse 2 – a blameless way of life (lit. 'walk'), righteous actions, and truth-speaking from the heart (this last by contrast with the wicked in, e.g., Pss. 10:7; 12:2-4).

Examples (rather than a comprehensive list) are given in 3-5a, focusing on:

(a) Speech (3), the truth-speaking of 2c expanded in three more lines – no slander spoken, no wrong done (by slander), no slur (bring shame on someone by false rumours).

(b) Value system (4a), who he despises and who he honours (contrast Rom. 1:32).

(c) Trustworthiness (4b), a man whose word is his bond.

(d) Absence of covetousness (5a), so that, positively, he lends generously and, negatively, his judgement is not distorted by the hope of gain (bribes and their many cousins in everyday life).

5b concludes that this person – and this person alone – 'will never be shaken,' is safe in a dangerous world. The word 'shaken' (sometimes translated 'moved') indicates the stability of standing on the Rock of the covenant God's Person and Law, not destroyed by the unstable chaotic waters of wickedness.

There are three mistaken responses to this Psalm and three right directions in which it should move us. The wrong ones are:

(a) The hypocrisy that comes from a shallow legalistic reading, which enables me to claim to be this person.

(b) Apathy, not grasping the importance of the question of verse 1.

(c) Moralistic religious zealotry, a self-generated determination to do my best to be this person.

Instead we ought:

(a) First to be filled with despair, as we realise that by nature we are utterly excluded from the only safe place on earth.

(b) Then to be overwhelmed with immense gratitude that Jesus Christ, the Righteous Man of Psalm 1 and now Psalm 15, is the King of Psalm 2 and has gone up – supremely in His Ascension – to this 'holy mountain' for us for, while David asks the question of verse 1, only Jesus finally answers it, in life as well as in teaching.

(c) Finally to find welling up within us by the Spirit of
     Jesus a longing and determination that our hearts
     and lives will increasingly be in practice what they
     are by grace in Christ our Righteous Head.

Psalm 16

[Vol. 1: 46-47, 76-85, 184]

In Psalm 15, David has taught us that the blameless
and godly one will be the unshaken one. In Psalm 16 he
develops this in terms of his desires. The key logic words
are 'for' (1b '*For* in you I take refuge') and 'Therefore' (9a
'*Therefore* my heart is glad…'). These link David's desires
with David's destiny. Desire shapes destiny: this is the
theme of the Psalm.

In verse 1 David prays to be kept safe *because* he seeks
refuge in 'my God' (a covenant expression). This picks up a
common theme in previous Psalms (e.g. 2:12; 5:11; 7:1; 9:9;
11:1; 12:7; 14:6).

In verses 2-8a he expresses fully and strongly how his
desires are entirely and exclusively focused on the God in
whom he seeks refuge. He wills to obey Him as his 'Lord/
Master' (2a); he looks for good nowhere else (2b); he admires
only those who share this desire (3); he really believes that
looking anywhere else leads to misery (4); he trusts that,
having the covenant God and Him alone is sufficient for all
truly desirable things (5,6); he listens to the counsel of the
covenant God and meditates on it at night (7); he keeps his
'eyes' (i.e. desires) solely focused on the covenant God (8a).

And, *because* his desire is single and pure, he is confident
that his destiny is secure (8b-11). He will not be shaken (8b,
cf. 15:5); he cannot die and stay dead but is sure of bodily life

with God forever in unblemished joy and pleasure, because his desire is to have the covenant God at his 'right hand' (8b, 11c), to walk with this God in 'the path of life' (11a), and to be always before his face ('in your presence' 11b).

Who can pray this? Not – in his own life and nature – David, for David's desires were very mixed up. Not us, for we would be terrible hypocrites if we claimed that our desires were focused on God *alone*. Could it be Jesus of Nazareth? He appeared to have his desires focused on God alone. But we cannot see his heart. The acid test for the Psalm 16 Man is that he cannot die and stay dead. For this reason, the bodily resurrection of Jesus is the proof positive that He, and He alone, is the Psalm 16 Man (Acts 2:25-32). This demonstrates that the desires of Jesus were entirely and intensely focused on the will and the presence of God His Father. In Acts 13 Paul says Jesus is both the Psalm 2 Man and the Psalm 16 Man (quoting Ps. 2:33 and Ps. 16:35). The King of Psalm 2 is the Lover of God of Psalm 16.

This calls out from us a double response. First, a wonderful thankfulness that Jesus has won this blessing for us. As Paul says in Acts 13, the fact that Jesus is who He is and did what He did means that forgiveness of sins is available in His name (Acts 13:38,39). When He prays for 'refuge' He does so for Himself and for all His people. When He is confident of bodily resurrection, His confidence extends to all His people. Jesus has won for us the blessings of Psalm 16.

But we must not stop there. For by the Spirit of Jesus – as in Psalm 15 – we too begin to long in our hearts to have more of this single-hearted love for God, that our desires may become more like Psalm 16 yearnings. Psalm 16 assures us of blessings in Christ and reconfigures our desires in Christ.

Psalm 17

[Vol. 1: 35, 108]

Psalm 17 should be read alongside Psalms 15 and 16. In each of them David speaks prophetically with the voice of the perfect and greater King whom he foreshadows. While in Psalm 16 David's confidence is based on his single-hearted desire, in Psalm 17 it is founded on his righteousness. Notice the words 'just' (1), 'vindication' (2a), 'what is right' (2b), 'vindicated' (15). David claims answered prayer because he is the Righteous King.

This Psalm comes in three sections, each beginning with a fresh prayer (1, 6, 13).

In verses 1-5 David prays because he has the right heart. As we saw in Vol.1, chapter 6 he claims a deep righteousness of heart expressed in a flawless life.

In verses 6-8 David prays because he is the right person. The clue is in words that echo the Exodus from Egypt. In verse 7 the words 'wonders', 'great love' and 'by your right hand' echo the same words in the Song after the crossing of the Red Sea, Exodus 15:11-13. David implies that he is in some way the personification of Israel, who were God's 'Son' (Exod. 4:22); as the anointed King, this is exactly who he is (Ps. 2:7). The words 'apple of your eye' and 'your wings' in verse 8 echo another Israel song, Deuteronomy 32:9-11. David is confident his prayers will be heard because he is the Representative Head of the covenant people, and therefore God's 'Son'.

Verses 9-12 describe the wicked and help us feel the mortal threat to God's King.

In verses 13-15 David prays because he has the right affections. That is to say, he implies that his enemies are

precisely God's enemies, with a one to one correspondence.
There is a translation question in verse 14b for which you
will need to consult a commentary.

David is confident because he has the right heart, is the
right person and has the right affections. All this is by the
Spirit of Jesus Christ, who has in His sinless nature a heart
of perfect righteousness, is in His divine-human person the
anointed King and Representative Head of the people of
God, and exhibits in all His affections a perfect harmony
with His Father, so that enemies of Jesus are precisely
enemies of God.

Just as Jesus is the Man with access to God's holy mountain in Psalm 15 and the Man assured of bodily resurrection
in Psalm 16, so He is the Righteous Man of Psalm 17 and
therefore assured of final joy with God (15). We have these
blessings only in Him; but we do have them, and in Christ
we may pray this psalm with that confidence that comes
from imputed righteousness.

> Accepted in the Well-beloved,
> And clothed in righteousness divine,
> I see the bar of heaven removed;
> And all Thy merits, Lord, are mine.[7]

Psalm 18

[Vol. 1: 47, 59, 106, 108, 151, 162, 171]

The importance of Psalm 18 is signalled by its length, its
superscription, and its language. It is by far the longest
psalm so far.[8] The superscription, echoed where the psalm

---

7. 'Tis finished! The Messiah dies' (Charles Wesley).

8. Even if Psalm 9 and 10 are put together, they fall 12 verses short of
   Psalm 18.

is repeated almost verbatim in 2 Sam. 22, speaks of a definitive time when David's kingdom was established and Saul's hostility ended. The struggles that have pervaded Psalms 3–17 are – for the moment – over. For the first time since Psalm 2 there is explicit reference (50) to the 'king' and the 'anointed' (Messiah, Christ); after Psalm 18, there are several more such references. Here, in David's experience, we learn enduring truths about God's Messiah.

Verses 1-6 begin with the Messiah's confidence, in deep distress (4, 5), in the trustworthiness of His God. Nowhere else in the Psalter are there so many words for God as in verses 1, 2 (strength, rock, fortress, deliverer, shield, horn of salvation, stronghold). Jesus the Messiah had just this confidence in the deepest possible distress.

Verses 7-19 dramatise the Messiah's rescue in terms which are both cosmic (the drama of 7-15) and personal (16-19). Notice the bracketing references to the 'foundations' of the world (vv. 7, 15). When God comes to rescue His Messiah, it is an event that impacts the world order. And yet in the context of a deeply personal relationship, in which He reaches down, takes hold, draws out, rescues, is the Messiah's support, brings him out, delights in him (16-19). When God the Father reached down to rescue His Son, Jesus Christ, it was a salvation that was both cosmic (for it touches the roots of the universe) and personal (for it arises out of an eternal bond of love).

The reason for the rescue is celebrated in verses 20-29 in two aspects. First, the righteousness of the Messiah (20-24), who will be – in Jesus Christ – utterly sinless. And, second, the consistent faithfulness of God (25-29) who will always act like this towards the blameless and pure man of Psalms 1, 15, and 17. It is not possible for the 'cords' of death to keep their hold on this righteous anointed one (Acts 2:24, echoing the 'cords of death' language of vv. 4, 5).

The victory drama of verses 30-45 moves the story forward from rescue to offensive warfare in which the king is first trained and equipped by the covenant God (30-36) and then acts in pursuit and triumph over his enemies (37-45). At the end of which, the promise of Psalm 2 will be fulfilled, and he will be 'the head of nations' (43).

This anointed King, who now rules the world, praises the faithful 'Rock' character of His utterly good Father God, and He praises Him 'among the nations'. The covenant God does indeed give His anointed King great victories and show His unfailing covenant love to Him for ever (46-50).

As we sing this psalm, we enter into the sufferings of the Messiah, we share His confidence in His Father God, we rejoice that in His salvation is our hope, we watch as He conquers the world, and we join – in all the world – in praising, with Him, the Rock-like goodness of His and our Father God. The key to our response to this psalm is found in Romans 15:9. Paul cites verse 49 of this psalm in support of his teaching that Christ's purpose is 'that the Gentiles might glorify God for his mercy' and therefore be humble members of their local church (the argument of Rom. 14:1-15:13[9]).

Psalm 19

[Vol. 1: 148, 157, 158, 184]

This is a Psalm of David. Verse 14a tells us it is the words of the anointed King's mouth flowing out of the meditation

---

9. See Christopher Ash, *Teaching Romans* ad loc.

of the anointed King's heart (the same word for meditation is used of the Righteous Man in Ps. 1:2). That is to say, it finds its full meaning when the Messiah speaks it. The King prays (14) that these words and this meditation may be pleasing in the sight of God. We may be confident that, by the Spirit of Christ, they were indeed pleasing to God the Father, supremely when Jesus Himself prayed them.

The words of the psalm segue from a spoken meditation (1-9) addressed to no-one in particular, to words addressed in the second person to God (10-14). The words 'your servant' in verse 11 signal the shift.

The spoken meditation (1-10) functions for us as Spirit-given instruction on the lips of our King, to which we listen with rapt attention. When we join in – as for other instructional material in the Psalms – we add our 'amen' to the truths expressed and signal that we agree with them.

We listen first as our King thinks about Creation (1-6). In Psalm 8 he wonders that the covenant God has set His 'glory' in the 'heavens' (Ps. 8:1) and considers the heavens and heavenly bodies (Ps. 8:3). Here He teaches that the 'heavens' declare the 'glory' of God (1) and thinks about the greatest heavenly body, the sun (4-6). Behind this lies the idea of a created order whose 'foundations' express the character and holy goodness of God. This order is universal, hinted at by the universal scope of the sun's daily journey and received warmth (6). The man who will govern creation (Ps. 8) thinks how creation reveals the glory of his Father God.

But, although the created order declares the glory of God, it is only in the scriptures that we read that glory in its full clarity and moral purity. This is why, in verses 7-9, the focus is on the moral goodness of the word of God. Six words are used of God's word – 'law' (torah, instruction), 'statutes', 'precepts', 'commands', 'fear' (pointing to our proper response), and 'decrees'. Its qualities are given in seven more words – 'perfect' (i.e. blameless, with integrity), 'trustworthy', 'right' (that is, morally upright), 'radiant' (shining out with truth), 'pure' (or clean), 'firm' and 'righteous'. Its benefits are repentance ('refreshing' is literally 'returning' or 'repenting'), wisdom, joy, and enlightenment.

As our King turns over these qualities in his mind and meditates on these benefits, he is moved to prayer (10-13). When the King prays we may perhaps take it that He leads us, his people, in prayer, both setting us an example and inviting us, by his Spirit, to join in. The meditation of the King's heart becomes the meditation of our hearts and the words of the King's mouth become the words of our mouths.

What matchless value have these words (10), not just because they reveal but also because they warn me, turn my heart from error and sin, and give me the very great rewards promised in Psalm 1 (11). Our King prays to be blameless, kept free both from the hidden faults that might lurk in the depths of his heart and the willful, deliberate, high-handed sins that might enslave Him (12, 13). One particular question raised here in verse 12 – as in other expressions of penitence in the Psalms – is whether and, if so, how, the sinless King can pray for forgiveness. (There is no difficulty with his praying v. 13, to be *kept* from willful sins.) I am not sure, but I think the answer is that in the spotless heart of the Lord Jesus, when faced with the purity of the Law (7-10) there was such a humble sense of human frailty that He fears lest, somewhere in the depths of his own heart, there might lurk hidden faults. There were none; but the fact that He prayed so humbly was – paradoxically – another piece in the jigsaw of evidence for his sinlessness.

We too pray with Him that scripture will warn and guard us and keep us in the way of life.

In words that echo Psalm 18 ('Rock') and the whole Exodus drama ('Redeemer'), our king prays that these words will be pleasing in God's sight. We may trust that they are, and pray that our joining in of these meditations will similarly be pleasing to God.

Psalm 20

[Vol. 1: 101-102]

Psalms 20 and 21 fit closely together. In Psalm 20 the people pray for the King, and in Psalm 21 they rejoice with the King. One feature to note is how closely the joy and blessing of the people are tied to the joy and blessing of the King. These psalms press home to us with especial power the depth and significance of our being in Christ our King.

In verses 1-5 we pray for someone. It becomes clear in verse 9 that it is the King for whom we are praying[10]. This is not (in the first instance) a prayer for your or my individual blessing, but for God's blessing on the King. We may sum up verses 1-5 by saying that we pray that the King's prayers will be heard. We want the covenant God to 'answer' Him (1, 2), to accept His sacrifices (3, i.e. hear His prayers, which is the result of right relationship with God through sacrifice), to give Him what His heart desires (v. 4, i.e. what He prays), and to grant all His requests (5).

---

10. It may be that verse 9 should be translated, 'LORD, give victory! May the King answer us when we call!' In this case the King, whose own prayers are answered (cf. John 11:41, 42) becomes the one who answers His people's prayers.

We know what the King prays, from Psalm 2, where he
is invited to pray to conquer and rule the world (Ps. 2:8, 9)!
It is this prayer we long to see finally answered. When the
King rules the world, we His people will be filled with joy
(5); in His victory is our delight.

In verses 6-8 we are invited to join in an expression of
confidence: 'Now this I know…' What do we know? That
Psalm 2 is true! That the covenant God gives victory (rescue,
salvation) to 'his anointed' – the anointed King, Messiah,
or Christ, of Psalm 2 and Psalm 18. And so we trust, not in
human power (the evocative super-weapon pairing of chariots
and horses, as in Exod. 15:1-18) but in the revealed 'name'
of the covenant God who has promised that His Messiah
will rule the world. This affects us deeply. For when He wins
(and His enemies 'fall') 'we will rise up and stand firm' (8).

And so the opening prayer 'May the LORD answer *you*'
(1) becomes the closing prayer, 'Answer *us* when we call!'
(9). We pray that the King's prayer will be answered, and
we add our 'Amen' to His prayers.

The prayer of Psalm 20 was definitively answered in the
incarnation, life, miracles, teaching, and supremely victorious
death, resurrection and ascension of Jesus the Messiah. And
yet we await the consummation of that victory, when the prayer
of the King is fully answered, every enemy is placed beneath
His feet, death the last enemy is destroyed, and He hands over
the kingdom to His Father (1 Cor. 15:24-28). Psalm 20 now
expresses for us this deep longing for the final victory of Jesus.

Psalm 21
See the introduction to Psalm 20. Psalm 21 echoes Psalm
20 closely. Again, the joy of the King's people is closely tied
to the joy of the King in the victories that the covenant God

gives Him. The King has prayed the prayer of Psalm 2 and now – in the final fulfilment of this psalm – He knows the joy of a full answer to His prayers. He is crowned with the public demonstration of worldwide rule (3), with eternal life that comes from victory even over death (4), with great glory (5). Above all, His joy comes from reigning in intimate fellowship with the covenant God, His Father (6); His victory is the fruit of His faith in the unfailing covenant love (*chesed*) of God the Father, the Most High God (7).

The King's victory is the same as God's victory and results in a total destruction of all enemies, a burning up in righteous wrath (8-12). In verse 13 we, the King's people, praise the covenant God for His power in giving victory to Jesus His King.

The dominant note in Psalm 21, in distinction to Psalm 20, is the joy that comes from confident anticipation of the future victory of the King. Though we do not now see Him, we trust that He is seated at the right hand of God, and are even now filled with an inexpressible and glorious joy because we know that our King's victory guarantees our salvation (1 Pet. 1:8, 9).

Psalm 22
[Vol. 1: 43, 46, 47, 163, 181, 213-214, 218]

The first part of Psalm 22 comes as a shock after the confident joy of Psalm 21. The King who 'trusts in the LORD' and 'will not be shaken' (Ps. 21:7) still 'trusts' (Ps. 22:9 and note the repetition of 'trust' in vv. 4, 5, 8); but He endures astonishing suffering.

The psalm divides after verse 21. In verses 1-21 we hear the King's agonized prayers (1-2, 11, 19-21) interwoven with descriptions of His terrible suffering (6-8, 12-18) and His expressions of trust (3-5, 9-10). From verses 22-31 the King whose cry for help has been answered (24; cf. Heb. 5:7) leads the assembly (22, 25) in praise.

Our Christ-centred readings of the Psalms are explicitly supported by the New Testament in this psalm. Both verses 1-21 and verses 22-31 are fulfilled in Jesus. He takes verse 1 on His lips on the cross (Matt. 27:46; Mark 15:34). The mockery and insults of verses 7, 8 are echoed at the cross (Matt. 27:39, 43; Mark 15:29; Luke 23:35,36). The thirst of verse 15 is fulfilled in John 19:28. The division of Jesus's clothes and casting of lots for a garment is recorded in Matthew 27:35, Mark 15:24, Luke 23:34, and John 19:24 (with explicit quotation of Ps. 22:18). And then, the first verse of the second part verse 22 is explicitly said by Hebrews 2:12 to be finally spoken by Jesus.

From verses 1-21 we learn that, before the King can lead God's assembled people in praise, He must endure terrible sufferings, and ultimately suffering fulfilled in crucifixion. We enter in our imaginations with the King into the depths of this lonely suffering; for loneliness is a strong motif. God ('My God' – the phrase of covenant relationship – comes three times in vv. 1, 2) is far away (1, 11) and silent (2), while He is surrounded by vicious evil enemies (6-8, and notice the repetition of 'surround' in 12 and 16). He does not endure this suffering with His people, but for them, as their substitute.

And yet the King is the supreme believer; He trusts. He has trusted from His mother's womb and still He trusts (9, 10). He is the fulfilment of believing Israel of old (4, 5). He trusts, finally, not simply in the face of death, but right into the lions' jaws of death.

And because His trust is vindicated – ultimately in bodily resurrection – King Jesus can declare the name of the faithful covenant God in the assembly of God's people (12, Heb. 2:12).

As we hear Him make this joyful proclamation we learn, not only that the covenant God has rescued this one afflicted man who trusted in Him, but that we may therefore be confident that He will rescue all those who follow in His footsteps; in verse 26 'the poor' is plural, i.e. all those who, like Jesus Christ, are afflicted.

We are also reassured that the promises of Psalm 2 are trustworthy. Verses 27 and 28 echo language both of Psalm 2 and of the covenant with Abraham. The covenant God will rule the world through His anointed King, who has been crucified and is now raised in glory.

Psalm 23
[Vol. 1: 32-33, 57, 94-95]

Before this much-loved psalm can become ours, we must remember that it is first David's, and then Jesus's. That is, it is a psalm of our King before it becomes ours in him. Coming after the terrors of Psalm 22, Psalm 23 is especially striking. We have just sung with our King of the lonely horrors of God-forsakenness. And yet, through this darkest of valleys, our King trusts that the covenant God is His Shepherd.

There are many echoes of the Exodus, when the 'Shepherd of Israel' (Ps. 80:1) ensured that His people would 'lack nothing' (Deut. 2:7), brought them to a 'holy *pasture*' (Exod. 15:13, translated 'holy dwelling' in the NIV), to a land described as His 'rest' (e.g. Ps. 95:11, the same word as 'quiet' in 'quiet waters'), and spread 'a table' for them in the wilderness (Ps. 78:19). The king who sings this psalm is the representative head of the people of God; he is the embodiment of redeemed Israel. He walks in intimate fellowship with the covenant God, his Shepherd, who guides him, as he guided Israel, 'for his name's sake', that is, because his reputation as a faithful promise-making, covenant-keeping God depends on this.

Jesus knew this confidence, and shared with David the assurance that, even though He walked through 'the darkest valley' (the valley of the shadow of death[11]), He need fear no evil, for His shepherd was with Him, His 'rod' to fend off attacks from wild beasts, His 'staff' or 'crook' to guide and lead Him in paths of righteousness.

The banquet of verse 5 is a victory meal ('in the presence of my enemies') in which the enemies can only look on while the King is anointed with oil (before the meal) and given an overflowing cup of blessing. Verse 6 is the climax, repeating 'the LORD' as an inclusio with verse 1, and expressing a beautiful confidence that the goodness and love (covenant love, *chesed*) follow the King all His life, so that He will dwell in the presence of God in His house all His days.

The King who inherits these covenant assurances is ultimately Jesus Christ. He is the singer of Psalm 23. What comfort this psalm must have brought to Him in His earthly sufferings! And now it is ours as we are 'in Christ'. Our King becomes, with God the Father, our Good Shepherd, leading us His sheep where He has gone before. With our King – and only with our King, never in isolated spirituality – we share this deep and beautiful

---

11. The 'deep darkness' word is used, in half its OT occurrences, in Job.

assurance, that as we follow Him through the valley of the shadow of death, we too need fear no evil, and we too will dwell with Jesus in the Father's house for ever.

Psalm 24
[Vol. 1: 153, 154, 181, 182-3]

David sings here, not of his own kingship, but of the Kingship of the Covenant God. The key to the psalm is the relationship between its three parts.

Part 1 (1, 2) affirms that the whole earth with all the people, animals, crops and everything else in it is the LORD's because – in language echoing Genesis 1:9,10 and echoed in 2 Peter 3:5 – He made it a safe, morally reliable place, a place of creation *order* in the midst of evil chaos.

Part 2 (3-6) echoes the question of Psalm 15:1. Who may enter and survive in the presence of this covenant God? The answer is moral: those who have clean hands (right actions) and a pure heart (right desires), who worship this God alone (echoing the 2nd and 9th commandments). These think right and behave right because they seek the face of the covenant God, desiring above all else His holy presence. These, and these alone, can enter.

Part 3 (7-10) celebrates, with vivid and memorable repetition, the triumphant return of the covenant God after military victory (echoing language used when the Ark of the Covenant returned from battle). The LORD returns to the LORD's own holy place.

Putting these together, we may start with part 1 and part 3. The Creator God is sovereign over all creation (1, 2). And yet He needs to win a war against evil to establish His Kingdom over all. When He does so He returns to His 'mountain', His 'holy place' of government (7-10). When He returns, He brings with Him those who are qualified to ascend this mountain to this holy place.

We may then read this in a moralistic way ('try to be those kinds of people') or a Christocentric way. Supremely, we need a human king who is qualified to enter with the covenant God in triumph to the place of supreme authority in heaven and on earth. This king needs to have clean hands and a pure heart. Thank God we have just such a king in Jesus Christ! Just as he is the man of Psalm 1 and the man of Psalm 15, so he is the man of Psalm 24. Only as His righteousness (his clean hands and pure heart) are given to us by grace are we qualified to enter with Him into this place of the presence of the victorious and sovereign Creator God. And then, by the Spirit of our King, we too are moved to seek His face (6) and to purify our hands and our hearts (4).

Psalm 25
[Vol. 1: 33, 188]

Before we consider the themes of this acrostic psalm, notice that, while the psalm is overwhelmingly individual (1-21), it ends with a corporate prayer (22). As we read the prayer of David the (individual) king, we remember that what he prays, we pray.

The four major interwoven motifs in David's prayer are trust, penitence, longing to live right, and prayer for rescue. Trust dominates at the start (1-3). David's faith is not blind, but based on covenant promises (made by the LORD, the covenant God). The desire to live right (4-15) picks up language both of wisdom (the two 'ways' of Psalm

1 echoed in the words 'way' and 'path') and of law (picking up law and covenant words from Ps. 19). Penitence appears strongly in verses 7, 11, and 18; the prayers for forgiveness are based on God's qualities of covenant mercy, love and faithfulness. David's prayers for rescue reflect the loneliness and troubles of his heart (especially in vv. 16-21).

The covenant words translated 'loving and faithful' (10) come into Greek as the phrase usually translated 'grace and truth' (grace being covenant love and truth being covenant faithfulness). When we read in John 1:14 that the incarnate Word is 'full of grace and truth' we grasp the wonderful truth that the covenant love of God the Father is incarnate in Jesus Christ. He is the King in whom covenant love and faithfulness are to be found and experienced[12].

Two questions arise when we ask how Jesus of Nazareth could pray this psalm. The first is what it might mean for Him to pray prayers of penitence for sin, since He had none. David could certainly pray these, but what about Jesus? Perhaps the best way to read this is that, as the king who bears our sins for us, Jesus can lead His people in penitence[13].

The second question is the relationship between the prayer of this individual (David, and finally Jesus) and the whole people of God. Verse 22 is the key here. Because the covenant God relieves the king of 'the troubles' of his heart (17), the whole people of God may be confident that He will deliver them from all their 'troubles' (22). In Christ we express our trust, as He did; by the Spirit of Christ we too voice a passionate desire to be led in ways of right living; led

12. See also Psalms 26:3 and 57:10.

13. See Vol. 1, pp. 61-63.

by Christ we confess our sins and pray for forgiveness; and in Christ we pray for a rescue in which we may be confident.

Psalm 26
[Vol. 1: 171, 222]

Before making this your psalm or my psalm, we need to remember the king who first prayed it, and the King who fulfilled it. There are two assemblies or congregations in the psalm, first 'the assembly of evildoers' (5) and finally 'the great congregation' of the righteous in the Temple (12). The King will be absent from the former (5) but leading the praise of the covenant God in the latter (12). We come into the drama as members of one or other of these congregations.

But first, let us hear our king. David claims to be a Psalm 1 man, a Psalm 15 man, and a Psalm 24 man. Twice he says, 'I have led (and I lead) a blameless life' (1, 11). The covenant love ('unfailing love') and faithfulness of God are at the heart of his life (3); as we saw in Psalm 25, covenant love and faithfulness translates into 'grace and truth' in the New Testament. David may, by grace, be accounted a Psalm 1 man; but he is not so by nature. Only Jesus Christ our King is 'full of grace and truth', the man who is entirely and perfectly the man of Psalms 1, 15, and 24. Jesus is so, not because of His outward law-keeping, but because in the deepest affections of His heart He 'loves' to be in the presence of God His Father (8) and He hates all wickedness (4-5, 9-10).

Jesus our King never 'faltered' (v. 1, lit. did not 'slip' morally); and so, at the end of this psalm, He can say that His feet (speaking of His life) 'stand on level ground' with perfect moral uprightness; and therefore He – and He alone –

can lead the praise of God in the great congregation of God's people (12). As we join with Jesus in His song, we rejoice in our imputed blamelessness in Christ, we resolve afresh for a godly aversion to the values of the wicked, and a godly affection for the Father, both of which we have in Christ.

Psalm 27

[Vol. 1: 43, 222]

Although the themes are intermingled, there is a broad movement in this psalm.

David begins by expressing a wonderful confidence in the midst of hostility (1-3). The opposition is emphatic ('the wicked advance against me to devour me' 'my enemies and my foes' 'an army besiege me' 'war break out against me') but three times David says he will not fear (1a, 1b, 3a).

The second theme (4) is David's single-hearted love for the covenant God. This is the one and only thing he wants; he wants it all the days of his life; his gaze is filled with 'the beauty of the LORD'.

In verse 5,6 he returns to confidence in trouble, but now he adds to safety the expectation of exaltation and victory over all his enemies.

The third theme is urgent prayer (7-14). Precisely because he is confident in troubles, David prays. Again, his one desire surfaces (8) in his exhorting himself to seek God's face. David prays on the basis of covenant (e.g. the word 'forsake' is a covenant word, vv. 9, 10, and the title 'your servant' is a covenant title, v. 9).

The endpoint of the psalm is a strong confidence (13) that issues in the exhortation (to himself? to us?) to go on waiting for the LORD in persevering prayer (14).

Our King Jesus Christ shared David's covenant confidence amidst yet deeper hostility. For His foes advanced against Him and it was as if an army laid siege to His life (2, 3); they desired His death and used false witness to work violence (12) against Him. And yet Jesus did not fear, but trusted ('confident' in v. 3 is the same word 'trust' as in Ps. 26:1). His one desire, utterly consistent and passionate, was for the presence and fellowship of the beautiful Father (4, 8). And so He prayed, with loud cries and tears, to the one who was able to save Him from death; and He was heard (Heb. 5:7). He said to Himself, as He prayed this psalm, 'Wait for the LORD; be strong and take heart and wait for the LORD'; He says the same to us. As we pray this psalm with Him we share His troubles, we learn His confidence, we purify our desire for God, and we persevere in prayer for our final rescue.

Psalm 28

The key to Psalm 28 is the relationship between the individual words of verses 1-7 and the references to the people of God in verses 8, 9. Because the covenant God is a fortress of salvation for David His 'anointed one' (8b) he is the one who saves His 'people' (9). So we listen carefully to the prayer of the anointed one, for what happens to him will happen to us.

Speaking and silence are the themes of verses 1, 2. David calls, cries for mercy and lifts up his hands in prayer. He does so 'towards your Most Holy Place,' the Holy of Holies, where the Ark of the Covenant is kept. That is, David prays on the basis of the covenant that God has with him (Ps. 2; 2 Sam. 7). All the Old Testament covenants are now focused on this covenant with the Messiah. And yet the covenant God is silent; there is no reply. If God never answers David's prayer, David might as well be in 'the pit,' the silent place of the dead (see Ps. 30:9). But covenant presupposes a real, living, unbreakable relationship (cf. Matt. 22:32). David's unanswered prayer threatens the covenant; this is why he prays so urgently.

In verses 6, 7 David rejoices, and praises God, that his prayers were heard. 'Hear my cry for mercy,' he prays in verse 2; 'he has heard my cry for mercy,' he celebrates in verse 6. There is no praise in 'the pit' (Ps. 30:9); but the Messiah is not in the pit!

In between verses 1-2 and verses 6-7 the focus is on 'the wicked' (3-5). There is an interplay between what they do ('those who *do* evil' 'their *deeds*' 'their evil *work*' 'what their hands have *done*') and what God does ('the *deeds* of the LORD' 'what his hands have *done*'). They are not genuine covenant people, for they speak 'cordially' (lit. *shalom*, peace, a covenant word) while harbouring malice. They do not care about what God does (to make and keep a covenant); and so they and all they have achieved will be torn down. Their covenant-breaking lives will end in failure; God's covenant-keeping activity will end with the king's prayers being answered (and Ps. 2 fulfilled).

And so (8, 9), precisely because the covenant God answered the prayers of the anointed king (the Messiah or Christ), we – the King's people – may pray with confidence that He will save and bless us, be our shepherd (cf. Ps. 23:1) and carry us forever.

As we sing this Psalm with Jesus Christ our Anointed King, we heed the warning not to be like the wicked; our natural tendency to be like them is counteracted by a deepening aversion to all they represent. But above all, we rejoice that our prayers are heard in the anointed King's name. In Him, we too are in unbreakable covenant with the living God.

Psalm 29
[Vol. 1: 149]

This is a very different psalm to most of those around it. While it sounds wonderful, it is not so easy to know how to appropriate it and pray it. Two observations may help get us started.

First, it begins (1) and ends (11) with references to the 'strength' that the covenant God has, and gives to His people. The blessing of 'peace' (11b) comes from the supremely strong God who gives His people strength. This is the over-arching theme.

Second, there are striking similarities with the 'Song by the Sea' sung by the people of God at the time of the Exodus (Exod. 15:1-18). Both have references to 'strength' (Ps. 29:1, 11; Exod. 15:2, 13); in each, the 'strength' of God is associated with His 'name' (Ps. 29:1, 2; Exod. 15:2,3), that is His revealed character; the cosmic governing assembly of the so-called 'sons of God' or 'angels' appears in both passages (Ps. 29:1 'heavenly beings'; Exod. 15:11 'the gods'); in each, God is King (Ps. 29:10; Exod. 15:18); in both, God's power over the hostile 'waters' is celebrated (Ps. 29:3, 10; Exod. 15:1-11); and God wins His people's victory in each passage through a storm (cf. Exod. 15:8, 10). When Old Testament believers sang Psalm 29, they could not help thinking of the great redemption won for them from the powers that enslaved them in Egypt.

Verses 1 and 2 exhort 'the sons of god', who are representative of all powers in the universe, both human and superhuman, to acknowledge that the covenant God reveals ('glory') His 'strength' by His 'name'; and that this revealed strength is seen in His 'holiness', that is, in the revelation of God focused on the Old Testament tabernacle or temple (9c).

Verses 3-9 make explicit, by emphatic repetition, that it is by 'the voice of the LORD' that God establishes and reveals His victory. He speaks and all creation, including the hostile powers symbolized by 'the waters' (3) or 'the flood' (10), submits to His word.

Because He is sovereign, by His spoken word, over all creation, in verses 10-11 His people celebrate that His supremacy means their (and our) strength and peace.

When Jesus sang this psalm of David, He affirmed His trust that the words of God, which are precisely the words He Himself spoke, as the incarnate Word of God (John 12:49,50), exercise the sovereign authority of God over all things and guarantee His people's peace. He won that victory over all the powers of evil at the cross (Col. 2:14,15) and can therefore assure His people that in Him we have peace, because He has overcome the world (John 16:33).

As we sing this psalm, we abandon all our puffed-up pretensions of strength (thinking ourselves to be like 'heavenly beings') and experience strong reassurance that in Christ, the Word of God, we find strength and peace in the midst of all the chaotic and terrifying powers of evil, that threaten to enslave us.

Psalm 30
[Vol. 1: 151, 181]

In this psalm David goes to the heart of a deep truth: the reason human beings are alive is to give glory to the God who gave us life. Humanity ought to be one glad chorus of praise to our Creator! The first and last words of the psalm (in Hebrew) are verbs of praise (1 '*I will exalt…*'; 12 'For ever *I will praise you*'); verbs of praise appear also in verses 4 and 9. Praise is what accompanies joyful restoration to life (11).

The two poles of the psalm are (a) life and joyful praise and (b) death and weeping. Death appears in verse 3 ('the realm of the dead' – i.e. Sheol – and 'the pit') and in verse 9 ('the pit… the dust…'). When people are close to death they weep (5) and wail (11).

The psalm is prompted by an escape from death, probably from illness, made worse by the ever-present enemies who will rejoice at David's death (1-3). Because the covenant God lifted David up, David will lift God up (exalt Him) in praise (1).

In verses 4-7 David exhorts all the faithful people of God (the *chasidim*, those who have both received and shown God's covenant love, His *chesed*) to join him in praise. David gives his testimony, which is that he has been restored to life and also forgiven for the self-confidence he had evidently felt when things were going well (6). For a while he thought he was the master of his own soul; he now knows that every breath comes only from the covenant God. Self-confidence leads down to the Pit!

Verses 8-10 tell more of David's story of healing. The key is the argument David uses in prayer: 'Will the dust …proclaim your faithfulness?' Only a living David will be audible proof that God is faithful to His covenant with His King. God has heard this prayer. In verses 11-12 David concludes with emphatic joy and praise.

King Hezekiah echoes this psalm in many ways (Isa. 38:9-20).

When Jesus sings this psalm, He too gladly acknowledges that every human breath He breathed came from His Father. Never Himself guilty of self-confidence, Jesus sings David's testimony in a new key, leading His people in confession and glad praise for every breath of our lives. This psalm is a powerful reminder to us that praise is the life-blood of the redeemed life of all Christ's people.

Psalm 31
[Vol. 1: 33, 37, 46, 207]

The key to understanding what David says in verses 1-22 is the exhortation he gives in verses 23,24. Here he addresses all the faithful people of God (the *chasidim*, those who have received and who show His covenant love, His *chesed*) and exhorts us to love God, to trust God, and to be strong of heart as we wait for Him in hope. The aim of what David says in the body of the psalm is that we will respond as he teaches us at the end.

David sings first (1-5) that he committed his spirit into the hands of the covenant God, who is his refuge, rock, and strong fortress. It is God to whom he goes for safety. He does so (6-8) because he gladly trusts in, or clings to (6) the covenant God; he trusts because he knows God's covenant love to him as the anointed king (7).

All this is in the midst of intense suffering. Verses 9-13 describe a deep and miserable distress, characterized by its desperate loneliness, despised by enemies and neighbours, shunned in horror by his closest friends. This distress is like a terrorist attack (v. 13 'Terror on every side'); David is surrounded by those who seek his life (13).

And yet David trusts (14-18). In covenant faithfulness David says, 'You are my God' (14). He trusts that all his times are in God's hands (15). He prays for the covenant blessings of Numbers 6:24-26 (echoed in v. 16 'Let your face shine...').

David affirms his glad and confident faith again in verses 19-20. He believes God has an abundance of good things stored up for those who fear him. He trust that there is protection to be found and safety from the 'accusing tongues' of the false witnesses who seek to bring him down.

And so he praises the covenant God for the wonders of His covenant love (21,22) and exhorts his people to do the same (23, 24).

Jesus speaks verse 5 on the cross (Luke 23:46). The first martyr, Stephen, echoes that sentiment (Acts 7:59). Peter exhorts Christian people likewise to entrust ourselves to our faithful Creator (1 Pet. 4:19) just as Jesus did (1 Pet. 2:23).

And so we join in as Jesus tells David's story, which becomes His own story in fulfilment, in verses 1-22. And then we heed our King's exhortation (23, 24) that we too should do as He has done, to love the covenant God the Father, to trust His covenant love for us in Christ our King, and therefore, in Christ, to be strong and take heart as we pray and wait and hope in Him.

Psalm 32

[Vol. 1: 100, 107, 109-114, 185, 188]

Here David declares a blessing (1, 2), tells his story (3-5) and exhorts the faithful as to how we should respond (6-11).

The blessing (1, 2) echoes the opening of Psalm 1 and the close of Psalm 2 (1:1; 2:12). There the blessing is on the one who loves God and His Law (Ps. 1) and the one who submits to God's King (Ps. 2). Here the blessing is on the man who is forgiven his sin. Using three different words for sin (NIV 'transgressions', 'sins', 'sin') and three ways of expressing forgiveness (NIV 'forgiven', 'covered', not 'counted') the richness of forgiveness for the full spectrum of sin is declared. The sting is in verse 2b – 'in whose spirit is no deceit'. Here is the rub: forgiveness comes only after open confession.

This sets us up to hear David's story, in two parts. First (3, 4) what happens when David seeks to cover up his own sin. The result is bodily and mental misery. But then (5) he stops the cover up, confesses his sins – and is immediately and wonderfully forgiven. Because David does not seek to cover up his own sins, the covenant God covers them in forgiveness.

The exhortation (v. 6 'Therefore…') is addressed to 'all the faithful' (lit. 'every *chasîd*', every recipient of God's *chesed*). They too are to do what David has done. In this context, to 'pray' (6) means openly to confess sins. This will lead to three blessings. The first (6b, 7) is safety in God's judgement; the 'rising of the mighty waters' uses terrifying flood imagery to speak of God's judgement. The one whose sins are confessed and forgiven may be assured of a 'hiding-place' in that day, both the intermediate days of partial judgement in this life and the terrible final day of reckoning.

The second blessing is given in verses 8, 9. David speaks with the voice of a prophet as God's spokesman: 'I, the King, as the representative of the covenant God, will instruct you…'. The promise comes with the exhortation not to be stubborn (9), which is the same spirit as the one who will not confess their sin earlier in the psalm.

The final blessing (10) is the assurance of God's covenant love surrounding the one who trusts in him.

Our response (11) should be – as sinners who have confessed our sins – great joy in the covenant God.

In Romans 4:6-8 Paul quotes from this psalm and teaches that David is declaring the blessedness of those 'to whom God credits righteousness apart from works' because of having the righteousness of Jesus Christ imputed to them. Echoing verse 5, 1 John 1:9 promises the same.

When Jesus sings this psalm He too declares this blessedness. Jesus says to us, take heed of David's testimony and believe David's words of blessing and exhortation. They come to us with Jesus Christ's authority, as the one who has won that blessing for us. As we join in the psalm we too affirm that we believe the blessing, will confess our sins, and trust the promises with great joy.

Psalm 33

[Vol. 1: 149, 232-233]

Very unusually for Book 1, there is no superscription. Some old manuscripts attach Psalm 33 to Psalm 32 as one long psalm. The major Greek translation adds 'of David'. We cannot be sure. It doesn't matter for, whether David or another, the voice that speaks it is an authorised, Spirit-inspired voice.

The psalm begins with an emphatic exhortation to wholehearted praise (1-3); it ends with our commitment to wait, hope, rejoice, and trust (20-22). In between (4-19) are the reasons to praise and to hope. These focus on the word of the LORD (4-9) and therefore the plans of the LORD (10-12) and the eyes of the LORD (13-19).

The word of the covenant God is described in its character (4, 5) and its creative power (6-9). Its character is the same as that of the God who speaks it – righteousness, faithfulness, justice, and unfailing love, all of them covenant words. What God has promised in His covenant, He will most surely do.

This is seen in the creation made when God spoke His word (6-9, cf. Gen. 1). The emphasis lies on its firmness (9b): in His unfailing love, God has made a world in which the waters of chaos are held at bay (7), evil is restrained, there is a habitable world in which we may know where we stand, both morally and physically. Moral order in creation comes from the powerful word of the morally loving and faithful God.

This Creator has not left the world to carry on without Him. On the contrary (10-12), He has 'plans' and 'purposes' which He is working out in sovereign love. All other purposes – the rebellious autonomous plotting of the nations in Psalm 2:1-3 – will be frustrated. But God's plans of covenant love will be fulfilled. So, whereas the rebellious nations will be thwarted, the nation or people whom He has chosen will be blessed (12).

Verses 13-19 focus on what God *sees* (v. 13 'looks down... sees...' v. 14 'watches...' v. 15 'considers...' v. 18 'the eyes of the LORD...'). Although He does not immediately act (and therefore His people have to wait), He always sees. With echoes of the tower of Babel (Gen. 11:1-9), God looks down and sees proud human plans. But He watches. Humans think we can do what we want by human strength (16, 17), but the covenant God's loving eyes are watching to rescue from death all those who fear Him and hope in His unfailing covenant love (18, 19).

God's promises are as firm as God's world. Old Covenant believers, like Simeon and Anna (Luke 2:25-38), could 'wait in hope' trusting in God's unfailing covenant

love (20-22) knowing that one day all those promises would
be fulfilled. And they were, when Jesus came, and all the
promises of God are 'Yes' in Him (2 Cor. 1:20). As the
Incarnate Word of God, He brought the saving power of
God into this world. When He returns, that rescue will
be completed. We may wait, hope, rejoice and trust in His
unfailing love with great confidence.

Psalm 34
[Vol. 1: 109, 127, 227]

Psalm 34 is an acrostic, as is Psalm 37.

To pray this psalm we need to grasp that in it one afflicted man exhorts other afflicted people to praise the covenant God because in his rescue lies the assurance of their
rescue.

David the anointed (1 Sam. 16) but rejected and hunted
king sings after his surprising rescue from Achish, the
Philistine King of Gath (here called by the title 'Abimelech',
lit. 'my father is king') as recorded in 1 Samuel 21:10-15.
He sings his personal praise (1, 2a) and gives his personal
testimony (4, 6).

The agenda for the psalm is set in verses 1-3: I am going
to praise the covenant God for what he has done for me;
now I want you too to join me in this praise, because you,
like me, will find the rescue only he can give. When David
exhorts 'the afflicted' (2) he uses the plural of the same
word he uses to describe himself in verse 6 'poor man'. One
needy man exhorts other needy people to come to the same
God for rescue.

Verses 4-7 alternate the king's experience (4, 6) with
what will be true for all who follow him and trust in the

same covenant God (5, 7). What I found to be true in my needy human experience you too will find to be true if you too look to him.

Verses 8-14 are full of exhortations: 'Taste... see... Fear... Come... listen... keep... Turn... do... seek... pursue...'. The two key words are 'good' and 'fear'. The LORD's guardian angel (Heb. 1:14) protects 'those who *fear* him' (7). '*Fear* the LORD,' says the king, 'for those who *fear* him lack nothing' (9). 'I will teach you the *fear* of the LORD' (ESV) (11). And the fear of the LORD means a changed life. Which is where 'good' comes in. The covenant God is '*good*' and you can taste His goodness (1 Pet. 2:3) (8); therefore those who seek Him 'lack no *good* thing' (10). If you want to see '*good* days' (v. 12, that is, to have your desires met) then you must 'turn from evil and do *good*' (14).

This bracing moral dimension[14] continues in verses 15-22, where the key word is 'righteous' (vv. 15, 17, 19, 21). This means those who seek the covenant God, come to Him for refuge, trust Him, and have their hearts shaped by His goodness into a changed life. Those who do 'evil' (another repeated word in the psalm, see vv. 13, 14, 16, 21 and also v. 19 'troubles' – lit. 'evils') will be condemned. But 'the righteous', although they may have many troubles and be sometimes crushed in spirit and broken-hearted (17, 18, 19), they may know that the covenant God is close to them in their troubles and will in the end rescue them from them all.

Jesus Christ the King, the great 'pioneer' of our faith (Heb. 12:2) has gone before us through deeper troubles than David; he felt his heart broken and his spirit crushed. But in it all He feared and loved God His Father and consistently

---

14. Echoed in 1 Peter 3:10-12, which quotes Psalm 34:12-16.

went about doing good (Acts 10:38). Jesus was not alone, for
the Father was close to Him (John 16:32), heard His prayers
(John 11:42,43) and rescued Him by bodily resurrection, so
that none of His bones were broken (v. 20, cf. John 19:36). As
we sing this psalm with Jesus, He exhorts us to walk in His
footsteps of trust, of righteousness of life, and of glad praise
for the good covenant Father who will most certainly rescue
us in the end. 'Just as we share abundantly in the sufferings
of Christ, so also our comfort abounds in Christ' (2 Cor. 1:5)

Psalm 35

[Vol. 1: 106-107, 133-134]

In Psalm 35 there is one singer, David, and two groups
around him. The most prominent group is those who seek
his life (4), they want to trap and destroy him (7), they bear
false witness against him (11), they repay him evil for good
(12) and are his enemies without any justifiable reason (19).
But there is an alternative; in verse 27 we meet 'those who
delight in (his) vindication'; these are 'the great assembly'
(or congregation, church) (18). You and I are not David; our
choice is to which of these two groups we will belong. Will
we be – as Augustine put it – those who mock our King or
those who praise with our King?

There is a tremendous and intense battle raging around
the king. Battle language is prominent, especially in verses 1-3. The king does not seek revenge, although his opponents deserve it. David prays for justice to be done[15]. He prays
for 'the angel of the LORD' (5, 6) to wage war on his behalf
(as in Ps. 34:7). Like hunters, they want to trap him in 'the

---

15. See vol. 1 chapter 8.

pit', which means death (cf. 30:10). As in Psalm 34, the King is one of 'the poor' or 'the afflicted' (35:10; 34:2, 6). Indeed, He is one who identifies closely with those in need; weeping with those who weep (Rom. 12:15), in verse 13 He 'humbled' Himself (lit. 'made himself poor/afflicted'). Anticipating a later and greater King, He made Himself poor in order to make others rich (2 Cor. 8:9). But He Himself is treated with utterly unjust hatred and malice. They hate Him 'without cause' (quoted in John 15:25 of Jesus).

As we sing this song with Jesus our King we enter into the depths of His innocent sufferings; we feel the injustice of the way He was treated; we repent that by nature we too would be among the mockers; we rejoice in His vindication (27) and are glad that we belong by grace to the 'great assembly' in which He gives the Father thanks for His rescue. Indeed, a very similar psalm is quoted by Paul of what happens when the gospel of Jesus is preached and believed all over the world (Rom. 15:9, quoting Ps. 18:49). Jesus leads all who belong to His church, His assembly, His choir, in praise to the Father.

But we must go one stage further. Although we are not the King, something of the overflow of the King's experience must necessarily be ours as we follow Him. Those who maliciously mocked and gnashed their teeth at Jesus (echoing v. 16) did the same to His first martyr Stephen (cf. Acts 7:54); we should not be surprised if they do the same to us.[16]

---

16. The Hebrew word 'nephesh' is prominent in this psalm; in verse 25 'what we wanted' uses the verb with the same root, for 'my soul' means 'myself in the aspect of my desires'. Although 'my soul' is disguised in some modern translations, it seems more frequent here. The 'desire' (soul) of the King triumphs over the desires of his enemies.

Psalm 36

Here we have a short, simple, and profound psalm. David begins with a meditation about 'the wicked' (1-4). He considers, and teaches us, about their 'eyes' which are so focused on self as to be blind to their faults (1b, 2). About their words which – coming from self-deceived eyes are inevitably deceitful (3a). About their actions which are neither wise (since they have no proper knowledge of themselves) nor good (3b), and about their hearts. Verse 4 demonstrates that their wrongdoing is not a few isolated mistakes but rather the set purpose of the committed will and premeditated heart. It is a devastating analysis and one that should drive us to our knees in confession. For Paul quotes from verse 1 in Romans 3:18 as part of his demonstration that each and every human being is by nature guilty before God.

But then our King moves our focus from human wickedness to divine perfection. The rest of the psalm celebrates the LORD's covenant love ('your love' 5; 'your unfailing love' 7; 'your love' 10) which is synonymous with his 'faithfulness' (5b), 'righteousness' (6a, 10b), and 'justice' (6b). In verses 5-9 he speaks in adoration to this covenant God. He rejoices that, because this God is the Creator, His goodness infuses the whole created order, from the highest of heights to the deepest of depths (5, 6); He – and He alone – is the fountain of all life, all delight, all safety, for any creature anywhere, both human beings and animals. The river of life that will be at the heart of the New Creation is the only source of life (cf. Rev. 21:6).

Verses 10-12 give the petition of the psalm. The king puts together the dreadful all-pervasiveness of wickedness with the wonderful ever-present glory of divine covenant love. We live in a world with wickedness everywhere and the covenant love of the Creator everywhere. So how should we pray? That the covenant love and righteousness of God will be actively and intentionally directed ('continue...') towards all who know God and are upright in heart (10), protecting them from the movements ('foot') and actions ('hand') of the wicked (11) who will most certainly not endure (12).

This psalm must have been both a sobering word to Jesus, as He sang verses 1-4 and remembered the world in which He lived, but also a glorious assurance to Him that the unfailing covenant love of His Father was ever-present (5-9). No doubt He too prayed verses 10-12 with a deep sense of how much He needed His Father's loving protection. Now He leads us in this same psalm. We shrink in horror from the wickedness from which Jesus is rescuing us, especially that wickedness in our own hearts. We celebrate with Jesus the ever-present unfailing love of the Father known to us in Jesus. We pray with Jesus for protection from evil, and most especially for protection from the evil that invades and threatens to capture our own hearts.

Psalm 37

[Vol. 1: 100, 108, 187, 188]

In this psalm we hear one voice teaching us – with the themes interwoven – about two ways, two times, and two responses. The voice is David's, the inspired teacher, speaking as a prophet, by the Spirit of Christ, to his people. Ultimately we hear the voice of Christ our Wisdom (1 Cor. 1:30), whose wisdom is the wisdom of the cross (as in 1 Cor. 1:1-2:5).

The two ways to live are – in brief – that of 'the wicked' and 'the righteous'. These are described in terms of their behavior, their interaction, and their success. The wicked, in their behaviour, are grabbers, always out for self; the righteous are givers (21, 26). The wicked are unjust; the righteous love justice. But the main focus is on their interaction. For the wicked actively hate and persecute the righteous (e.g. 12-15, 32). And – by and large – they succeed in what they do (e.g. 35).

The two times are the present and the imminent future. In the present the wicked succeed and the righteous are oppressed. Very soon – and, although it may seem a long wait, it is not long in God's eyes (2 'soon'; 10 'a little while') – the wicked will be cut off from the promised land and the righteous will inherit the land. In an echo of Psalm 2, the covenant God 'laughs at the wicked' (13). The covenant blessings on the righteous will be poured out; the covenant curses on the wicked will take effect. Language of 'inheritance' and 'the land' (the promised land) is frequent (3, 9, 11, 18, 22, 27, 29, 34). There is 'a future' for the 'blameless' (i.e. believers with integrity), but 'no future for the wicked' (37, 38). In the end, the promised land is fulfilled in the new heavens and new earth, for the 'meek' (i.e. afflicted, poor, knowing their need) will inherit the earth (v. 11, Matt. 5:5)[17].

All this leads to the purpose of this teaching psalm, which is to warn the people of God against one attitude and inculcate in us another. Verses 1-11 lead with this purpose and spell out these two responses. The very natural but wrong response to unfair persecution is to get angry. Three

---

17. See vol. 1, chapter 13.

times the teacher tells us not to 'fret' (1, 7, 8, i.e. get angry), once to refrain from 'anger' and 'wrath' (8). The reason is that meeting evil with evil is a surrender to evil (8b). Instead we are to trust in the covenant God (3, 5), to focus our hope on the LORD (34), take delight in Him (4), be still and quiet in our hearts before Him (v. 7, the opposite of anger) and entrust ourselves to the one who judges justly, which is just what Jesus our Wisdom Teacher did when treated with terrible unfairness (1 Pet. 2:23). The wisdom David teaches here is ultimately the wisdom of the cross, that to suffer injustice entrusting ourselves to the covenant God in whom we delight is to overcome evil with good. As we pray this psalm we commit ourselves to hearing and heeding the wise voice of Christ our teacher who has lived this way before us.

Psalm 38

There is a puzzle in this psalm, the resolution of which goes to the heart of the universe. It is the song of a man who appears, at the same time, to be both guilty and innocent!

It begins however (1-12) with a straightforward, if widely neglected truth: all suffering is the result of sin. David laments deeply the misery of his suffering: it is deeply invasive (v. 3, it goes from his 'body', lit. 'flesh', right into his 'bones'), overwhelmingly heavy (4), disgusting (5), draining of inward joy (6), all-consuming in its desperate pain (7), unsettling in the inward turmoil it causes (8, 'anguish' is literally 'tumult'), draining of all hope (9,10, longings and sighing with no satisfaction, the 'eyes' as symbols of desire and hope), lonely (11) and frightening (12). He knows it is the result of his 'sin' (3), 'guilt' (4), 'sinful folly' (5), and 'iniquity' (18); he understands that this suffering is the expression of the 'anger', 'wrath' (1, 3), 'arrows', and heavy 'hand' (2) of the covenant God. Echoing Psalm 32:3,4, David is – in the language of the Book of Common Prayer – 'grieved and wearied by the burden of his sins'. The first thing this psalm does, as we sing it, is to help us reconnect sin and suffering, to understand that the sin which brought death into the world (Rom. 5:12) also brought the shadow of death in every experience of suffering and sadness. Suffering is sin made visible.

But then the puzzle: this David is not simply you or me, in at least two ways. He has enemies (12) in a way that will not always fit with our experience (though sometimes it may). And – and this is the really significant fact – he is at the same time guilty and innocent! As we read verses 13-20 we see a man who refuses to hit back and defend himself, but entrusts himself to the God who judges justly (13-16), and claims that his enemies have no valid reason for their hatred (17-20), since he himself acts with 'good' and 'seek(s) only to do what is good' (20).

So what can be happening here? The answer – ultimately – is a foreshadowing of the sufferings of great David's greater Son. Jesus felt every facet of the misery caused by sins, though not His own. From the start of His public ministry he was numbered with the transgressors (Matt. 3:13-17); the shadow of the punishment for His people's sins fell upon Him. Verses 1-12 open for us a window supremely onto His sufferings, before they in some ways express ours.

But then verses 13-20 open up for us the prayer of the Son of God as He cries out to the Father for rescue from bearing the burden of sins. Silent before Pontius Pilate (Matt. 27:14, cf. vv. 13, 14) he cries out to the Father for vindication. Verses 21 and 22 are a final prayer of the sinless Son of God, a prayer that the Father heard and answered at the Resurrection. As we are grieved and wearied by the burden of our sufferings, we are helped by this psalm to grasp deeply that this burden is the overflow of the weight of our sin. And we take heart, as we pray this psalm, that God the Father heard the cry of His Son as the Son suffers for His sinful people. Because He has done this, David before Him could be hopeful of rescue, and we after Him may know great assurance that we will not in the end be forsaken (21), but our God will come 'quickly' to save us (22).

Psalm 39

This is a most unusual psalm, perhaps arising out of the awareness of old age or impending death. The key may be to notice that the Hebrew word *hebel* appears three times. More than half the occurrences of this word in the Old Testament are in Ecclesiastes, where it is usually translated 'vanity'. In this psalm it appears in verse 5 ('but a breath'), verse 6 ('in vain' i.e. in emptiness, pointlessness), and verse 11 ('but a breath'). The word conveys the futility or frustration (cf. Rom. 8:20) experienced in a world under God's righteous curse upon sinners, a world overshadowed by death.

The inner workings of David's heart that generated this psalm are told in verses 1-3. David is 'in the presence of the wicked' (1) and it appears that their wickedness makes him naturally angry. (The expression 'my heart grew hot' is used in Deuteronomy 19:6 of someone whose close relative has been killed.) David seeks to heed his own admonition not to fret by remaining silent (Ps. 37:1-8; cf. James 1:26). In the end he must vocalise his troubled meditation; he does so, not angrily and sinfully to the wicked, but in prayer to God.

In verses 4-6 he asks for a fresh apprehension of the transitoriness of his own – and all – human life, how it is shadowed by emptiness and pointlessness. Perhaps especially he has the wicked in mind, whose successes have troubled him so much. He wants to grasp deeply that their rushing around is all in vain (6). They and he together are just 'a breath' in this age.

Verse 7 is the centre and heart of the psalm. I naturally seek things in this life; but when I grasp that it is empty, I seek only the living God. In verses 8-11 David considers, no longer the sin of the wicked, but his own sin. He considers that his sufferings come because he is a sinner in a world under God's righteous curse. That's why we are all 'but a breath' (11).

In verse 12 David weeps and cries because he grasps more deeply that this world is not his home. Like the patriarchs, he was one passing through the 'land' of this world, as one with no rights ('a foreigner', 'a stranger', cf. Heb. 11:9-13). He prays, sadly, in verse 13, that God will look away from him with His face of discipline (cf. Job 7:19) so that he may have some enjoyment in life yet. For he knows he must depart soon and be no more on this earth.

Jesus prayed this psalm as a fully human being troubled by wickedness, struggling against the temptation to lash out at them (1-3), feeling the breath-like brevity and frustration of living as one identified with sinners in a world under the curse, as one hoping in and seeking only God (7) and not setting his delight on the things of this age (11). We too may pray all these things in Him (cf. 1 Pet. 2:11).

Psalm 40

[Vol. 1: 47-48, 61, 187, 207]

This psalm opens up when we look carefully for the relationship between the one king who prays it and the great assembly (= 'congregation' or 'church') he leads. Most of the psalm is intensely singular ('I', 'me', 'my'...). But – and this is the critical point to note – this one man is deeply significant for many: verse 3 '...*our* God. *Many* will see... put *their* trust in him; verse 5 '*Many*... wonders... too *many* to declare' – because these wonders are poured out on many people; verses 9, 10 '..in *the great assembly*... *the great assembly*'; verse 16 '*all* who seek you... *those* who long...' What happens to this one man has a massive impact on his many people.

In verses 1-3 the king tells his story of waiting, of being lifted out of the 'pit' of destruction, of singing a new song of praise. All this happens as 'many' watch and learn from what happens to him that the God who rescued him is the one in whom they too can 'put their trust'.

In verses 4-5 the king declares a blessing on all who will follow him by trusting the covenant God. The word 'wonders' is often used of the redemption at the Exodus. In the same way there are many 'Exodus redemptions', one for each man and woman who shares the trust of the king.

When we come to verses 6-8, however, the king is acting alone. He understands that what God wants is not in the end sacrifices but the perfect obedient self-offering that sacrifices signify. He comes – as is written in the scroll of the scriptures (from Gen. 3:15 onwards) – willingly to do the will of God in offering Himself as the sacrifice for His people's sins. Hebrews 10:5-10 explicitly teach us that these words are finally spoken, and fulfilled, not by David but by Jesus as He goes obediently to the cross. Truly the King will offer Himself for the many.

In verses 9-10 the scene changes from the perfect, but lonely, self-offering of the king to his victorious proclamation in 'the great assembly' of his church. God the Father has kept all His covenant promises by saving the King and, with Him, all His people. The words 'righteousness', 'faithfulness', 'saving help' (= salvation), and 'love' are all covenant words.

Verses 11-17 repeat the same grand sequence so that we feel it more deeply. The King prays urgently that He will be full of the 'love and faithfulness' (11) of God (aka 'grace and truth', cf. John 1:14) and be rescued from the penalty for 'my sins' (12) – the sins that were David's in reality, but Christ's only by imputation, as He 'became sin' for us (2 Cor. 5:21). The result of the King's salvation is (v. 16) that 'all who seek' God will rejoice.

As we sing this psalm with Jesus our King we learn of His sufferings, His perfect self-offering on the cross, and His being saved by the Father in the resurrection. And we sign up for being part of that 'great assembly' in which we hear His proclamation of the grace and truth of the covenant God incarnated in Him. Verse 16 sums up our response – a joyful declaration that the covenant God is very great!

Psalm 41
[Vol. 1: 206]

Verse 13 is the conclusion, not just to Psalm 41, but to all of Book I. The 'Amen and Amen' show that the congregation of God's people were expected, not simply to listen to the

Psalms, but to join in and – as it were – add their signatures to them, to affirm all that is asked of us as we join in, not simply this psalm, but all of Psalms 1-41.

The contrast running through this psalm is life and death. All the negative words and phrases express the shadow of death: verse 1 'the weak…times of trouble'; verse 3 'sick-bed…bed of illness'; verse 5 'When will he die and his name perish?'; verse 8 'a vile disease…he will never get up…'. By contrast, life is indicated in several ways: verse 2 'preserves' (lit. 'keeps him alive'); verse 3 'sustains… restores'; verse 4 'heal me'; verse 10 'raise me up'; verse 12 'you uphold me and set me in your presence…'

First (1-3) the king affirms a foundational truth: the covenant God will give life to the one who cares for the weak (v. 1; cf. Matt. 5:7), that is, the man who acts as God does, with covenant care. In the Hebrew, this blessing is given to 'the man' (singular) who does these things. This man will have times of trouble; he will become weak and sick; but in the end his life will be preserved. God who cares for the poor and needy man who himself cares for the poor and needy one; this connection of salvation and godliness is unbreakable.

Verses 4-9 convey, in a frightening atmosphere, the life-threatening experience of this righteous man. He bears the penalty of sins (4), which are his – in David's case, in actuality, in Jesus's case, by imputation. His enemies seek his life. And the particular horror of their hostility is the deceit and hypocrisy. They pretend to be his friends (6): they come to see him and 'speak falsely' – i.e. saying kind things to him. But in reality they want the righteous king dead. The sharpest pain of this enmity is the betrayal by a 'close friend' (a 'man of peace') who shares fellowship

meals with the king. Perhaps for David this was his
trusted counsellor Ahitophel, who betrayed him in Absalom's rebellion (2 Sam. 15:12, 31). Finally, this was Judas
Iscariot (John 13:18, quoting part of v. 9; cf. Mark 14:18;
Luke 22:21; Acts 1:16).

In verses 10-12 the king prays again that his life will be
raised up so that the king's enemies do not finally triumph
and justice is done in the universe. The king trusts that the
blessing he has pronounced in verses 1-3 is true; he will be
set in God's presence for ever (12).

King Jesus sings this psalm, which concludes Book I,
and brings us right back to core truths: the King is mortally
opposed and will suffer deeply; but in the end He will be
given life and His enemies will not triumph. All this is true
– but only for the Psalm 2 king who is also the Psalm 1
man of godliness (the one who cares for the weak). What
David affirmed was finally shown to be true of Jesus Christ,
the man of Psalm 1 and the King of Psalm 2.

As we sing this song with our King, verse 13 encourages
us to 'add our signatures' to the praise of the covenant God,
who does keep all His promises to His anointed King –
and will therefore keep all His promises of eternal life to
us, in Christ. For we too live in the shadow of death and
cry to Him for preservation from death and every shadow
of death.

BOOK 2

Introduction to Book 2

Book 2 ends (72:20) with 'This concludes the prayers of David son of Jesse'. This marks Books 1 and 2 as the original 'of David' collection, although a number of other 'of David' psalms have now been inserted into the later books.

Book 2 begins, however, with a group of 'sons of Korah' psalms (42/3-49, from the Korahite psalm-writing group) and one 'of Asaph' (50). With these we do not make the 'David-king-Jesus Christ' connection; the authors were Spirit-inspired people, but not the Spirit-inspired king. This will change the way we read them from the way we have read Book 1.

The structure of Psalms 42-50 is as follows. The group begins with two psalms of distress, by an individual (42/3) and the whole people (44). The next four (45-48) celebrate the wonder of the covenant God and His King in Zion. Finally, in Psalms 49 and 50 there are two appeals and challenges, to the people of God and the world.

After this, they are all headed 'of David' except for 71 (anonymous) and 72 ('of Solomon').

One feature of Book 2 (and some others) is a tendency to use the general noun 'God' (Hebrew *Elohim*) more often than the particular covenant name 'the LORD' (Hebrew *YHWH*) – or more than in other parts of the Psalter. We do not know why this is so. One thoughtful suggestion[1] is that there is a focus on reaching out to speak to 'the nations' (which feature a little more in this part of the Psalter) and perhaps the general word 'God' is more accessible to them.

---

1. O. Palmer Robertson, *The flow of the Psalms*, pp. 95-102.

Psalms 42 and 43

[Vol. 1: 150]

These are often taken together. Psalm 43 has no super-scription; this may suggest it is to be read closely with Psalm 42. The refrain of 42:5 and 42:11 is repeated verbatim in 43:5. And 42:9b is the same as 43:2b. While there is nothing to stop us praying them separately, I will take them together.

Some of the features to watch for are two voices (fear and faith), two places (Jerusalem and far away by Mt. Hermon), two groups (the assembly of God's people and the enemies), and the different effects of water (42:1 refreshment; 42:3 tears; 42:7 chaotic destruction).

Perhaps the most prominent feature is the repeated refrain (42:5, 11; 43:5) in which this believer speaks to himself. On the one hand is the voice of experience, his low spirits ('downcast') and inner turmoil ('disturbed'). On the other, this believer can preach to himself with the voice of faith, to exhort himself to set his hope in God his Saviour. This same voice of faith is heard in 42:8, affirming the 'song' of the steadfast covenant love of God for him. This inner dialogue gives a window into the interior struggles of the life of faith, and supremely the life of faith as lived by Jesus the pre-eminent believer.

But although the psalm keeps coming back to this personal and inward dialogue, it is far from just an individual psalm. For the struggles of this believer are caused by the tension between two places and therefore two groups of people. He is far away from 'the house of God' in Jerusalem where the 'festive throng' of God's people gather (42:4), he is far away by the headwaters of the River Jordan in the Hermon mountain range (42:6), and he longs to return to 'your holy mountain' (43:3) in Jerusalem, the place of God's anointed king (Ps. 2:6). And he is surrounded by mocking people (42:3), 'the enemy' (42:9; 43:2), 'my foes' (42:10), 'an unfaithful nation' who are 'deceitful and wicked' (43:1).

His troubles are social (mocked by unbelievers, 42:3), experiential (suffering disasters, 42:7, and pain in his bones, 42:10), and judicial (longing for vindication, 43:1). Jesus Christ knew all these, and they will be the common experience of His followers, who will be at the same time 'in Christ' (the fulfilment of 'your holy mountain') and 'in the world', surrounded by skeptical people and experiencing all these dimensions of suffering.

Just as the Lord Jesus will have prayed this psalm and, by it, preached faith to Himself, so we – as we experience the same tensions – may do the same in Him.

Psalm 44

[Vol. 1: 37]

Where psalm 42/43 is an individual lament, Psalm 44 is corporate. And yet in it we hear also the voice of the individual psalmist. This alternation between singular (4a, 6, 15, 16) and plural (1-3, 5, 7-14, 17-26) is very significant. The experience of the whole people of God is focused on this representative member, who speaks rather as a leader of the believing remnant of Israel. Like all the psalmists, he does so by the Spirit of the Christ to come.

Verses 1-8 express his – and their – trust (6, 7). Specifically, he trusts the God who made the covenant with Abraham that the promised land (2, 3) will be the inheritance of Abraham's 'seed' (singular as representative of corporate whole, Gal. 3:16, 29). The conflict throughout the psalm focuses on this land, that finds its fulfilment in the new heavens and new earth[1].

Verses 9-16 express the agony of rejection, experienced both corporately (e.g. 'rejected and humbled *us*' v. 9a) and in the disgrace of this one representative believer (15, 16).

The surprise in verses 17-22 is that, by contrast with many other psalms that admit Israel's sin (e.g. 106), this rejection has fallen also on the believing remnant of Israel who have not been false to the covenant and yet 'for (God's) sake… face death all day long' and 'are considered as sheep to be slaughtered' (22). The language of suffering is the intense language of the abattoir; and this suffering is undeserved!

Verses 23-26 conclude with an urgent appeal for God – in the covenant language of Numbers 10:35 – to 'Rise up' and rescue His people.

In the context of strong assurance for the people of Christ, who need this assurance because they share in the sufferings of Christ (Rom. 8:17), Romans 8:36 quotes verse 22 of this psalm. Jesus leads His believing people in singing this psalm. For in it we express our trust that the new heavens and new earth, promised by covenant to Abraham's 'seed'

---

1. See vol. 1, chapter 13.

(e.g. Rom. 4:13) will be our inheritance in Christ. With Him we lament His, and our, present sufferings in all the intensity experienced by the persecuted church. And with Him we cry with confidence for final rescue.

Psalm 45
[Vol. 1: 102]

The king in David's line has not been explicitly present in Psalms 42-44. He reappears here in a unique psalm, sung by one of the 'sons of Korah' – as a kind of Old Testament Poet Laureate – for the wedding of a king. This 'poet' is stirred (by the Spirit of Christ) as he contemplates the nobility of his theme (1). For the bridegroom-king he addresses in verses 1-9 is a truly wonderful man, excelling by far the reality of King David and all his heirs down Old Testament history.

This bridegroom-king is 'the most excellent (lit. doubly beautiful) of men' (2a). The singer celebrates the beauty of the king's lips (2) for he speaks as never man spoke (John 7:46). The 'poet' sings the beauty of his war (3-5), for he is a warrior-bridegroom, who will overcome evil with good and win the victory for 'truth, humility, and justice' (how different from human wars!). In the end, he will win this victory when he rides in majesty, in lowly pomp, to die on the cross[2]. He lauds the beauty of his throne and his court (6-9), which will bring justice to rule for ever. In this king, the kingdom of God merges with the kingdom of David, just as David's 'son' is finally 'Son of God' and indeed even 'God the Son'. Hebrews 1:8, 9 quotes verses 6, 7 of

---

2. The hymn 'Ride on, ride on, in majesty' was inspired by psalm 45.

the psalm in its demonstration of the divine greatness of Jesus. What a bridegroom! What a king! You could only sing this psalm amid the realities of Old Testament history if you believed that one day a very great King would come in David's line to be the divine bridegroom of the people of God.

In verses 10-12 our poet turns briefly to the bride, who appears for the first time. Surprisingly, she is not the main focus of this wedding celebration! He exhorts her, firmly and urgently, to leave behind her former allegiances and give all her loyalty and submissive love to her husband and king, who is enthralled by her wonderful loveliness. She may worry about the good things she is leaving behind, but she will not lose out (12), for the fabulously wealthy Tyrians, the legendary billionaires of the ancient East, will pour their wealth out upon her. Verses 13-15 celebrate the beauty of the bride and her bridesmaids in their procession to the king. This bride, we later learn, has been given a stupendous inward beauty through good deeds given to her by grace (Rev. 19:7,8).

In verses 16, 17, the poet turns again to the king; we know this from the return to masculine indicators in the Hebrew (for 'your... your... you... your... you'). In vivid blessing, this king is promised such a dynasty as will rule the world for ever. All this is fulfilled in Jesus Christ, the beautiful divine bridegroom of the people of God, who will govern the new creation with him (e.g. 1 Cor. 6:2).

As we join in this song for the wedding of Jesus our Bridegroom, our hearts are ravished by His loveliness, and especially the beauty of His victory at the cross (2-9); we hear the admonition to leave behind all the loyalties and allegiances of the world so that we may be presented to

Jesus 'as a pure virgin' with single-hearted worship and purity of life (10, 11, 2 Cor. 11:2); we marvel at the inward beauty that will be ours by grace; and we rejoice in the cosmic dynastic promise we will inherit with Him (16, 17).

Psalm 46

[Vol. 1: 150, 155, 190, 193]

In this psalm we exhort one another to cease our rebellion and to take refuge in Christ alone from the just judgements of God.

The psalm is divided by the refrain in verse 7 and at the end, verse 11. Verses 1-7 state a fact; verses 8-11 exhort to a response. The fact (1-7) is that there is one, and only one, safe place in a world under the judgement of God. There is an alternation between safety (1, 4 and 5, 7) and danger (2 and 3, 6). Danger comes – in familiar psalms imagery – from the chaotic flood waters that 'roar and foam' in terrifying threat to the moral stability of the world. The solid earth, and supremely the rock-solid mountains, signify the place of creation order, where you know where you stand. But we live in a world where this good order is threatened by waters of chaos. The concrete expression of these powers of chaos is rebellious kingdoms (v. 6, cf. Ps. 2:1-3 and Luke 21:25) and – in Israel's history – the enslaving power of the ancient Pharaoh of the Exodus. However these forces of chaos are not independent of the sovereign Creator God, the 'LORD Almighty' (the LORD of hosts, the God with unbeatable armies). When all these troubles come, it is because '*he* lifts his voice' (6b). Like the flood in Noah's day, the irruption of waters of chaos upon the world is the judgement of God.

In this world under judgement, there is one safe place. This is the place on earth where God may be known as 'refuge', 'the city of God, the holy place where the Most High dwells' (1, 4). This is where the covenant God ('the LORD'), the God of covenant history ('the God of Jacob') dwells. These covenant promises find their final 'Yes!' in Jesus Christ (2 Cor. 1:20). Christ is the safe 'place' in a world under judgement. In this 'place' the waters of chaos are transformed into life-giving waters of the river of life (v. 4, cf. Rev. 22:1,2).

Verses 8-10 have plural imperatives to all who will heed them: 'Come...see...Be still...know...' We invite one another to see, with the eye of faith, the final destruction of all powers of rebellion, the climactic fulfilment of Psalm 2, the utter defeat of all evil powers in the universe (cf. Rev. 12:18). In response, we are to 'be still and know' that this God is the true God. 'Be still...' is not an invitation to quiet meditation, but rather to the silence of awestruck surrender.

As Jesus leads us in the singing of this corporate psalm, we tell one another that Jesus Christ Himself is the only safe place in a dangerous world under judgement. And we exhort one another to surrender our rebellious hearts to Him as we bow in awe before the assurance of His final victory. For this conquering Christ is the presence of the Almighty God 'with us'.

Psalm 47

[Vol. 1: 160, 162, 181]

This is an evangelistic psalm, in which 'the nations' (the rest of the world) are repeatedly exhorted to acclaim the ascended King. This king is 'Most High' (2), 'has ascended' (5) and 'is greatly exalted' (9). For this reason the church has traditionally, and rightly, seen these acclamations as finding their fulfilment in our praise of the ascended Christ (and therefore sung on Ascension Day). For Christ is the one in whom the kingdom of David merges with the kingdom of God, and in whose person all the fullness of the deity dwells bodily (Col. 1:19; 2:9).

The appeal comes right at the start (1): all nations are told to 'clap your hands' and 'shout' (in acclamation). We see exactly this in 2 Kings 11:12 where the people who acknowledged the rightful king clapped their hands and shouted, 'Long live the king!'. Every man and woman faces this choice: will they join the loyal applause, or remain silent in dumb rebellion?

The first reason is given in verses 2-5. They are to acclaim the ascended Christ because he loves the church. This 'great King over all the earth' (2) demonstrates His greatness by keeping His covenant promises to the people upon whom He has set His love (3, 4), 'Jacob' in Old Covenant language, fulfilled in the new covenant people of Christ, Jew and gentile. The 'inheritance' is fulfilled in the new heavens and new earth. As the people of King David's day shouted and sounded trumpets when the Ark of the Covenant came up to Jerusalem (v. 5, and see 2 Sam. 6:12,15), so the world is exhorted to praise the King who fulfils the covenant when He ascends to His kingly throne.

The emphatic appeal comes five times again in verses 6, 7, with five identical plural imperatives: 'Sing praises…!' Join in the applause with all your heart!

The second reason develops from the first and reaches its climax in verse 9. This people, whom he loves and to whom he gives the new heavens and new earth, is the fulfilment of 'Jacob' (4); but, more deeply, they are the fulfilment of the covenant with Abraham, that all nations will be blessed through him. We are to acclaim the ascended Jesus, not just because He loves the church, but because through the church He will gather the world. In the logic of Colossians 1:15-20, this great Head of the Church will reconcile to Himself the whole redeemed created order. All who share the faith of Abraham, be they Jew or gentile, will inherit the blessings given to Abraham's 'seed' the Lord Jesus Christ (Rom. 4:11,12; Gal. 3:7-9).

As we join Jesus in singing this psalm, we rejoice in the ascended Lord Jesus. But – and this is the challenging part – we commit ourselves to speaking the challenge of this psalm to outsiders, to invite and exhort them to join with us in the loyal applause for Jesus our great King over all the earth.

Psalm 48
[Vol. 1: 193]

In this psalm we delight in the security that we have by the covenant love of God in Christ, who is the fulfilment of all that Zion foreshadowed[3]. The psalm is emphatically focused on Zion, and bracketed (1, 14) by references to 'our God', which means the God to whom we, His people, belong by covenant.

Verses 1-3 celebrate the beauty of the city. This 'city of God' was celebrated in Psalm 46:4; its 'great king' was praised in Psalm 47:2; it is the 'holy mountain' on which the king

---

3. Vol. 1, chapter 13.

in David's line is enthroned (Ps. 2:6) and separation from which caused such heartache to the psalmist in Psalm 43:3. Because God the 'Great King' is in her, it is an impregnably high and 'beautiful' (2) city. The 'whole earth' rejoices in her (2) because she is the one place of safety in a dangerous world. 'Zaphon' (2) means 'North' and the 'mountain in the north' means, in the ancient near east, something like Mount Olympus meant to the Greeks and Romans, an impregnably high mountain from which God – or, for polytheists, the gods – rule the world. She is beautiful because she is unchangeably safe and shines with the presence of God.

Verses 4-8 develop the words 'citadels' and 'fortress' in verse 3. The focus now is on the majestic safety of this beautiful city. She is attacked (4), by the worldwide coalition of rebellious humanity we met in Psalm 2:1-3. But – in the faith-filled vision of the psalmist – the attack fails the moment the rebels see the city in her astounding majesty. She is 'secure for ever' (8).

In verses 9-11 we come – with the eyes of faith – to 'the temple', the heart of the city's beauty and security. Here is the focus of the covenant; here we meditate on the 'unfailing love' (*chesed*, covenant love), the 'righteousness' (God acting to do the right thing in rescuing His people), and the 'judgements' of God (His judicial decisions for His people and against their enemies). The joy of Mount Zion and the surrounding villages (lit. 'daughters') is rooted in steadfast covenant love.

In the vision of verses 1-11 we sing the beauty, the safety, and above all the covenant love that causes the beauty and the safety of the place where God dwells on earth. All of which finds its fulfilment when Emmanuel, 'God with us' walks the earth and all that Zion foreshadowed is fulfilled.

The psalm ends with an exhortation to one another to 'Walk about Zion...' to think hard about just how beautiful, how safe, and how full of covenant love she is (12-14). The great mistake was to think this applied to the outward form of Jerusalem. Jeremiah warned against that mistake (e.g. Jer. 7) and was proved right when the Babylonians destroyed the city. Jesus too warned against the same mistake (e.g. Mark 13:1, 2) and was proved right when the Romans sacked the city. No, this psalm was to be sung with the eyes of faith, trusting that one day the place where God dwelt on earth would fulfil and transcend the beauty, the safety and supremely the astonishing love praised in this psalm. In Christ that is so. The psalm invites us to 'walk about' Christ, to 'consider well' the beauty, the safety, and the love of God that is ours in Christ, and to take heart in the midst of a dangerous world.

Psalm 49

[Vol. 1: 151, 188]

Who speaks this psalm? To whom? Why? And how does it fit with the theme of these 'sons of Korah' psalms (42-49)?

Verses 1-4 tell us this is – at least at the start – an urgent appeal to all human beings. Here is the voice of wisdom, (cf. Prov. 8:1-11). The psalmist speaks, by the Spirit of Christ our Wisdom, with an urgent, universal message. In the 'meditation' of his heart there is the wise meditation of Psalm 1:2 and not the foolish plotting (lit. 'meditation') of Psalm 2:1. He will expound to us a 'proverb' or 'riddle', something not immediately obvious but that needs thought. He will expound it 'with the harp' – traditionally an instrument of joy (cf. Ps. 137:2, 3). This sober psalm has a joyful message! The psalm ends with another reference to 'understanding' (20), bookending the psalm with this theme.

Verses 5 and 6 unlock the question of why the psalmist sings. Notice the singular 'I'; one wise man speaks to all the world, to himself, and – especially – to the people of God. The issue is 'fear', fear prompted by being surrounded by 'wicked deceivers' who make his life a misery. This ties us in to the familiar theme of a leader of the people of God, and the people of God as a whole, surrounded by the wicked (e.g. Pss. 11,14). Verse 6 goes to the heart of why these people are wicked: they trust in 'their wealth'. They are successful, self-confident, arrogant, and oppressive to the people of God. Is it really better to be godly than rich and ungodly?

The voice of wisdom (ultimately Christ our Wisdom) gives us two subtly different answers to the question, 'Why need I not fear in these circumstances?' Each ends with a similar refrain (v. 12 and v. 20). The first (7-12) is that human life is so valuable, and so deeply in debt because of sin, that no humanly procured ransom will be sufficient to save us from death, which is the wages of sin. Left to ourselves we all die like animals. This is how it is with these self-confident wicked; we need not fear them, but should remember that one day, for all their pomp, and no matter how grand their tomb, they will rot in the grave just like a dead animal.

The second answer (13-20) contains the surprising good news. Although all of us by nature die like animals, some of us will not, by grace! The same theme of the helplessness of proud humanity continues in verses 13 and 14, with the deep irony that – continuing the animal language – they are like sheep, but with death, like our proverbial Grim

Reaper, as 'their shepherd'; what a contrast to the covenant
God, the Shepherd of the King and all His people (Ps. 23)!
But there is a 'morning' coming (14), when 'the upright will
prevail', no matter how oppressed they may be in this life;
and on that day 'God will redeem me from the realm of the
dead' and '*take* me to himself' (15, cf. Enoch, Gen. 5:24 and
Elisha, 2 Kings 2:3-5). This wise representative Israelite
knows he cannot redeem himself from the wages of sin, and
trusts the covenant God to redeem him from death.

And so, in verse 16, he addresses the whole people of
God: 'Do not be overawed…' (lit. 'do not fear', echoing
what he said of himself in v. 5). As we listen to Christ our
Wisdom expounding this proverbial understanding, we
hear Him teaching Himself, in His earthly life, not to be
cowed or seduced by 'the kingdoms of the world and their
glory' (Matt. 4:8); and we heed His encouragement to us,
accompanied by a joyful harp, not to be overawed by them
ourselves.

Psalm 50
[Vol.I:149]

The 'sons of Korah' group of psalms ends with 49. Before
we return to a large group of David psalms, there is this one
psalm 'of Asaph'. In it we hear the voice of God; the psalmist
speaks as a prophet, God's mouthpiece. Just as in Psalm 49
we heard, in its fulfilment, the voice of Christ our Wisdom,
so in Psalm 50 we hear the teaching voice of Christ our
Prophet summoning His people to covenant faithfulness.

Verses 1-6 declare a solemn summons to a covenant
assembly of the people of God (cf. Deut. 31:10-13). Names
for God are piled up, one upon another, for solemnity (v. 1a,

cf. Josh. 22:22). The whole earth (1) and the heavens (4) are
summoned as witnesses, to see the covenant God 'judge his
people', who 'gather' to him in a great congregation or church
(5). In language that combines the beauty of Mount Zion
(v. 2, echoing Ps. 48 and echoed sadly in Lam. 2:15) with the
awesome holiness of Mount Sinai (v. 3, echoing Exod. 19:16-
19), God 'shines forth' (2) with the searing, all-consuming
light of His holy covenant love. It is an awesome scene as
judgement begins with the people of God (1 Pet. 4:17).

And then God speaks two words. The first (7-15)
rebukes His people for acting, in formal religion, as though
they were doing something for God when they offered
sacrifices (which they were doing a great deal, v. 8 'ever
before me'!) before instructing them how to act (14,15).
No, says God, I do not need you (cf. Acts 17:25); but you
need me. All 'the world is mine' (v. 12, echoing Ps. 24:1).
You need to offer 'thank-offerings' and 'fulfil your vows'
as an expression of grateful dependence (14), and to pray
urgently (15a) as a vital acknowledgment of your need.
Then I promise 'I will deliver you' (15b).

The second word is an urgent warning to 'the wicked'
within Israel (16-21). To those who say they belong to the
covenant (16b) but actually break the covenant commandments (vv. 17-20, citing commandments 8, 7, and 9). When
I do not immediately speak and act in judgement ('I kept
silent') you think that means I don't really mind, that I am
'exactly like you', with flexible moral standards (v. 21a). But
judgement will come. I was 'silent' (21) but now I 'will not
be silent' (3).

Like Psalm 2, this psalm ends with a warning (22) and
a promise (23). Again 'thank-offerings' are the mark of true
religion (23, 14, cf. Rom. 1:21 'nor gave thanks...').

The believing Jew, Jesus of Nazareth, heard this summons, believed this promise and heeded this warning. God in heaven used this warning to keep Him from falling into sin, and this promise to guard His heart in intimate thankful dependence upon His Father. Now, by His Spirit, He speaks this promise and warning to us His people. When we join in this psalm we add our 'Amen' both the warning, committing ourselves to be warned by it; and we join with Jesus in thanksgiving, as Hebrews exhorts us: 'Through Jesus…let us continually offer to God a sacrifice of praise…' (Heb. 13:15). God makes the promises; Christ speaks them to us and we chorus the 'Amen' to the glory of God (2 Cor. 1:20).

Psalm 51

[Vol. 1: 61, 182]

Psalm 51 is the best-known psalm of penitence. But it comes with a big question: how do we pray it in Christ?

The original context is clear and terrible, signalled in the heading, and recorded for us in 2 Samuel 12:1-14. In Psalm 51:1-12 David prays deeply and intensely for forgiveness. He does so (v. 1) on the basis of the covenant 'mercy' and 'unfailing love' (*chesed*) that he already knows; that is to say, his confession is not an attempt to gain a relationship with God, but arises out of that gracious relationship. David admits that his sin is deep in its direction, being fundamentally against God who is right to condemn (4, partly quoted in Rom. 3:4), that it is deep in its origin (5), being the sinful nature he has inherited as a human being in Adam's line ('Original Sin'), and that it is deep in its nature, being rooted, not just in words, deeds, or even thoughts, but in the depths of his heart and needing an act of new creation to make within him a 'pure heart' (6-12); the verb 'create' (10) is a strong word used only of the direct action of God.

Significant for our praying of the psalm in Christ is that, in verses 13-19, David goes on to commit himself to speak to the people of God, to 'teach transgressors' God's ways, so that 'sinners will return to you' as he has done. He brings to God the acceptable sacrifice of 'a broken and contrite heart' (17) and knows that a congregation of such broken hearts will lead to a built-up church ('Zion' v. 18) in which sins are forgiven and the moral distinction between the church and the world (symbolized by the 'walls of Jerusalem') will be clear and right.

David therefore, as the pre-eminent Israelite and – here – the supremely horrible sinner, leads his people in repentance. He shows them how to repent deeply and well, assuring them of full forgiveness even for the very worst sin of the most prominent sinner (and therefore for the more mundane sins of his very ordinary people).

It is usual to go on to say that David only finds forgiveness because of Christ. This is true, but involves what seems like an arbitrary 'add on' to the psalm. Forgiveness in Christ does not arise out of the psalm when read like this. Is it possible, however, that Jesus Christ was so identified with His sinful people, as the one who was 'made sin for us' (2 Cor. 5:21) that, as He bore our sins in His own person on the cross, He – the pre-eminent Israelite and, by imputation, the supremely horrible sinner – could actually lead us in repentance, knowing and feeling the horrible burden of our sins in His own sinless heart? In some strange and terrifying way, Jesus had His sin (which was our sin) 'always before Him'; He knew the misery of a sin-laden conscience; He felt the depth of our depravity and cried with desperate urgency for a new heart, that in His vindication and resurrection might be the 'new creation' (2 Cor. 5:17) that gives us pure hearts in Him. I think it is. But, if I am right, the agony and misery of our sin must have impacted the heart of Jesus more deeply than most of us have ever considered. If this is so, we join our wonderful representative substitute Head in praying this psalm with a heart cry that comes from the Spirit of Jesus Himself.

A Note on Psalms 52-59

We come now to a collection of Psalms that are associated with the period when David had been anointed King (1 Sam. 16) but was hunted by Saul. Psalms 52, 54, 56, 57, and 59 have headings tying them to this distressing period. It may be that the other psalms also come from this time.

Psalm 52

[Vol. 1: 108-109]

Psalm 49 has warned us about those who 'trust in their wealth and boast of their great riches' (49:6). Psalm 50 rebukes those who 'use your mouth for evil and harness your tongue to deceit' (50:19). In Psalm 52 we meet just such a man, Doeg the Edomite, Saul's chief shepherd, who betrayed David to Saul. The terrible story is told in 1 Samuel 21:1-9 and 22:9-23.

In verses 1-7 the king speaks to this wicked opponent; 'you' means the enemy. We cannot be sure that this particular opponent ever heard these words. But, in future ages, others of us who are by nature enemies of the king have heard these words and taken warning from them. Then in verses 8 and 9, the king speaks to God in heaven; 'you' now means God.

The key to the psalm is the contrasts between the portrait of this enemy (1-7) and what the king says of himself (8,9). These focus first on desires and faith and then culminate in destiny. This enemy is called ironically 'you mighty hero' (1) because that is what he thinks himself to be. He 'boasts of' (= praises) 'evil' (1), the evil this enemy has succeeded in doing. His 'love' is for 'evil' and therefore he uses his tongue to do evil, by speaking twisted, deceitful, malicious, destructive words (2-4). Words are very powerful; all this man does is speak, and yet his words wreak havoc, as did Doeg's in 1 Samuel 22. He desires evil and he boasts of his evil deeds, because at heart he trusts in himself. But his destiny is to be brought down into eternal punishment, uprooted from the land of the living (5). Echoing God's laughter (Ps. 2:4), those who are righteous by faith will laugh at how foolish he has been (6). His terrible epitaph (7) focuses on the root of his error: he did not trust in God, but 'trusted in his great wealth…'. His desires (for evil, with himself at the centre) shaped his faith (in himself) and will lead to his destiny (the destruction of his self).

In shining contrast (8, 9), the king is confident that his destiny – like the righteous one of Psalm 1 – is to be a flourishing green tree in the house (presence) of God for ever. His trust is 'in God's unfailing love' (*chesed*) and therefore it is God whom he praises, rather than himself. His desire is for God's 'name' for he knows that this, and this alone, is 'good'.

And, whereas the evil opponent ends up terribly alone, this righteous King will be in the midst of a great congregation, 'your faithful people' (9). Which is where we come in, as the congregation of the King. In his desire for God's presence and his trust in God's covenant promises, David foreshadows the Lord Jesus Christ; in his destiny as the flourishing leader of God's assembled church, the figure of David likewise finds its fulfilment in Christ the Head of the Church. As we sing this very personal psalm with our King, we take warning not to walk in the evil man's footsteps, not to share his desires, not to imitate his faith in himself. And we find ourselves longing, with our King, for the presence of God, and trusting in the unfailing love of God, given to us in Christ our King.

Psalm 53

This is almost word for word the same as Psalm 14, with some substitutions of 'God' for 'the LORD' (see Introduction to Book 2); also Psalm 53:5 differs from Psalm 14:5b,6. We do not know why it has been included twice. In both places it fits well. Here the context is psalms from the time when David was a fugitive from Saul. (It is also the period during which he meets Nabal, the fool, 1 Sam. 25!) While Jesus Christ, God's King, is anointed but not yet publicly acclaimed, it is very appropriate to lament the troubles His people experience from a godless world (4) and to long for the day when God's King will rule the world from all that 'Zion' signifies in biblical theology (6).

Psalm 54

The heading of Psalm 54 is remarkably similar to that of Psalm 52. Each is 'a maskil of David'; in each someone has betrayed David by going to Saul and telling him where David is. But the focus of David's song here is different.

Here the key word, at start and end, is the 'name' of the covenant God (1, 6), who is given His name 'the LORD' (6) unusually in Book 2. The 'name' of the covenant God is equivalent to His 'might' (1) and signifies His personal and powerful action on earth on behalf of the one with whom He is in covenant. David the king is that man, which is why he can pray like this.

Verses 1 and 2 are an urgent prayer. Verses 3 and 4 repeat the word 'me' (lit. 'my soul' or 'my life') and contrast the enemies who seek to kill 'my soul' with the God who upholds or sustains 'my soul'. In the historical context, the former is Saul (1 Sam. 23:15 '...to take his life/soul'); but Saul is only the immediate concrete expression of all who will not have God's anointed King rule over them. The king trusts the God whose 'name' rests upon him by covenant to be his 'help' and save his life. He prays, on the basis of this same covenant 'faithfulness' that the tables will be turned and the harm his enemies speak (their 'slander') will turn back on them (5). He anticipates the great day when he will praise this 'name', celebrate his 'good' nature, having experienced final rescue from all his troubles (6, 7).

The day will come when one of David's heirs will pray for his people, 'Holy Father, protect them by the power of your name, the name that you gave me...' (John 17:11). As Jesus goes to the cross, he trusts that in His resurrection He will praise the 'name' of the Father who has vindicated Him and given Him to 'look in triumph on all his foes' (7). As we His people sing this psalm with our King, we too trust that the Father will indeed protect us by the power of that same 'name', given to Jesus our covenant King, and given to us in Him.

Psalm 55

This psalm is extraordinary in its intensity and corres-
pondingly wonderful in its comfort. It is set in the context
of other psalms from the long period when David was the
anointed but unrecognized and persecuted king; perhaps it
too comes from this time.

In verses 1-8 David feels the hellishness of evil and longs
to escape. Urgent repeated cries (vv. 1, 2a 'listen... do not
ignore ...hear ...answer') are followed by a heart-rending
description of David's sufferings. He is 'distraught' (as of
a defeated army running hither and thither); his enemies
threaten him and 'bring down suffering on' him (like waves
crashing down). In verses 4 and 5 the words 'anguish...
terrors of death...fear...trembling...horror' smell of hell.
David understands that behind the hostility directed at
God's anointed king (cf. Ps. 2:1-3) lies the devil, who is a
deceitful murderer (John 8:44). And so (6-8) David wishes
that he could escape and dreams about it. As a prophet, we
hear through his voice the voice of a later King; we begin to
feel the supernatural terrors of hell directed against Christ,
the agony of Gethsemane, the darkness of the cross. As
the people of Christ, we too smell the stink of hell in the
troubles we face.

And yet (9-15), so long as the king is on earth, these
sufferings are inescapable. In general terms (9-11) 'the city'
(wherever people live and the king seeks to rule) there are
'wicked' people speaking 'words' that must be 'confounded'
(as at Babel, Gen. 11:9). 'The city' has seven evils: violence
(people hurting people) and 'strife' (people fighting people)
are the paradoxical watchmen of the city, making sure no
peace and harmony creep in! Inside are 'malice' (people

hating people), 'abuse' (people making trouble for people), 'destructive forces' (people tearing people apart), 'threats' (people manipulating people) and 'lies' (people deceiving people). Wherever there are people, these evils abound. How hard for the king to govern such a 'city'!

But the worst is yet to come: betrayal by a close friend, one of the king's inner circle (12-14). We do not know when and by whom this was David's experience, but we know exactly how it came to Jesus through Judas Iscariot. And how it hurt! And so the king prays (15), as only the king can pray, for his enemies – who are not just personal enemies, but traitors to the rule of God in the world – to be defeated.

The main thrust of verses 16-23 is that the King is unshakeable. In the midst of such hostility (18), and the renewed presence of betrayal (20, 21), he knows he is safe. Verse 22 is almost a motto verse for the psalm. It is in the singular, as God in heaven says to His King, 'Cast your (singular) cares on me, the covenant God, and I will sustain you (singular); I will never let the righteous (singular – the Righteous one) be shaken.' God promises that his King will be unshakeable, and (23a) the king's enemies defeated. And so (23b) the King says, 'But as for me, I trust in you.'

This 'unshakeability' finds its fulfilment, not in David, who did die, but in Jesus Christ our King. Christ is unshakeable. And we are secure in him, and only in him. 1 Peter 5:7, echoing Psalm 55:22, is our promise surely, but only, because we are in Christ. We too face the hellishness of evil; like Jesus, we long to escape, but know we cannot until the resurrection day; but we cling with confidence to the unshakeable Christ.

Psalm 56

This psalm expresses vividly what Calvin calls the 'strenuous contest' there is in the heart of the king – and the king's people – between fear and faith. Pursued by Saul, David has fled to Gath, Goliath's city (1 Sam. 21:10); how desperate must he have been – in such mortal danger in his own land that he flees to the city of his most famous enemy! In verses 1 and 2, David cries desperately to God, keenly aware of his incessant ('all day long...all day long'), insistent ('hot pursuit...press their attack'), overwhelming ('many'), and self-confident ('in their pride') foes.

And yet, alternating with these reasons for fear are repeated expressions of trust, in the refrain of verses 3-4 and verses 10-11. He is simultaneously 'afraid' (3) and 'not afraid' (4, 11), the latter because he trusts and praises the 'word' of covenant promise that God has given him, as the anointed king (Ps. 2:6-9). His opponents are powerful but 'mere mortals' (v. 4, lit. 'flesh') or 'man' (v. 11, lit. 'adam').

And yet the pressure continues in verses 5, 6. Again 'all day long' (for the third time), the pressure is relentless, deceitful ('they twist my words'), malicious ('for my ruin... hoping to take my life'), and inescapable ('conspire...lurk... watch my steps...'). Hated and hunted, it is a terrible predicament. Who would not fear? And all this time, our thoughts move forward 1000 years to a greater King, hated and hunted (e.g. Luke 11:53, 54; Mark 3:2), and yet learning – perhaps from this psalm – to trust the covenant promise of God to his King and so to be unafraid even as He was afraid.

Verse 7 is a prayer only the king can pray, for he asks that 'the nations' (the rest of the world) will be defeated in their rebellion. David understands that his present predicament is the local expression of a worldwide hostility to God's anointed king (Ps. 2:1-3 again). He knows that God is 'for' him (9) and that every tear David sheds is recorded or kept by God, both because God cares and as mounting evidence of the guilt of the nations. That is true for every tear drop shed by the Son of God (e.g. Heb. 5:7); how much more for every drop of blood He shed, and then for every drop of blood shed by His martyrs down the centuries. They too will 'know that God is for' them, because God is 'for' their King.

After the renewed refrain of trust (10, 11), the King ends with thanksgiving (12, 13). He has promised ('vows') that when He is rescued, He will offer 'thank-offerings' to God for rescuing him from death (finally in resurrection) that He may spend eternity, with all the King's people, walking before God the Father 'in the light of life'. As we sing this psalm with our King, we too cry urgently in our fear; we too take comfort in His covenant promise to His king; and we too know what it is to be both afraid and unafraid (in that strange tension of Christian experience), while confident of final life.

Psalm 57

Psalms 57, 58, and 59 share the same author (David), the same designation (a miktam) and the same tune ('Do not destroy').

The axis upon which the drama of this psalm is enacted runs from heaven to earth. David is in 'the cave', probably the cave of Adullam (1 Sam. 22:1), again during that period when he is the anointed but persecuted king (as in Pss. 52,

54, 56 and 59 and probably others in this series). David has with him several hundred debt-ridden, troubled, friends (1 Sam. 22:2). As we sing this psalm, we remember than none of us is the king, but any or all of us may be among this unimpressive group of the king's friends. Ultimately, to be 'in Christ' is to be one of the rather motley and un-distinguished group whose only hope is that they are friends of the anointed king.

This is a song of the king from a dark, trapped, cramped place on earth, where he is surrounded by men who are like ravenous beasts, especially in what they say (4), in danger from hunters setting traps for him (6). There is also much language of height: 'heaven', the 'heavens' or 'skies' (3, 5, 10, 10, 11), 'God Most High' (2). This contrast between God Most High in heaven and the king in the cave on earth, threatened by a hunter's 'pit' (6) runs through the psalm.

Two other keys to singing this psalm are the word 'glory' (5, 11) and the pair of words 'love' and 'faithfulness' (3, 10). Glory is the visible manifestation of the presence and power of the invisible God from heaven. In the refrain, David prays that the God exalted in heaven, who is invisible, will make His presence visible and felt on earth in all its darkness. This is what 'glory...over all the earth' means. 'Love' is *chesed*, covenant love, steadfast gracious love, grace. 'Faithfulness' is covenant faithfulness, being true to His promises, truth. The expression 'love and faithfulness' is equivalent to what we meet in the New Testament as 'grace and truth' (John 1:14). David sings that 'God sends forth his love and faithfulness' to himself, the king in the darkness of the cave. This 'love' and 'faithfulness' characterise the God who dwells in 'the heavens...the skies' (10). And he sends it to rest upon His king. In its fulfilment, this 'love and faithfulness', this 'covenant grace of God and truthfulness of God to his promises' rests in all its fullness on Jesus Christ the incarnate Son of God; he is the one upon whom God in heaven sends His 'love and faithfulness'. In the same verse, John writes that he and his fellow-apostles 'have seen his glory' (John 1:14). In this final King the invisible God makes Himself visible upon earth (cf. John 1:18 'made (the Father) known').

As we sing this psalm with David the Old Covenant King, and finally with Jesus Christ the King, we sit with him in the darkness of the cave knowing that because of our association with the king, upon whom the love and faithfulness of God rests in all its fullness, we too may trust and sing with steadfast hearts (7, 8). What is more, our king promises that one day he will praise God 'among the nations...among the peoples' (9), a promise fulfilled in the gentile mission of the church as, all over the world, Christ our King sings the praises of God the Father in heaven, through the lips of men and women who become His friends. (A very similar verse, Ps. 18:49, is quoted of Christ in Rom. 15:9.)

Psalm 58

Psalm 58 shares with Psalms 57 and 59 the same author ('David'), designation ('a miktam') and tune ('Do not destroy'). Since 57 and 59 come from when David was persecuted by Saul, it seems likely that 58 comes from the same period.

In verses 1 and 2 David feels the violence of injustice. He asks of the 'rulers' (almost 'gods', men with god-like power) whether they exercise their power fairly. It is like an inspection question. The emphatic answer is 'No!'; from their 'heart' (the origin) to their 'hands' (actions) they use their power unfairly and therefore turn power into 'violence'. David experiences this violence from King Saul. Jesus felt this keenly from the powerful people of His day. We too, as Jesus' people, ought to feel the horror of this.

But it gets worse. In verses 3-5 David laments the persistence and incurability of injustice. Its source is the 'heart' (2), its origin from conception (3), its methods deceitful (3b), its consequences deathly (v. 4 'venom') and – worst of all – its remedy non-existent. Like a snake with headphones, they cannot be stopped. There is no cure for injustice in human affairs. David laments this. Jesus laments this, for the violent greed of the Pharisees (e.g. Luke 20:47) is made deaf by hypocrisy. We too lament this and are realistic that no social programmes can cure injustice on earth.

In verses 6-9 David longs deeply for the total removal of injustice. He uses a vivid succession of images united by their focus on the final and total removal of unfairness – like wild animals whose broken teeth render them powerless, like water that flows away and is gone, like weapons that fail, like a slug or snail that melts away and, most terribly, like a stillborn child (for what has been conceived is a monster, v. 3). David longs for injustice to be gone forever; so does Jesus; so do we.

And so David, and Jesus, and we in Christ, rejoice in the sure hope of final justice (9-11). Verse 10 is battle language; when you win, the only way you know you have definitively won is from the spilt blood of the enemy; this is why such a terrible scene is finally glad, for injustice is gone for ever (cf. Rev. 18:20). Upon 'the earth' (v. 3, echoed in v. 11) human judges (powerful people) use power violently for their own ends; but finally we shall all know that 'there is a God who judges the earth'.

By nature, we all come under the condemnation of this psalm. Only by grace may we find this psalm a source of joy, as men and women made righteous in Christ.

Psalm 59

Psalms 57, 58, and 59 share the same author (David), the same designation (a miktam) and the same tune ('Do not destroy'). The story behind Psalm 59 is recorded in 1 Sam. 19:11-17. It was a frightening time for David.

There are three facets that remind us this psalm is a song of the king, and not of any old random individual believer. The first is the references to the 'nations' (5,8) and 'the ends of the earth' (13); the scope of this battle is universal (as in Ps. 2). The second is the reference to the laughter of the covenant God (8), which again echoes Psalm 2. The third is the designation of the wicked as 'traitors' (5), for treachery is directed especially against the rightful king, and threatens the whole order of God's people.

Unusually, this psalm has two contrasting refrains. The positive one comes in verses 9, 10 and again at the end in verses 16, 17. The key word, present also in verse 1, is perhaps 'fortress' which comes four times, at the beginning, middle and end (twice). David is, at the same time, in a house surrounded by enemies, and 'in' the covenant God, his fortress. When we join in the psalm, one strand woven into its texture is to pray with our King that the covenant God will keep for Him His covenant promise that He will be kept safe to rule the world. Verses 11-13 teach us to pray for the *visible* victory of the King. The king prays that his enemies

will not just quietly die or disappear (11), but that they will
be so demonstrably and publicly defeated that all the world
will know 'that God rules over Jacob' by His anointed king.

The negative refrain, strange and haunting, is in
verses 6, 7 and verses 14, 15, in each case beginning with
the shivering terror in the words, 'they return at evening…
like dogs…'; evening is the time 'when darkness reigns', and
therefore of lowering mood and rising fears (cf. Luke 22:53).
What David experiences, God's anointed King Jesus knew,
the mortal terror of being surrounded by enemies (e.g.
Mark 3:1-6; Luke 20:20; John 5:16-18). The devil came and
went and then returned 'at an opportune time' (Luke 4:13);
he will do the same with us. As we sing this psalm with
our King, we too shiver at the lurking threat of evil that is
determined to destroy our King and all his people. That
this 'return at evening' comes back as a refrain reminds us
that the life of faith is not a simple upward movement from
fear to faith, but a roller-coaster of inward struggle between
fear and faith; as it was for David, as it was for Jesus, so it
will be for us in Christ.

As we pray this psalm, we learn to shiver at the lurking
terror of evil and, at the same time, to pray with confidence
for the present safety of our King's people ('fortress') and
for the visible victory of Jesus our King when He returns.

Psalm 60

[Vol. 1: 37]

This psalm teaches the people of God how to pray, and
how then to act, in 'desperate times'. It is very timely for the
church of Christ today. Where at least some of Psalms 52-59
come from that early period when the king was anointed but

unrecognized, this comes from a generally successful time in David's reign, recorded in 2 Sam. 8:13,14. He is up in the north (the two 'Aram' regions) when – it would seem – the Edomites attack in the south with, to start with, devastating success. Later Joab defeats them, but not yet.

The psalm is all plural except for verse 9, which makes it clear that David the King is leading the people in prayer.

Verses 1-5 help us to feel the desperate weakness of the people of God, and therefore of the church of God. Like a land in an earthquake (2), or people staggering around dazed and confused (3), God has shown them 'desperate times' (3). If there is 'a banner' (4) it may well be a banner to retreat to (as in Jer. 4:6). The people of God were in desperate straits at this point in David's reign. They were in 'desperate times' when Jesus of Nazareth walked this earth, harassed and helpless, a desperately lost and confused people, 'like sheep without a shepherd' (Matt. 9:36). We are in 'desperate times' today, divided, retreating, weak and helpless. Feel it with the help of this psalm.

But then, verses 6-8, the psalm invites us to hear the promise to the people of God. God speaks 'from his sanctuary', for this is a promise from his Holiness, a true holy war promise. The places in verses 6-7 speak of the whole of the promised land, Shechem west of the Jordan, Sukkoth east of the Jordan (both places Jacob visited, Gen. 33:17,18), Gilead west of the Jordan, Manasseh east of the Jordan, Ephraim perhaps the largest tribal territory west of the Jordan. And Judah, the 'sceptre', the tribe from which the promised Ruler will come (Gen. 49:10). God will rule by His king, in His holiness, over the whole of the promised land. And all evil powers will be defeated (8); the ancient enemies Moab to the south, Edom to the east, and

Philistia to the west, symbolise all hostile forces. Fulfilled
in the final 'inheritance' of the new heavens and new earth,
this promise finds its goal when God will rule the new
creation in holiness by His promised King (e.g. Rom. 4:13;
1 Pet. 1:4-9; Acts 20:32).

Finally – and this is where the psalm is leading us –
in verses 9-12 we pledge ourselves to go with our King
in a venture of faith to the very heartland of evil. The
'fortified city' is the rock fortress of Edom, legendary for its
impregnability (e.g. Jer. 49:16; Obad. 3, 4), like Helm's Deep
in The Lord of the Rings. The song moves from a posture
of defense to an initiative of faith, as the king commits
himself to lead a gospel expedition to the 'strongholds' of
evil, in human societies and finally in the human heart
(2 Cor. 10:3-5). The king trusts, and invites us his people to
trust, that as we go with him into the heartlands of evil, 'we
shall gain the victory' (12) with our King.

In desperate times, we feel the weakness of the people of
God, but we also hear the promise to the people of God and go
in faith, our own great weakness feeling, with the King of the
people of God, in gospel initiatives and with gospel confidence.

Psalm 61

From now to the end of Book 2 there is no explicit context
in David's life (except for a brief cryptic reference in the
heading to Psalm 63).

This is a singular psalm, a song of the king, but with a
significant reference to his people in verse 5b ('the heritage
of those who fear your name').

Perhaps the key to the psalm is the need for the king
to be in covenant relationship in the presence of God.

Verses 1-4 end with this longing to be in God's covenant 'tent', to be safe 'in the shelter' of the 'wings' of the cherubim over the Ark of the Covenant. In verse 7 we pray that the king will be 'enthroned in God's presence'. If we belong to the King who is secure in the presence of God, then all is well for us.

In verses 1-4 we join with our King in praying, in the king's weakness, and therefore in the weakness of his church, for the king and his church to be safe in the presence of God. David cries 'from the ends of the earth' (whether literal or metaphorical); he is in exile, distant and separated from his God, and therefore his 'heart grows faint' within him, for life and vitality come only from the living presence of God. Surrounded by chaotic waters of evil, he prays to be led upwards to the 'rock' of God's secure mountain presence, a rock he cannot reach by his own efforts, but to which God must bring him by grace.

In each of verses 5 and 8 the king speaks of his 'vows' (his promise to give praise to the God who keeps covenant by rescuing him) and of God's 'name', His living presence given to His king on earth and, through Him, to the people (the church) who are the king's 'heritage' (inheritance). The king prays with confidence now, trusting the promises; in the weakness of his exile (1-4) he is strong in faith. In between verse 5 and verse 8 a voice (vv. 6, 7, perhaps the king still, speaking in the third person, but more likely the people) prays for the king to reign for ever, ruling in the presence of God, with God's covenant love or grace and God's covenant faithfulness or truth to protect him. This prayer, partially answered in part of David's reign, is finally answered when a king comes who is 'full of grace and truth' (John 1:14, that is, love and faithfulness) and who, after his weakness, is appointed 'Son of God with power' (Rom. 1:4), ascended and enthroned at the Father's right hand.

As we sing this psalm today, we sing with the King's church in our weakness and exile, and we sing with our King in his power, rejoicing that our King is enthroned in the presence of God the Father for us, and longing for the day when all His church ('the heritage of those who fear your name') will join Him there.

Psalm 62

This is an emphatic psalm. Six times the word translated 'surely', 'truly', 'yes', 'only', or 'alone' begins a verse (1, 2, 4, 5, 6, 9). The psalm is about security, first, the king's security, and then his people's security in him.

In verses 1-7 the king speaks of the God in whom he has found security. The section begins (1, 2) and ends (5, 6, 7) with very similar affirmations. Will the king be saved? Yes, his 'salvation' comes from God (1, 2, 6,7). Is the king's position secure? Will the king be unshaken? Yes, for God is his 'rock' (as in Ps. 61:2) and he will 'never be shaken' (2, 6). Will the king be glorious? Yes, for his 'honour' (lit. 'glory') depends on God (7). And so he waits quietly, at rest in his heart, for this God to act and save him (1a, 5a).

In between (3, 4), we hear the king rebuke those who 'assault' him (lit. 'assault a man' – but the man is clearly the king) and think they can 'topple' him from his 'lofty place' (his high position shows this is not just any one of us, but the king). They think the king is just a 'leaning wall' or a 'tottering fence', easily toppled. They are wrong! He is secure.

Now, in verses 8-10, the king turns to address his people, who face the same choice the king has faced. Will they 'trust' in the God whom the king has trusted (8)? He exhorts them to, for the God who is 'my refuge' for the king (7) is 'our refuge' as his people (8). They need not be afraid, for the people who seek to topple the king (3,4), and who seek to unsettle the king's people, are weightless, insubstantial, empty people (9). So the people must not 'trust' (10) what these godless people trust, the riches they acquire by their deceitful words (4b) and violent methods (9). The king calls the people to make the same decision of faith that he has made, to rest quietly in their hearts as they wait for God to save them.

Verses 11 and 12 are the king's punchline. The 'one... two...' formula stresses the certainty of what he now says. God 'has spoken' it, and he has 'heard' it. There is a God who is strong ('power belongs...'), unfailing in His covenant love to the king and His people ('unfailing love' is *chesed*, covenant love), and utterly fair (lit. 'You reward a man' - as in v. 4 – 'according to what he has done'). This is good news ultimately only when the King is a king better than David, who does only good and is rewarded with covenant love and power on behalf of all his people. This is our great and good King Jesus, who trusted the Father when threatened, and exhorts us in this psalm to find security with Him in the Father God whom He trusted for us.

Psalm 63

[Vol. 1: 86-92, 109]

I have covered this psalm quite fully in volume 1 and will not repeat it here.

Psalm 64

Perhaps what is most striking in this psalm is the precision of the reversals (between vv. 1-6 and vv. 7-10) and the appropriateness of God's judgement. The wicked have sharpened 'tongues' (3a); but 'their own tongues' will be turned against them (8a). They aim their words like 'arrows' (3b); but God will shoot them with His 'arrows' (7a). They 'shoot' at God's king (4a); but God will 'shoot' them (7a). They have no 'fear' (4b); but when they are destroyed 'all people will fear' (9a), looking with God-fearing awe at what God has done in judgement. The wicked are marked by a 'cunning' cleverness of 'mind and *heart*' (6c); but in the end it is the 'upright in *heart*' who will be cheering. The king begins full of dread in the face of 'the threat of the enemy' (1b); in the end he will 'rejoice' (10a).

But we should also notice – as in other psalms – the implicit combination of singular and plural. This is a prayer of the king, who speaks in the singular (1, 2 'Hear *me*, *my* God, as *I* voice *my* complaint; protect *my* life…Hide *me*…'). Verse 10ab is in the singular, lit. 'The righteous one will rejoice in the LORD…'. Supremely this song is about the attacks on the king and God's judgement on those who attack the king. And yet everything the wicked do to attack the king, they do to attack the king's people. And so it is not only the 'righteous one' who rejoices at the end (10ab) but '*all* the upright in heart' (10c).

As Old Covenant Israel sang this song with David their king, so we New Covenant believers sing it with Jesus our King; we too meditate on 'the threat of the enemy' whose attacks upon the king were plural (the emphasis on their plots and encouragement of one another, fulfilled in the hostility of a whole culture set against the king), 'sudden' and unexpected ('ambush'), confident ('who will see it?') and very clever ('cunning'). Their attacks on the king's church will be the same. We too must expect a hostile culture, confident, clever, and dangerous to faith.

When David experienced a rescue (from Saul, from Absalom, from external enemies) people looked on with awe and proclaimed what God had done for him (9). When we look at the bodily resurrection of Jesus we are awe-struck at this astonishing and wonderful reversal. We take comfort that one day the same reversal will be done for 'all the upright in heart' on the day we are raised in the body from the dead.

Psalm 65

Psalms 65, 66, 67, and 68 are all called 'a song'; this may indicate that they are linked. Each of them has a focus on the fulfilment of the promise to Abraham (Gen. 12:1-3) that through his seed blessing will come to the world.

The motif of awe from Psalm 64 continues in Psalm 65 (see vv. 5, 8). But now it is an emphatically corporate awe, as David leads his people in a shared song of harvest joy. This is not, however, a song of generalized so-called spirituality. Verses 1-4 give a clear pointer to the source of harvest joy. We join our King (1, in 'Zion' the place of the king and temple) in a restful quiet readiness to praise God (the word 'awaits' translates the same word 'rest' or 'silence' in 62:1). We will praise Him supremely because He answers prayer (2), and most deeply answers prayer for the forgiveness of sins (3), answering this prayer with a wonderful reconciliation, bringing us near to his presence

(4a) and therefore into the place of covenant blessings (4b). For all the blessings of harvest are – in their Old Covenant context – blessings of being in right covenant relationship with God (e.g. Deut. 28:1-14). In their New Covenant fulfilment, all the blessings of God are found in what Zion foreshadows, under the shadow of God's King, in the blessings of the new heavens and new earth.

Verses 5-8 broaden the canvas from 'our' particular experience to what God does in the whole cosmos. Using vivid creation imagery, our King leads us in praising God for keeping the chaotic 'waters' at bay, stilling their storms (7), forming 'mountains' as solid places of order (6), and therefore giving hope (5) and joy (8) to a world threatened by evil. This is by the gospel foreshadowed in Zion. The 'wonders' by which God brings order out of chaos and good out of evil are to be found in God's King.

Verses 9-13 lead us in a jubilant celebration of the abundant goodness of God. Notice how He takes the chaotic storm waters (v. 7, symbolising evil) and turns them into life-giving river waters (9, 10). The awesome goodness of the covenant God is experienced in part in every harvest, every mouthful of food, every breath we breathe; it will be fulfilled in the abundant life of the resurrection in the new heavens and new earth. This psalm helps us to celebrate with full hearts in response to the abundant fullness of God's grace to us in Christ our King.

Psalm 66
[Vol. 1: 102]

Psalms 65, 66, 67, and 68 are all called 'a song'; this may indicate that they are linked.

This is the one of the first clearly evangelistic psalms. An anonymous prophetic voice leads his people in song (vv. 9-12, 'our... us... we...') and then speaks for himself (vv. 13-19, 'I... my... me...'). He and they address the rest of the world; the psalm is full of plural exhortations ('Shout... sing... praise... come and see...'). The psalm begins (1-5) with an emphatic invitation to join in cheerful praise of God. The focus is on His 'name' (2, 4), His 'glory' (v. 2a 'glory', v. 2b 'glorious'), and His deeds (v. 3 'deeds', v. 5 'what God has done...his awesome deeds'). Put together, 'name', 'glory', and 'deeds' speak of the invisible God making Himself known on earth.

When we ask how He has done this, the answer is given in verse 6: through the redemption of a people for Himself in the Exodus ('the sea into dry land') and the gift of the promised land ('through the waters' – lit. river - 'on foot', referring to crossing the Jordan). The invitation at the end of verse 6 is perhaps the key to the psalm: 'come, let *us*' – any of us all over the earth in any age – 'rejoice in him.' That is, the redemption of a particular people from slavery and the gift to this particular people of a place of rest is good news for any man or woman all over the world who is grafted into this people by faith (cf. Rom. 11:13-24; Eph. 2:11-13). This redemption is a potential blessing for all who will join in the praise of this redeeming God.

But (7) it is also a warning, a demonstration that He is stronger than all the gods of this age (including those of the Pharaohs of ancient Egypt); do not rebel! (cf. Ps. 2:10-12).

Verses 8-12 repeat this invitation (8) and base it again on the wonders of redemption. In language that echoes the later exile in Babylon, the people say, 'we were in terrible need and God redeemed us; you too are in more desperate need than you perhaps realise; he can be your redeemer too'.

From verse 13 the voice speaks, not so much as a leader of the people ('we… our… us…') but as an individual who has experienced salvation ('I…my…me…'). He promises to offer sacrifices as a sign of his thankfulness and devotion (13-15) and invites us all (v. 16 'Come and hear…') as he tells us 'what he has done for me'. He claims that because he walked with a clear conscience before God, not cherishing sin in his heart, God has heard and answered his prayer for rescue (17-19). The covenant 'love' of God (*chesed*) is with this man (20).

So who is he? We do not know his name, in Israel's history; he is anonymous. But he sings and leads Israel by the Spirit of a later believing psalm-singer, one who never cherished sin in his heart, one whose prayers were always heard (cf. John 11:41, 42), a man whom God took 'through fire and water' and brought – in His bodily resurrection and ascension – 'to a place of abundance' (12). This man is the leader and spokesman for a redeemed people. In this psalm he leads them – leads us – in a joyful invitation to the rest of the world to move from rebellion (7) to praise. This psalm should be sung with outsiders in our midst, inviting them to see how the invisible God has made Himself visible in Jesus, how the resurrection of Jesus is proof that redemption is available to all who will join the praise, and a warning that rebellion is doomed (cf. Acts 17:31).

Psalm 67
[Vol. 1: 163]

When God works in grace to bless a people, there is something deeply attractive about what others see (cf. the logic of Rom. 11).

Each of Psalms 65, 66, 67, and 68 is called 'a song'; this may indicate that they are linked. Psalm 67 shares with Psalm 65 the theme of harvest, and with Psalms 65 and 66 the logic that when people see what God has done 'for us' they too will want to join His people. This logic is explicit in the words 'so that' (2a, 7b) and implicit in the refrain of verse 3 and verse 5. The whole purpose of this psalm is that there will be praise of God's saving grace from men and women all over the world. In this way the promise to Abraham (Gen. 12:1-3) will be fulfilled.

The structure is nicely balanced, so that verses 1, 2 and verses 6, 7 bookend the psalm praying for God's blessing on Israel in order that the rest of the world will know His saving ways (2 'your salvation' – this is about undeserved blessing) and 'fear him' with reverent fear (7b). Inside these brackets, the refrain of verses 3 is balanced by the refrain of verses 5, expressing forcibly and emphatically our longing that 'the peoples', indeed 'all the peoples' will praise the God of Israel.

At the heart of the psalm, verse 4 (the only three-line verse) gives the reason why the rest of the world should praise Him: He rules 'with equity' and guides the nations. That is, He is the God who is sovereign (He guides) and fair ('equity'). In some way His blessing of Israel must demonstrate this. There is a play on the word translated 'earth' (2, 7) or 'land' (6); what happens in the 'land' (the promised land) demonstrates something that applies in all the 'earth'. It shows that when a people live in faithful covenant with the good Creator, they will be blessed. This psalm is a celebration of the blessings of covenant faithfulness. And therein lies a problem; for Israel was not faithful.

To pray Psalm 67 Christianly it is vital to grasp that the blessings being prayed for (v. 1 'bless us', v. 6 'blesses us', v. 7 'bless us'), and celebrated, are covenant blessings. The words 'be gracious to us...make his face shine on us' (1b) come from the priestly covenant blessing of Numbers 6:24-26; and the blessings of 'harvest' (6) for 'the land' (i.e. the promised land) are the blessings promised in the covenant (e.g. Deut. 28:1-14). The Old Covenant logic is that when 'the peoples' or 'the nations' (i.e. the rest of the world) see the people of Israel, the Old Covenant 'church' (e.g. Acts 7:38) being blessed with rich harvests in the promised land, they too will join in the praise of the God of Israel.

This can reach its fulfilment only when a man does what Israel was called to do but failed: a man who lives in consistent faithfulness to the God of the covenant and makes the ways of God the Father known on earth (v. 2a, cf. John 1:18; Luke 2:29-32). In this man – and this man alone – all the covenant blessings are to be found (cf. Eph. 1:3). When we pray this psalm in Christ, we long that God will so bless us in Christ with these spiritual blessings, and above all with the godliness that is consistent with God's 'equity', that others, seeing the beauty of this blessing, will be moved to join in the praise of this great God.

Psalm 68

[Vol. 1: 98, 171, 181, 189, 231]

Psalms 65, 66, 67, and 68 are all called 'a song'; this may indicate that they are linked. Psalm 68 shares with these others the motif of universality (e.g. 68:31, 32).

In this psalm we hear the voice of David encouraging those who are 'righteous' by faith to be very glad in the

warrior God who rescues. The psalm begins with this
(1-4, v. 1 'arise' echoing Num. 10:35) adding a headline
summary of why (5, 6): in the stories that follow God
will prove that He cares for orphans, widows, the lonely,
and prisoners – which are all ways of describing us in our
essential neediness. The story of Israel is the story of the
God who rescues those who know their need of Him; this
is what it is to be 'righteous' (3).

At the heart of this long psalm is a jubilant cascade of
victory stories (v. 7, beginning 'when you…') from Israel's
history (7-18). With echoes of the Exodus (see Exod. 15),
the travels in the wilderness (7), Mount Sinai (8), the
conquest of the promised land (14), and at least one later
rescue (Judg. 4, 5, echoed in vv. 8-10 and 'the sheepfolds'
v. 13, Judg. 5:16), the story is shaped around two mountains.
The God of the covenant moves from Mount Sinai (7, 8) to
'the mountain where God chooses to reign' (16, i.e. Zion,
cf. Ps. 2; see also v. 29) where we find 'his sanctuary' (17, 24,
35). This mountain is the envy of 'Mount Bashan', perhaps
symbolising the highest achievements of human pride (cf.
Isa. 2:2). To this mountain (Zion) God ascends on high
in a victory procession (18), accompanied by an invincible
army (17) and followed by 'many captives'. The kingdom of
God merges with the kingdom of David's heir on Mount
Zion. This great victory of the King, in whose person God
and man are found together in perfect harmony, is fulfilled
in the death, resurrection, and ascension of Jesus Christ the
King, and His receiving and giving of victory gifts to His
people (Eph. 4:7-13). In this victory the law of God (from
Mt. Sinai) is enthroned to govern the world, but ultimately
in the better covenant of 'Zion' in which sins are forgiven
(cf. Heb. 12:18-24).

Verses 19-27 build on these victories to celebrate the present grace we may expect from God (19), rescue from 'death' itself (20, cf. 1 Cor. 15:54-57), and – above all – the final gathering of God's people (21-27), who will be gathered (22) 'from Bashan' (the high places) and 'from the depths of the sea' (the lowest places). When the final victory procession of God (24) comes into the reality that Zion foreshadowed, there will be 'a great congregation... the assembly of Israel' (26) fulfilled in the church of Jesus the King, Jew and gentile (cf. Rev. 7:4-9).

The song closes (28-35) with a prayer that God will do for His people what He has done before (28), prayed in glad confidence that one day all that Zion foreshadows will be fulfilled in an international gathering, bowing in glad submission to Jesus the God-man who is king.

As we join in this triumphant song we too feel something of the gladness that comes to the people of God from knowing, not only past victories in Old Testament history, but the great rescue fulfilled in the ascension of Jesus our King, and the assurance this gives us of final rescue even from death itself. For God has won, by Jesus; we can trust God, in Jesus; God will gather, around Jesus.

Psalm 69

[Vol. 1: 48, 123, 129]

This psalm begins with the king's deep suffering and ends with the people's gladness because the king is rescued. Before the king's exaltation in Psalm 68 must come the king's sufferings in Psalm 69, fulfilled in an extraordinary concentration of New Testament references about Jesus. In verses 1-29 we hear the voice of David, speaking by

the Spirit of Christ, crying with the urgent prayer of the
suffering king. His plight is desperate (vv. 1-3, piling up
language of waters) and undeserved (vv. 4, 5 – where v. 5
is either a very sensitive conscience or the king bearing the
sin of his people). This King is hated without any justifiable
reason (v. 4, quoted by Jesus of Himself in John 15:25).

In some ways, verse 6 is the key to hearing this psalm.
There is one man, a king (singular) and there are people
(plural) 'who hope in' God, 'who seek' God. What happens to the king affects deeply what happens to these
believing people. Only if the suffering king is vindicated,
will the people not be disgraced. We come back to this in
verses 32, 33.

The reason what happens to the king matters so much
is that he is being treated as God is treated; it is 'zeal' for
God's 'house' (the temple, i.e. God's presence and covenant)
that provokes this scorn (7-12). Verse 9a is quoted of Jesus
in John 2:17; verse 9b is quoted of Jesus in Romans 15:3.
Here is a zealous king who is mocked, as David was mocked
(v. 12 echoed and fulfilled in Matt. 27:27-30 and the other
gospels).

The persecution of this king tests the covenant
faithfulness of God. Verses 13-18 are replete with covenant
language – God's 'favour... great love... salvation' (13),
'the goodness of your love... your great mercy' (16), 'your
servant' (17). If the covenant God fails to rescue His king,
then His promises are seen to fail.

The sufferings of this king are heartbreaking (19-21).
Verse 21 is echoed at the cross of Jesus (Matt. 27:34,38). In
His sufferings he is deeply alone.

In verses 22-29 the king prays – as only a righteous king
can pray – for justice to be done. Verses 22,23 are quoted

of hardened Israel in Romans 11:9, 10. Verse 24 is echoed in Revelation 16:1. Verse 25 is quoted by Peter about Judas Iscariot in Acts 1:20. The king can only be saved (29) if those who persist in hostility to him are finally judged (22-28).

As we join in verses 1-29 we gain an insight into the suffering heart of David, fulfilled in the broken heart of Jesus. We feel the agony; and yet at the same time we cry for the king's vindication, a vindication achieved at the resurrection of Jesus and to be consummated at His return.

The short final section (30-36) changes key dramatically from lament to glad thanksgiving. As the king rejoices, by faith, in the assurance of his salvation, so the people of verse 6 who 'seek God' 'will see' what has happened to our King and 'be glad' (32); God's rescue of the suffering king is the guarantee that the covenant God 'hears the needy and does not despise his captive people' (33). As we join in the glad ending of the psalm we affirm our glad confidence that, because our King is exalted, so the whole people of God ('Zion... the cities of Judah') will prosper in the end.

Psalm 70

In this psalm we meet one individual and two groups. The individual is David the king, who is in urgent need. The urgency of his need brackets the psalm: 'Hasten... come quickly...' (1); 'come quickly...do not delay' (5). The suffering king of Psalm 69, who will be the victorious king of Psalm 68, needs rescuing very soon.

In the middle of the psalm there are two groups, described in terms of what they want. The first (2, 3) 'want' to take the king's 'life'; they 'desire' his 'ruin'. The king prays that they will be put to 'shame' (2a, 3b), be publicly seen to

be on the losing side (cf. Ps. 2). The second group (4) 'seek'
God and 'long for' his 'saving help'. These are those we met
in Psalm 69 ('those who seek you' v. 6; 'you who seek God'
v. 32). One group desires the king's demise, the other seeks
the God who is in covenant with this king. The king prays
that this second group will 'rejoice and be glad in you' and
always say how 'great' God is; this will happen (as in Ps. 69)
when they see the suffering king vindicated.

And yet, as the king prays against one group and for the
other, he himself is still in desperate need (5). All this was
true for king David, whose rescue deeply affected all who
sought God's face. It was supremely true of King Jesus,
who prays against His enemies and for all who truly love
God, since they are Christ's people. It is true too for the
whole church of Christ; when the first group persecute us,
they persecute Jesus (Acts 9:4; Matt. 25:40); even as we
seek God and know that our King has prayed for us to see
the greatness of God (4), we are yet in urgent need of God
to be our 'help' and 'deliverer' (5).

Psalm 71

[Vol. 1: 181]

It is at first difficult to see what is the point of this anonymous and not very clearly structured psalm, that echoes so
much of the language, and so many of the themes, of earlier
psalms (e.g. vv. 1-3a are almost verbatim from Ps. 31:1, 2).
It will be helpful to note three motifs, as we see what a
wonderfully appropriate psalm this is, near the end of
Books 1 and 2.

First, there are many references to time. These are of
three kinds: the psalmist's youth (v. 5 'since my youth'; v. 6

'from my birth... from my mother's womb'; v. 17 'since my youth'), all of time continuing (v. 3 'always'; v. 6 'ever'; v. 8 'all day long'; v. 14 'always'; v. 15 'all day long'; v. 17 'to this day'; v. 24 'all day long'), and old age (v. 9 'when I am old... when my strength is gone'; v. 18 'Even when I am old and grey'). This is the song of a man conscious of his ageing and thinking about all of his life, from the womb to the old age that may lie ahead.

Second, there is much about the great deeds God has done and does: verse 15 'your righteous deeds... your saving acts'; verse 16 'your mighty acts... your righteous deeds'; verse 17 'your marvelous deeds'; verse 18 'your mighty acts'; verse 24 'your righteous acts'. These deeds are actions of 'righteousness', God doing the right thing by rescuing the man with whom he is in covenant. People say that God 'has forsaken him' (11), but he prays confidently that God will not 'forsake' him (9, 18). Despite many 'troubles' he is sure God will 'restore' his 'life' and 'bring' him 'up' even from 'the depths of the earth', i.e. death (19, 20).

Third, the psalmist is zealous to proclaim these righteous deeds to the next generation. Despite being 'a sign to many' (v. 7a, a portent of God's judgement, in his frailty and perhaps worse), he insistently and persistently praises God (6, 8, 14, 22, 23). In what is almost a refrain, he repeats his determination to '*tell* of your righteous deeds' (15, 24). He will '*proclaim* your mighty acts...*proclaim* your righteous deeds...*declare* your marvelous deeds...*declare* your power to the next generation, your mighty acts to all who are to come' (16-18). Verse 19 is just such a declaration.

Near the end of Books 1 and 2 an ageing believer reflects on the faithfulness of the covenant God to him through all of life and the confidence this gives him in troubles and as he looks to the future. His grand purpose in what remains of his life is to proclaim this righteous wonderful faithfulness to the generations to come. Through the voice of this anonymous Old Covenant believer we hear the voice of a greater believer leading his people in reflective praise. This young man had his life cut off early, and yet even in youth he was conscious of ageing and confident that, whatever lay ahead for him, even many and bitter troubles and a descent to 'the depths of the earth' (20), the God and Father who had been faithful to him since Mary's womb would remain his refuge to the end. This faithfulness he proclaimed to his people in generations to come, including us. As we too reflect on our ageing and proclaim the Father's faithfulness, Jesus's song becomes ours.

Psalm 72

[Vol. 1: 102, 157, 162, 199, 206]

Books 1 and 2 conclude with a rich prayer that the king in David's line will indeed be the Psalm 1 man and Psalm 2 king with whom the Psalter began. This psalm 'concludes the prayers of David…' (20) and so the heading 'Of Solomon' may mean 'For Solomon', perhaps a prayer written by David that the people can pray for Solomon and his successors.

The themes are partly interwoven, but major on the following longings.

First and foremost, we pray that the character of the king and of his rule will be 'righteousness' and 'justice' (1, 2); that is, that he will be the 'righteous' man of Psalm 1.

Second (3-7), we desire that the fruit of his righteous rule will be blessings that extend to all creation (v. 3 'mountains…

hills..'; v. 6 'rain…showers…) and last as long as creation itself (5, 7). Just government is the prerequisite for a harmonious and prosperous creation; the stakes could not be higher. The word *shalom* ('prosperity', harmony, wholeness) brackets this section (3, 7).

Third (8-11) we ask that his kingdom will extend from the whole of the promised land (v. 8 'from (the Dead) Sea to (the Mediterranean) Sea and from the (Euphrates) River to the ends of the earth'), stretching out to eventual worldwide government (11). That is, we pray that this king will be the fulfilment of Psalm 2.

Fourth (12-14) we long for a king who will rescue the afflicted; for a deep neediness is the core characteristic of this king's people. Only those who know their need can be blessed by his rule; the proud oppressors will be excluded.

Fifth (15-17a) we yearn for a king supported by a willing prayerful people who want nothing more than his long reign, his riches, and 'his name' (his great reputation) to be celebrated for ever. To pray for this king's reign is to align one's heart's desires with the character and purposes of this king.

When these prayers are answered, the covenant promise to Abraham will be fulfilled, and blessing will come throughout all the world (v. 17b echoing Gen. 12:2, 3).

When all this happens, the finale to Book 2 (18, 19) will be a great celebration of the 'glorious name' of the covenant God, who has given the wonder of His 'name' to his King (notice the two uses of 'name', in verse 17 of the king, and verse 19 of the covenant God).

We join this song by thanking God that this King has come, the righteous man of Psalm 1 and the great covenant King of Psalm 2, and that in Jesus we have the assurance

of all these things. We pray for his return, when the whole
earth will be filled with God's glory (19b) and creation
itself will be restored to 'prosperity'. It is a grand and fitting
ending to Books 1 and 2.

BOOK 3

Introduction to Book 3

Books 1 and 2 are the main collection of psalms of David. Although they include a significant collection of others (42-50) and there are psalms of David later in the Psalter, Books 1 and 2 are dominated by the figure of the King. This is not true, or at least not in the same way of Book 3, which smells of exile. Several of the psalms from this short book contain clear indications of this; it is probable that the others are included because of their relevance to exile, whether or not they were actually written at that time.

Psalm 73

[Vol. 1: 40, 100, 183, 199]

This distressing and thoughtful psalm appears to have been placed at the start of Book 3 to set the tone. The exile poses acutely to believers the problem of the prosperity of the wicked – the victorious Babylonians or, a century or so before, Assyrians – and the sufferings of the righteous.

As with some other psalms, the key to reading Psalm 73 in Christ is to note that there is one individual ('Asaph') singing the psalm, and two groups of people in view. The most obvious group are the prosperous wicked, described vividly in verses 3-12. But there is another group, called 'Israel...those who are pure in heart' in verse 1 and 'your children' in verse 15 (and probably also '*his* people' in v. 10, see ESV). Perhaps the words that unlock the secret of the psalm are in verse 15: 'If I had spoken out like that (vv. 13, 14), I would have betrayed your children.' The way this one representative, this one Spirit-inspired believer grapples with the problem matters deeply to all God's children.

The issue with which he grapples is summed up in the word 'good' which brackets the psalm (v. 1 'good to Israel'; v. 28 'for me, it is good to be near God'). Asaph begins with his conclusion: 'God is good to Israel'; he ends by telling all the deeds of this good God and reaffirming his goodness (28). In his proclamation he is like the writer of Psalm 71 (where we saw that proclamation was a significant theme); this is a striking point of continuity between the end of Book 2 and the start of Book 3.

Is the covenant God of Israel good? It doesn't appear so, for those who care nothing for God in their proud arrogance trample on others and do very well for themselves (2-12). The temptation is therefore to say, with our psalmist in verses 13, 14, that it is 'in vain' to be faithful to God with a pure heart; there is no profit in it, but rather suffering. But – and this is why verse 15 is so important – had he concluded this, and therefore joined the wicked, he would have betrayed the children of God, who in some way depend on him to maintain faithfulness under pressure.

So when he describes his struggles (16) and their resolution (17), we watch with interest, knowing how much his faith will mean for us. As he sees, in God's 'sanctuary' – the place of his law and covenant – that there is a terrible judgement for the wicked (18-20) and it is 'ignorant' to become embittered by the prosperity of the wicked (21, 22), we watch enthralled; for the faith of this believer, speaking by the Spirit of a later and greater believer, is the voice of the 'pioneer and perfecter' of our own faith (Heb. 12:2).

As we sing this psalm, we watch with Asaph, and finally with Jesus, the prosperity of the wicked (2-11), feeling, as he must have felt, the perplexity of it all; we hear in our hearts the temptation he must have felt in his heart, that walking by faith with God is pointless (13,14); we go with him into the 'sanctuary' (17) and see with him the certainty of judgement (18-20), the folly of b ecoming embittered (21, 22), and finally the wonder and joyful satisfaction of walking in covenant fellowship with God (23-28). The wicked may lay claim to 'heaven' and 'earth' (9), but to have God as our Father, as Jesus does, is worth more than 'heaven' and 'earth' (25).

Psalm 74

[Vol. 1: 152, 171, 174-175, 177, 199, 202]

If Psalm 73 has us watching an individual's struggle of faith, Psalm 74 calls us to lament with the ravaged church of God as we grieve corporately. In words that help us feel keenly the misery of a ruined church, verses 1-11 cry out to the God of 'Mount Zion' with the memory of the temple being trashed by the Babylonians. With them, we are to hold together the promises implicit in verses 1, 2 (the sheep of God's pasture, the people God redeemed at the Exodus, Zion with all the promises of Ps. 2) with the pain of seeing the place of God's presence on earth sacked (3-8) and the perplexity of wondering if the pain will ever end (9-11). Here was a garden sanctuary with a touch of the beauty of Eden on earth (1 Kings 6:23-35). It is desperately, achingly painful. And it goes on and on and on (v. 1 'for ever'; v. 3 'everlasting ruins'; v. 9 'how long'; v. 10 'How long... for ever').

Five-hundred years later believers waited for 'the consolation of Jerusalem' (Luke 2:25). As they held the baby Jesus in their arms they saw this consolation embodied. But then this man, this living presence of God on earth, wept over Jerusalem (Luke 19:41-44) in a not dissimilar lament, as the place where God dwelt on earth was about to be destroyed (John 2:19) in an agony deeper still. Still today, as we sing this psalm, we feel keenly the desperate state of Christ's church on earth, vandalized, despised, in ruins.

In verses 12-17 there is an extraordinary change of key and subject. The psalmist, by the Spirit of Christ, goes right back to creation, when God demonstrated his power over the forces of chaos, supremely Leviathan (i.e. Satan, Rev. 12:9) and placed physical and moral order in the world. He made a covenant with creation that undergirds and guarantees his covenant of redemption (cf. Jer. 33:19-26). Every sunrise is a sign that God will restore the church of Christ, which cannot be destroyed, any more than Leviathan can destroy creation. When we grasp this imagery, these verses become a powerful tonic for hearts troubled at the state of Christ's church.

In response to this, Jesus leads us in praying urgently for that restoration (18-23). These final verses are full of pleas: 'Remember… Do not hand over… do not forget… Have regard… Do not let… Rise up… remember… Do not ignore….'

The voice we hear in this psalm is the Spirit of Christ, who teaches us to feel keenly the misery of a ruined church (1-11), to remember daily the Creator's power to bring order from disorder (12-17) and to pray urgently for the glory of God in the restoration of Christ's ruined church (18-23).

Psalm 75

The exile was a time when 'the earth and all its people quake' (3) and when arrogant victors boasted of their strength (their 'horns') (4, 5). This psalm was therefore appropriate for that time; and it is suitable for every time in which the church of God is troubled.

As so often, it includes both the corporate plural (v. 1 'We… we…') and the voice of the singular leader (v. 9 me…

I... I...'). The Spirit-inspired psalmist leads the people of God in this song. It begins with corporate praise because God's 'Name' is near and his 'wonderful deeds' are sure (1); close to the end the leader declares this praise before the people (9).

Most of the psalm, however, is a declaration of what God says (2-8, 10). There is an appointed time for judgement (2a) although it may not be yet. On that day God will judge (2b, 7a). In words echoing the songs of Hannah (1 Sam. 2:1-10) and Mary (Luke 1:46-55), the dominant motif is of lifting up and putting down. God rebukes those who 'lift up' themselves in their own strength ('horn') (4, 5), for we cannot successfully exalt ourselves (6). God alone brings down (the proud) and exalts (the humble) (7). There is a terrible 'cup' of God's righteous anger and the wicked will drink it (v. 8, echoed in e.g. Rev. 4:10). Verse 10 sums up this double-edged message of judgement – a cutting off of the 'horns' of the wicked, and a lifting up of the 'horns' of the righteous.

To join in this psalm at the time of exile means to sign up for corporate trust in the future judgement of God. For Jesus to sing this psalm (as the one whose Spirit first voiced it) means all this and more; for Jesus Himself would drink that terrible cup (Luke 22:42) on behalf of his people, becoming sin for them (2 Cor. 5:21). When we sing this psalm with Jesus, we take comfort that He has drunk that cup for us, who deserve it; and we take comfort also that Christ's oppressed and ravaged church will one day be lifted up in strength, when all proud human pretensions are cut off, and those who proudly oppress the church of Christ will have to drink that cup of judgement for themselves.

Psalm 76

This psalm shares with Psalm 75 the words 'For the director of music. A psalm of Asaph. A song'. They certainly read well together. At a time of exile and suffering for Christ's church, when weapons of hostile warfare have been seen, experienced, and deeply feared in the land, this psalm is a vigorous antidote.

Verses 1-6 portray the God of Israel, the God who dwells in 'Salem' (Jerusalem, place of peace) or 'Zion' as an all-conquering warrior. He is like a lion (v. 2, where the words for 'tent' and 'dwelling-place' are used in Hebrew of the lair and den of a predator), a warrior who breaks all the enemy weapons (3), one for whom the enemy are no more than 'game' to be hunted on the mountains (4); like the chariots and horsemen of Pharaoh (Exod. 15), all his powerful enemies lie still (5, 6). There will be a 'still'-ness (6b) in the world; it will not be the stillness of mystical experience, but rather of total defeat.

This is vigorous and – to our over-sensitised pallets – uncongenial language. But remember that what is being conquered is horrible arrogant evil, those who have failed to respond to the urgent warnings, both of Psalm 2:10-12 and Psalm 75:4, 5, 8. Those who persist in troubling Christ's church, whether from outside or from within, will be utterly defeated. One day the King of Psalm 2 will come, 'conquering and to conquer' (Rev. 6:2) and will win total victory.

If verses 1-6 portray total victory, verses 7-12 focus on the proper response, which is fear. The word 'feared' comes four times (7a, 8b, 11c, 12b). Do not fear those who can kill only the body, but fear him who can cast you into hell (Luke 12:5). God will act to save 'all the afflicted' (9b), those who look to him for salvation and experience troubles in this life from their persecutors.

When the church of Christ feels the pain and hopelessness of being exiles or 'foreigners' in this world, our Messiah leads us in this song of confident hope in his final victory. As the grand truths of this psalm sink into our outlook, we too are enabled to 'live out your time as foreigners here in reverent fear,' knowing that we 'call on a Father who judges each person's work impartially' (1 Pet. 1:17).

Psalm 77
[Vol. 1: 171, 177, 181, 200]

In verses 1-6 we hear the intense, dark, agonised voice of a representative of the people of God, leading the people in a deep expression of grief. This is not the private grief of an individual, but an individual expressing the corporate grief of a desolate people, in a way that is most appropriate at a time of exile. One single question is put six times in verses 7-9. It voices the most fearful anxiety a soul can harbour: was I right – were we right – to believe that the God of covenant love (8a 'unfailing love') is faithful to his promises? We thought his promise, the gospel promise (Gal. 3:8) that in Abraham's seed the whole world would be blessed, was a definite promise, and not just God's general intention. But now it has failed, and shows no sign of being reignited; notice the emphatic 'for ever... never... for ever... for all time'.

As this song-writer, singing by the Spirit of Christ, leads us his people in verses 1-9, we feel more deeply the

terrible mismatch between the promise and the actual state
of Christ's church on earth. We refuse to get used to it, to
adapt to it, to live with compromise; we insist on urgent
persistent prayer (v. 2 'stretched out untiring hands').

As we move from verses 1-9 into verses 10-20, we change
key from restless faith to reassured faith. Led by the Spirit
of Christ, we remember that the church of Christ was
brought into existence by a work of sovereign evil-defeating
grace. The song-writer rehearses intentionally, deliberately
remembering 'the years when the Most High stretched out
his right hand' (10), by which he means the astonishing
redemption of the Exodus. These are described in general
terms in verses 10-15 as wonderful, powerful, and holy,
and as deeds of redemption for 'your people' (15). They
culminate (16-19) in the crossing of the Red Sea, when the
chaotic waters of darkness, both literal and as symbolizing
supernatural evil, were parted to let God's people escape.
(There are echoes of the song of Exod. 15 in vv. 13-20.) The
people of Israel were formed as a redeemed people by this
act of sovereign grace. The Redeemer had no help from the
people, who were at least as weak then as the church of
Christ is today; he simply acted by his power to save.

And He did it, while Himself invisible (v. 19c 'your foot-
prints were unseen'), by an imperfect human leader (Moses)
and a flawed human priest (Aaron), by whose priesthood
the people had access to God (20). As Jesus sings this
psalm over half a millennium later He begins to know that
He Himself will be the perfect leader anticipated by Moses
and the flawless high priest foreshadowed by Aaron. Just
as the Old Covenant people were formed by the Exodus
redemption, a work of sovereign evil-defeating grace, so the
New Covenant church of Christ will be formed by a work

of sovereign evil-defeating grace at the cross of Christ; Jesus
our leader and priest guarantees to us that, weak and exiled
as we are, we do yet have the future promised us by God in
his covenant with Abraham. The answer, in Christ, to the
agonized six-fold question of verses 7-9 is a resounding No!

As we pray this psalm we learn to mourn and pray more
grievously and – at the same time – to know more deeply
the comfort of sovereign grace.

Psalm 78
[Vol. 1: 49, 100, 154, 171-172, 177 181-182, 188, 201]

A prophetic voice speaks, addressing God's people as '*my
people*' (1). It is all addressed to the people of God and
contains no 'upward' voice of prayer or praise. The voice
speaks; we listen. This voice speaks a long parable, in this
second longest of all the psalms (2). A 'parable' or 'hidden
thing' means something less than obvious, a truth that
requires personal engagement to uncover and understand
it. It is indeed a less than obvious psalm.

The 'what' of the psalm is given in verses 1-6. It is a retelling of stories of God's dealings with his people of old, retold
by one generation to the next and then the next and so on.
Notice the words 'told… tell… tell…' (3, 4, 6). It is 'teaching'
(v. 1, *tōrah*) about the 'law' (v. 5, *tōrah*), which includes what
we think of as law and also the whole story of God's promises
and rescue. This is what it is. The 'why' is hinted at in verse 6
('so that the next generation will know them…and…tell
their children') and explicit in verses 7, 8: 'Then they would
put their trust in God…' and 'not be like their ancestors…'.
That is, the purpose of the psalm is to produce obedient faith
in the present generation of the people of God.

The 'parable' runs from verse 9 to the end. It covers, with appropriate repetitions and flashbacks, the whole period from slavery in Egypt (12b, 43), through the plagues (12a, 44-49) and Passover (50, 51), across the Red Sea (13), through the wilderness wanderings led by the fiery cloudy pillar (14), with all the grumbling and provision of water from the rock (15, 16) and then quail (17-31), into the promised land (52-55), through early judgements (56-64), and then – fast forwarding several centuries – to the destruction of the northern kingdom of Israel by the Assyrians (67). The story ends (68-72) with God's choice of David and his line to rule from Zion (cf. Ps. 2); and this is the puzzle and irony if – as the context in Book 3 suggests – this psalm is to be sung in exile, when there is no longer a king in David's line and no longer a realistic Jerusalem. It is a tremendous sweep; and yet it ends before the end, and this is why it calls for an engaged believing thoughtfulness from us the present generation of hearers.

The question in the hearts of exilic believers must have been this: how do these 'things from of old' (2) instruct us, who face the end (as it seems) of David's line and of Zion? The answer must be hinted at by the dominant motifs of the story, which are the alternation and interplay of Israel's repeated unfaithfulness to the covenant, with consequent just judgements (8-11, 17-20, 30-33,36-37, 40-42, 56-64, 67) and God's persistent sovereign grace and his faithfulness to the covenant (12-16, 23-28, 38-39, 52-55, 65-66, 68-72). So the question is this: which will carry the day, our sin or God's covenant grace? Especially now we – in exile, with no king – are under the most terribly unsettling judgement so far?

The beginning of the psalm hints at the answer, for it focuses repeatedly on 'the praiseworthy deeds of the LORD, his power, and the wonders he has done' (4). This is in the end a story about God's power to save and not about our propensity towards unbelief. The end of the psalm likewise hints at the answer, for a story that rests so confidently with God's choice (vv. 68, 70 'chose... chose...') of Zion and David surely cannot end with the destruction of Zion and the ending of David's line.

Centuries later another prophetic voice spoke parables of the kingdom of God. And in his comment on this teaching, Matthew says it 'fulfilled what was spoken through the prophet' (the prophetic voice of Ps. 78): 'I will open my mouth in parables...' (quoting Ps. 78:2). Psalm 78 is a parable of the kingdom of God, for it ends with Zion and David. Jesus also told parables (Matt. 13) about the kingdom of God. Although the parables of Jesus are not identical to the historical 'parable' of Psalm 78, they draw us in to the same narrative, the story of how the sovereign choice and grace of God will build the kingdom of God in the face of all the unbelief and disobedience that we human beings can throw against his purposes.

In this psalm we hear the voice of Jesus our prophet and teacher retelling the story of the covenant God with his people and drawing us in to a similar penitence for our folly and a comparable trust in his sovereign grace. For there will come one who is the true manna from heaven (v. 24 quoted in John 6:31), who is the true 'rock' from which life-giving water flows (1 Cor. 10:3-5 echoing parts of vv. 15, 23-35), the true 'Zion' and the true 'Son of David'.

Psalm 79
[Vol. 1: 199, 201]
If Psalm 74 reassures the ruined church of Christ from the truth of creation, Psalm 79 brings comfort to that

same troubled church from the springs of atonement. In unravelling the core logic of this psalm we should note that there are three participants. First, of course, is God, the covenant God (the LORD). Second, there is his people, drawing their life from his 'holy temple' (1); they are called (2) '*your* servants... *your* own people' (lit. your faithful ones, those who receive and show your *chesed*), or 'Jacob' (v. 7, that is, the whole people of God, all 12 tribes), 'your servants' (10), 'the prisoners...those condemned to die' (11), 'your people, the sheep of your pasture' (13). Third, there are 'the nations' (i.e. the gentiles, 1, 6, 10, 10) also called 'our neighbours' (i.e. the hostile neighbouring nations, vv. 4, 12) or 'the kingdoms' (6).

Verses 1-4 lament, most movingly and intensely, how the unbelieving world ('that do not call on your name' v. 6) has utterly ravaged God's place and God's people, in the destruction of Jerusalem by the Babylonians – and again and again (e.g. Luke 21:24; Rev. 11:2; 16:6). Verse 5 acknowledges that this must be the outpouring of the jealous anger of God against his people, who have been unfaithful to Him, as an adulterous wife to a faithful husband. Verse 6 prays that this anger, God's 'wrath' will be turned instead against the unbelieving and persecuting world (with verse 7 repeating the lament of vv. 1-4).

We reach the heart of the psalm in verses 8-10a. The fundamental question is 'sins' (8) and the need for atonement ('forgive our sins' in v. 9 is literally 'make atonement for our sins'). The grounds on which the people of God pray for this are the 'name' of God (v. 9 'for the glory of your *name*... for your *name's* sake'). The reputation of God is tied to what happens to the people to whom He has promised blessing and salvation. Only if He atones for their sin and rescues them will the rest of the world be silenced when they ask, mockingly, 'Where is your God?' (10a); this taunt reveals a very low opinion of God. It is on these grounds, the glory of God, that we pray (10b-12) for a great reversal (note how v. 12 reverses v. 4 and 'the outpoured blood of your servants' in v. 10b echoes 'your servants' in v. 2 and 'poured out blood' in v. 3). This prayer is echoed in Rev. 6:10 and its answer celebrated in Rev. 19:2.

The end result and goal of the prayer is (13) a chorus of endless praise to God from his rescued people (cf. Rev. 19:1-8). The psalm is therefore most deeply about the name and honour of the covenant God. The Saviour who leads us in singing this song today is the one upon whom the fire of God's jealous righteous anger (5) burned with infinite ferocity as He took upon Himself the sins of His people in order that this necessary wrath might be drained to the dregs in His substitutionary sufferings. Then – and only then – the sins of His people would be atoned for (9) and the name of God be vindicated as His church is rescued. We still await the consummation of this rescue; but in Christ, confident in his atoning death, we pray this psalm with heartfelt feeling and Christ-rooted confidence.

Psalm 80

[Vol. 1: 172, 177, 200, 228]

Like Psalm 74, this psalm shows us how to pray for a ravaged church. Israel, the 'vine' of this psalm, the people of God, are the only hope for a wilderness world. The dominant image is of Israel as an abundant and fruitful vine, replacing the morally wild and death-dealing society of the nations in the promised land with a life-giving community of moral order and beauty (8-19; cf. Isa. 5:1-7; 27:2-6).

But the 'vine' has been ravaged (12, 13) because it has failed to be the life-giving plant it was meant to be (cf. Isa. 5:7). If the dominant image is of the 'vine', the prevailing prayer focuses on a double 'turning'. The people of God cry to God repeatedly to 'restore' them (lit. 'cause them to turn', that is, give them the gift of repentance). They ask this in three of the four refrains (3, 7, 19) and promise that, if God does this, they 'will not turn away' (18). When God gives them repentance, he too will 'return' to them (14) and make his 'face' shine upon them (vv. 3, 7, 19, echoing the blessing of Num. 6:25).

The underlying cause of the vine's ruin is a relationship broken by sin, so that their prayers are not heard (4). It does not matter whether, in the original history of the psalm, this was the exile of the ten northern tribes or the final exile of the southern kingdom; the point is that only a restored relationship with God will enable the vine to be the life-giving plant it is purposed to be. Only then will 'Israel' be – as it were – God's 'right hand man' (17) in the world.

As the people of God pray for God to do this double-turning work (of them to Him in repentance, of Him to them in grace), they emphasise his great power. Four times He is called 'Almighty' (4, 7, 14, 19), lit. '...of hosts', the God whose sovereign dynamic power is like that of a superpower with invincible armies. Only this sweeping power of God can achieve the supernatural victory of a restored relationship with a sinful people.

For centuries, Israel waited, through the long deep sadness of promises as yet unfulfilled. The vine was a treasured symbol of their national identity, but the reality fell very far short. Until a young man said to his followers, 'I am the true vine' – the fulfilment in my own person of all that Israel is called to be (John 15:1-8). By his sin-bearing death, and then through his Spirit's indwelling life, in vital union with Him, men and women are finally brought into restored fellowship with the Father, as children of God sharing the Son's intimate sonship. Then, and only then, can a community be created by grace, the church of Christ, through and in whom a morally wild world can gradually be reclaimed for the fruit of righteousness. As we now pray this psalm in Christ, we cry for daily grace to repent ('Restore us…'), and for daily life-transforming and church-shaping relationship ('Return to us… make your face shine on us…') until the day when the true Vine that is Jesus and his people finally fills, not just the Old Covenant promised land (11) but the whole of the new creation.

Psalm 81

[Vol. 1: 172, 177-178, 201]

In this psalm the people of God hear a voice of a great prophet. The voice (1-5a) summons the people of God to assemble joyfully for one of the great Old Covenant festivals, perhaps Tabernacles (see the reference to the 'full moon', v. 3). We gather to remember the great events of our Redemption (v. 5 'When God went out against Egypt…').

But, when we gather, we are surprised by another voice. Suddenly the one who summons us hears 'an unknown voice' (5b), that is, a voice that is not merely human, but the voice of God coming with authority from above. Speaking as a prophet, the psalmist then tells us what God says to his assembled people (6-16). This message is a reminder, a rebuke, and a gospel invitation.

In words that are replete with echoes from Exodus 17-20 and beyond, verses 6-10 remind us that we were formed as an assembled people (a church) when we cried in distress (v. 7a; Exod. 2:23,24), and owe our existence to a great redemption, that is tied to a great revelation of God's law (v. 7b the 'thundercloud' at Sinai, Exod. 19:6; v. 9 the first commandment, Exod. 20:3; v. 10a the preface to the Ten Commandments, Exod. 20:2).

Verses 11 and 12 are the core of the rebuke, that has been anticipated in verse 8a. Echoing many episodes in Exodus and Numbers, God says his people 'would not listen' to Him and so He 'gave them over' (cf. Rom. 1:26) to the stubbornness of their hearts. The word 'stubborn' (12) appears most commonly in Jeremiah, where it implicitly links the stubbornness of the people of God at the time of the Exodus with the stubbornness of the people of God at the time of the Babylonian exile. It is an enduring stubbornness, until the New Covenant work of the Spirit.

The gospel invitation is anticipated in verse 8b and explicit in verses 13-16. Despite past failure, God invites his people to come into great blessing (16).

The theme that unites the reminder, the rebuke and the invitation is that of listening to God's word (v. 8 *'Hear* me... if only you would *listen* to me'; v. 11 'But my people would not *listen* to me'; v. 13 'If my people would only *listen* to me'). To 'listen' means not just to hear the words; it means to 'follow God's ways' in loving obedience (13b). It is, in old fashioned language, to hear and to heed.

We have in this psalm one man who has listened speaking to a gathered people who need to listen. The psalmist is the one who 'heard an unknown voice' (5b) and passed it on. It is likely that verse 10b ('Open wide your mouth and I will fill it') is telling the prophet to open his mouth metaphorically so that God can fill it with His words; this is the usual meaning of language of 'filling' the 'mouth' (e.g. Jer. 1:9). The prophetic psalmist is the one who hears and internalizes God's words before speaking them. He listens; he exhorts us to listen.

The prophetic psalmist speaks by the Spirit of Jesus Christ. We, the assembled people of Christ, in this psalm hear the voice of Christ our great Prophet. He is the man who supremely has listened to the Father with an ever-open ear, who has listened and lovingly obeyed. He is the one who speaks to rebuke us for not listening and invites us afresh to listen, to repent, to believe and to obey. When we join in this psalm, we implicitly commit ourselves to hearing and heeding the word of God. For those of us who also teach that word, the commitment first to listen is particularly strong.

Psalm 82

[Vol. 1: 157, 163]

In this psalm we hear a prophetic voice (1-7) and then a prayer in response (8). The key verb is 'judge' which comes four times: verse 1 'renders judgement'; verse 2 'defend...' (= 'judge for'); verse 3 'Defend...'; verse 8 'judge'.

God presides in 'the great assembly' (lit. 'the council of God') and speaks in judgement on the 'gods' (1). What is this 'assembly' and who are these 'gods'? Jesus quotes verse 6 in John 10:34 and clearly indicates that they are human beings 'to whom the word of God came' (John 10:35). It seems most likely, therefore, that 'the great assembly' is the people of God, the people of Israel, and the 'gods' are their leaders. God speaks through the Asaphite prophet to condemn these leaders for their favouritism towards the wicked (2) and their failure to defend the weak (3, 4); this is the opposite of what the ideal king of Psalm 72 would do. As a result, God condemns them for their wilful ignorance (5a) and for the shattering effect they have on the moral foundations of the earth (5b).

God has given them the great dignity of being god-like creatures, 'sons of the Most High', made in the image and likeness of God (6). When Jesus claimed to be the Son of God the Father, he was claiming to be the human being perfectly in the image of God and therefore participating in God's divine nature (cf. John 10:30-38; Col. 1:15, 19; 2:9). But these leaders are condemned to mere mortality; far from being enduring god-like rulers of the people of God, they will perish just like any gentile ruler (7).

The prophet concludes with a prayer that God will 'rise up' (cf. Num. 10:35) and 'judge the earth'. He prays that God will do what He has promised to do, because 'all the nations are your inheritance' in fulfilment of the covenant with Abraham (Gen. 12:1-3).

The psalm finds its fulfilment when Jesus our great Prophet declares the judgement of God on the wicked rulers and leaders of the people of God. In the days of His earthly ministry they used to 'devour widows' houses' (Mark 12:40) and routinely abuse their positions of power (Matt. 23:1-36). Jesus declares God's judgement on them. When we join in this psalm we too commit ourselves to being Christlike leaders (if we are entrusted with leadership) and to praying for God's cleansing judgement on unworthy leaders and pastors of His people. Our prayer extends beyond this to people who exercise power in all the world, since 'all the nations' will be God's 'inheritance'.

Psalm 83
[Vol. 1: 132-133, 224]

An individual representative of the people of God ('Asaph', v. 13 'my God') leads the church of God in prayer under terrible pressure. The three lines of verse 1 express intense yearning that God will no longer be silent. Verses 2-8 describe the danger; verse 2 begins with 'Behold!' (NIV 'See…'). Verses 2-4 sound a crescendo of hostility to God, expressed in hostility to His people (3 'your people…those you cherish'), and culminating in the terrible goal of total destruction (4), so that 'Israel's *name* is remembered no more'. But Israel's 'name' represents God's 'name' on earth; so this hostility is of cosmic seriousness.

Verses 5-8 speak of a worldwide 'alliance' (lit. 'covenant') against the people of God, with a litany of ancient enemies, mostly close at hand, in all directions, and backed by 'Assyria' the superpower (hence '*Even* Assyria…'). This may suggest the period before Assyria destroyed the northern tribes; or perhaps 'Assyria' is a generic shorthand for worldwide superpower hostility in a later age.

The threat is terrible, not just for the people of God, but for the 'name' or reputation of God on earth and for His rule. There are echoes here of Psalm 2:1-3.

The intense prayer of verse 1 is made explicit in verses 9-18. It begins with remembering two of the great rescues in the days of the Judges, that from Midian (9a) and their leaders Oreb, Zeeb, Zebah and Zalmunna, (11) and that from Sisera (9b, 10). These are recorded in Judges chapters 4–7. Notice that their malicious goal in history (v. 12 'Let us take possession of the pasture-lands of God') echoes the contemporary aim expressed so terribly in verse 4 ('Come… let us destroy them…'). The God who rescued His people then is called upon to save them today.

The strong language of verses 13-18 are a cry for the total defeat of these enemies of the church. This is necessary because, so long as they are roaring their hostility, the church is surrounded by those who will not rest until they are totally destroyed. Either the church survives or the world survives; they cannot coexist forever. But notice the goal of the prayer (standing in contrast to the malicious goals of v. 4 and v. 12). This is expressed in verse 16b ('so that they will seek your *name*') and verse 18 ('Let them know that you, whose *name* is the LORD – that you alone are the Most High over all the earth'). Either by conversion – so that God's enemies are destroyed by becoming his friends – or by destruction, they must know and honour the 'name' of God as Most High. God's rescue of His church is the defining proof of the greatness of His 'name'.

The time came when the remnant of faithful Israel focused itself on the one true Israelite, Jesus Christ, who defined and lived out all that Israel was called to be. He supremely was surrounded by enemies on every side, who were determined to destroy His 'name' from off the earth (e.g. Acts 4:25-27). They killed Him, but God raised Him (e.g. Acts 4:10). God did for Jesus Christ what this prayer prays for the people of God; He was surrounded by malicious enemies on every side, and yet, at the moment of His death on the cross, God defeated all these enemies; and on Easter morning God declared Him Lord and Christ. When this message was first proclaimed, the hearers asked in alarm, 'What shall we do?' (Acts 2:37). Some of them sought and found and lived 'for the sake of the Name' (3 John 7).

Today the church of Jesus Christ is surrounded by a hostile world, and can pray this psalm in Christ, confident that the God who rescued Israel from Midian and Sisera, the God who saved His people from all its ancient enemies, the God who saved Jesus Christ from death and the one who held the power of death, this same God will rescue all the church of Christ.

Psalm 84

[Vol 1: 193]

This psalm teaches us to delight in the blessing given to 'the one who trusts in you' (12); supremely this blessing is given to Jesus, who trusted unfailingly in the Father; it is ours in Him.

This song expresses a deep heart longing for the sheer incomparable beauty of the covenant God of the Bible, who is desired for Himself alone. In verses 1-4 a Spirit-inspired representative of the people of God voices this yearning. He longs for home, the place where his heart belongs: verse 1 'your dwelling place'; verse 2 'the courts…'; verse 3 'a home…a nest…a place…'; verse 4 'your house'. It is the dwelling-place of 'the LORD Almighty' (1,3), the all-powerful covenant God, a place where insignificantly small creatures find a home (3), a place where the 'altar' (3) speaks of atonement and restored relationship with the holy God. For this place, this incomparably lovely God, his heart yearns.

But he is not there. Perhaps he is in exile in Babylon. Wherever he is, he sings a song for all the people of God living as exiles (1 Pet. 1:1) in a world far from the heavenly Jerusalem. And so, after speaking of the loveliness of home (1-4), he speaks about the journey home (5-7). There will be 'blessing' (4) when we reach home; but there is 'blessing' also (5) for us when our 'hearts are set on pilgrimage', when 'the highways' to Zion are in our hearts. All of life is a longing for home and a journey home. Verses 5-7 are a wonderful promise. We will need to pass through 'the Valley of Baca' (an unknown place, but clearly a dry and hard place); but even there we will find 'springs...pools' (6) of life-giving grace sufficient for the journey. Although our bodies and minds may fail, inwardly we will be renewed by the Spirit of God all the way to 'Zion' (7, cf. 2 Cor. 3:16).

Verses 8 and 9 are the puzzle. Suddenly, seemingly out of nowhere, the psalmist ('my prayer') leads the people of God ('...our...') in praying for God's 'favour' (that is, grace) on 'your anointed one' (the Messiah or King). Why? Because all blessing for the people of God depends upon God's blessing on the Messiah, in whom 'every spiritual blessing' is found (Eph. 1:3). And so a psalm that echoes much of Psalm 1 is tied also to Psalm 2.

The word 'favour' (grace) is repeated in verse 11. The 'favour and honour (glory)' that the covenant God bestows all comes in and through the 'favour' bestowed upon His Messiah. Verses 10-12 reprise the themes of the psalm. Along with 'blessed' (v. 12, echoing v. 4 and v. 5), perhaps the word 'good' (v. 10 'better' = '(more) good than...'; v. 11) sums up the theme. In addition, the moral element of goodness is introduced by the contrast with 'the tents of the wicked' (10) and 'those whose way of life is blameless' (11). Goodness of blessing comes only through the moral goodness of our Messiah and the moral goodness both imputed to us in Him and gradually given to us by His Spirit in progressive sanctification.

When we sing this song, led by Jesus our Messiah, we begin to share His heart love for His Father, the sustaining grace He knew in His earthly life of pilgrimage, and the assurance that every blessing is found in the Father through Him.

Psalm 85

The people of God in this psalm begin with a significant re-membrance (1-3), respond with a heartfelt petition (4-7) and listen to a sustained promise (8-13). The prayer is plural ('us.. us..'); only in verse 8 do we hear the solo Spirit-inspired psalmist leader's voice ('I…'). It is as though the people pray corporately and then listen as our leader teaches us the promise of God.

The memory is of some past time when God 'showed favour' to His 'land'. The promised land stands for the covenant people of God in His place. Verses 2 and 3 signifi-cantly define what 'favour' means. It is deeper than more comfortable circumstances. For it involves an acknowledg-ment of God's righteous 'wrath', His 'fierce anger' against sinners; only forgiveness, sins being 'covered' by an atoning sacrifice, can turn away His anger.

It is precisely this for which we pray in verses 4-7. The words 'restore' and 'anger' echo verses 1-3. When we pray for 'unfailing love' (*chesed*) and 'salvation' (7) it is atoning sacrifice that turns away the wrath of God for which we pray.

In response to this heartfelt prayer, the leader, speaking by the Spirit of Christ, tells us the promise he has heard from God the Father (8-13). All the blessings cascading down here come when his people no longer 'turn to folly' (8). The 'turn' verb comes five times in this psalm (1, 3, 4, 6, 8) and speaks of God's turning to his people: 'restored…

turned from... anger... Restore... revive (lit. turn to life); and also of his people's not turning away to folly.

The cascade of blessings comes in the following overlapping words: 'unfailing love' (7); 'peace' (8); 'salvation... glory...' (9); 'love' (= *chesed* again, v. 10); 'faithfulness... righteousness...peace' (10); 'faithfulness...righteousness...' (11); 'good...harvest' (12); 'righteousness' (13a) and above all 'his steps' (13b), that is, the presence of the living God. These blessings come from above, from below, and from in front ('before him' v. 13). They are all-encompassing and fill the promised 'land' (vv. 9, 11 'earth', v. 12). The new heavens and new earth – which the promised land foreshadows – will be filled full of the covenant mercies of God.

All these mercies are found in Christ, the one in whom 'grace and truth' (which is the Greek translation of 'love and faithfulness', John 1:14,17) is found in all its fullness. Christ is our peace, our salvation, our glory, our grace and love, our truth and faithfulness, our righteousness, our only and all-sufficient good.

When the anonymous 'son of Korah' sings this psalm by the Spirit of Christ, we hear the voice of the one who will bring, in His own person and by His own atoning death, all the blessings promised in this psalm. When we pray this psalm with Him, we thank God for every spiritual blessing found in Him (Eph. 1:3) and cry to God our heavenly Father for more and more of the fruit of these blessings in His forgiven church.

Psalm 86

[Vol. 1: 149, 151, 163, 185, 200, 225]

This is the only 'of David' psalm in Book 3. It cuts in on the 'sons of Korah' group from 84 to 88. It breathes the atmosphere of Books 1 and 2, with numerous echoes. Why is this older psalm included here? We cannot be sure. But perhaps it is a timely reminder, at a time of exile, that all the old truths of the anointed king and his covenant God are as relevant now – when there is no king – as they ever were. For they are timeless in their significance for the people of God.

The song focuses intensely on the relationship between the king and his covenant God. It is instructive to trace the nine uses of the word 'for' or 'because' (1, 2, 3, 4, 5 – which lit. begins 'For…' – 7, 10, 13, 17). In verses 1-4 the focus is on the king, his need (v. 1 'poor and needy') and his faith: he is 'faithful' (v. 2a; the word means 'the recipient of God's faithful love' and someone who demonstrates that faithfulness); he is God's 'servant' (a covenant relationship word) who 'trusts' in God (2b); he calls to God in prayer (3); and he puts his trust in God (4). All the faith of this devout king is directed to the covenant God.

Verses 5-7 shift the focus towards the character of God. In words that echo the most-quoted verses in the Old Testament, Exodus 34:6, 7, in verse 5 David says he calls on God because He is forgiving, good, and abounding in steadfast love (*chesed*). Therefore he is confident (7) that when he, the trusting servant king, calls in prayer, his prayer will be answered.

In verses 8-10 the king sings in wonder about the unique and glorious character of his God. There is 'none like' Him (8); He 'alone' is the true God (10). Three times David uses words from the verb 'to do': '*deeds*' (8), 'the nations you have *made*' (9), and '*do* marvellous deeds' (10). What this God *does* expresses who He *is*, in His wonderful covenant love and grace. The reference to 'the nations' (9) hints at the fulfilment of the Abrahamic covenant, that worldwide worship will result from God's covenant with this faithful one.

In verses 11-12 the king shows that his devotion is untainted by presumption. He prays to be taught to walk in God's ways (11a) and for 'an undivided heart' so that he will serve and praise 'with all my heart' (12a) without a trace of double-mindedness (cf. James 1:8).

Verses 13-17 reiterate and emphasise the themes of the prayer. Verse 13 makes it clear that the troubles from which this king needs rescuing take him all the way down to 'the realm of the dead'. Again, verse 15 echoes Exodus 34:6,7.

While it is moving to consider David praying such an intimate prayer of urgent need and humble devotion, it is all the more deeply moving to trace this song on the lips of Jesus of Nazareth. It focuses our attention intensely on the unbreakable covenant bond between Jesus Christ the Son of God and God His heavenly Father. You and I scarcely feature in the song at all. The only hint is in verse 9; for the worldwide people of this king are 'the nations' who 'will come and worship' and 'bring glory to your name' because of the faithfulness of the Son to the Father and the steadfast love of the Father to the Son.

As we sing this prayer with Jesus, we too are drawn in to this intimate relationship, in Christ, of need, of trust, of faithfulness, of resting our destiny with Christ on the covenant love of the Father. We too pray to be taught the Father's way and to have an undivided heart (11).

Psalm 87

[Vol. 1: 193-196]

This is an extraordinary song to sing during or after the exile, at times when Zion had little or no visible glory. This 'son of Korah' leads us, by the Spirit of Christ, to sing a song of a glory that will come to Zion only when Christ comes. The older 'of David' Psalm 86 says that when the king is established 'All the nations you have made will come and worship before you, Lord; they will bring glory to your name' (Ps. 86:9). Psalm 87 tells us what that glory will be. Zion, the city 'on the holy mountain', the city of the king (Ps. 2:6). The city 'founded' (1) and 'established' (6) by God. The spring from which its glory flows is the love of the covenant God who 'loves the gates of Zion' (2).

Verses 4-6 sing of an international and very surprising glory. Men and women within the great ancient enemies, Egypt (nicknamed 'Rahab' the sea monster) and Babylon, will bow the knee to the God of Zion; so will the ancient irritants the Philistines, the great idolaters of wealth, the Tyrians, the distant and ethnically remote inhabitants of Cush. Zion's citizens were deeply hostile to God, were full of idolatry, and are astonishingly diverse. These very surprising men and women will be given citizenship in Zion and even – more than just citizenship – an honorary birth certificate: 'This one was born there!' And this one; and that one, all over the world. These (new) birth certificates will be personally written, one by one, by the covenant God (6). These men and women, who by nature rejoiced in many natural privileges or talents or pleasures, will now acknowledge that there is one, and only one, privilege in which they deeply rejoice (7): 'All my fountains are in you' – in Zion, in the fellowship and city of God's king.

As the Lord Jesus leads His church in singing of the glory of the heavenly Zion, we rejoice with Him at this new birth by which we are made citizens of heaven (Phil. 3:20). When we meet with Christ's church we have come to Mount Zion (Heb. 12:22), that 'the Jerusalem that is above…is our mother' (Gal. 4:26), in anticipation of that final gathering of men and women, 'a great multitude that no one could count, from every nation, tribe, people, and language' (Rev. 7:9), when we will see 'the Lamb, standing on Mount Zion, and with him' every single one of His gathered people (Rev. 14:1).

We are challenged to value our new birth and therefore our membership of the church of Christ above all other privileges, and to rejoice at the multi-ethnic, multi-cultural, multi-national gathering that is the local church of Christ, with all its problems. For it is precisely its cultural non-homogeneity that is its glory. It is also a song to sing when we are discouraged by the church of Christ; for it has within its brief verses the promise of a great glory to be revealed.

Psalm 88
[Vol. 1: 34, 114-123]

How can we pray this darkest of all psalms? An otherwise unknown Old Covenant believer sings with persistent faith in deep suffering made deeper by God-forsakeness; and – on first reading - he appears to end without hope.

The persistence of his faith is demonstrated in the repeated expressions of prayer. In verses 1 and 2 he declares 'you are the God who saves me' and therefore he prays 'day and night'. This headline affirmation stands, no matter how deep the darkness that follows. He comes back to urgent prayer in verse 9 'every day' and again in verse 13 'in the morning'.

But perhaps the most impressive feature of the psalm is the evocation of deep suffering. Verses 3-5 begin with 'I…' and speak of the shadow of imminent death. Like the demoniac of Mark 5:2, living among the tombs, this man lives already very close to Sheol. The worst fact, however, comes from verse 5b to verse 8a, where the subject changes from 'I...' to 'You...' God is the agent of these sufferings; he has put this believer in these depths. This man is God-forsaken.

After the prayer of verse 9, verses 10-12 express the perplexity of faith with a series of questions. He believes God works 'wonders,' shows 'love' (*chesed*, covenant love) and 'faithfulness' and does 'righteous deeds'. It is vital for the health of the universe that the good God be praised for His goodness, that these 'wonders' should be 'known'. He is the God of the living, not of the dead (cf. Matt. 22:32). This believer's death cannot be the end of the story. Nothing short of bodily resurrection can answer these questions.

After the prayer of verse 13, verses 14-18 reprise the themes of the song. But how can we pray it? There are several answers. We enter empathetically into the sufferings of this unknown believer, perhaps representative of the struggles of believers at the time of, and after, the exile. Supremely they open for us a window into the darkness of the cross of Christ. But they also speak for us as the suffering church of Christ in every age. For the attacks of death and the one who holds the power of death upon Christ's church are attacks upon Christ. We pray this for ourselves, in especial identification with the persecuted church, and to shape in our own affections a realism in facing darkness, an intense perplexity of faith, and yet – under it all – a persistence in praying and a continuation in believing, however deep the darkness.

Psalm 89

[Vol. 1: 40, 152, 199, 206]

In this paradoxical and climactic psalm of Book 3 we are invited to rejoice in a wonderful love precisely as we lament with a terrible grief and wait in suffering hope. Time and again in Book 3 we are taken into the sadness of exile: Psalms 74, 77, 79, 80, 83 and 88 are perhaps the clearest examples. The whole book smells of exile; Psalm 89 is a fitting conclusion. The psalm begins (1, 2) and ends (46-51) on a very personal note, as this otherwise unknown man, 'Ethan the Ezrahite', sings ('I... I... my... my...') by the Spirit of God, who is the Spirit of Christ.

In verses 1-37 he invites us to rejoice deeply in a wonderful faithful love. The words 'love' (*chesed*, covenant steadfast love) and 'faithfulness' (to covenant promises) dominate, occurring fourteen times (in vv. 1, 2, 5, 8, 14, 23, 28, 33). He begins (1-4) by singing of the love and faithfulness of God, that is established in heaven for all time, by which God made a covenant with David that his 'line' (lit. 'seed') would endure for ever.

In verses 5-8 he expands on the words 'in heaven itself' (2): this faithfulness (that brackets the section, vv. 5, 8) is integral to, and inseparable from, the almighty power of God. In verses 9-13 he expands on this strength to praise God that this power really is almighty: it encompasses the whole created order, including the chaotic forces of evil, symbolized by 'the surging sea'. Nothing can defeat it. Verse 14 sums up the psalm to this point: it is by righteousness, justice, love, and faithfulness (more or less synonymous covenant words) that God rules the world.

And so, in verses 15-18, we sing with a joyful people, who rejoice precisely because of the covenant with David, that God has given us a 'horn' (a strong one, to defeat our enemies), a 'shield' (to protect us) and a 'king' (to rule over us with the kingship of God). Verses 19-29 retell the glory of the covenant with this king. The three notes that are sounded are His strength and victory (bringing the power of God to bear on the world), His intimate relationship as Son to the Father, and His everlasting reign (because He rules with the eternal God). He will rule for God over everything; God's rule over the 'sea' (9, 10) will be executed by this king (25). Verses 30-37 praise God that this covenant cannot be defeated by human sin. It really is an eternal covenant, rooted in the solidity of creation itself (v. 37 'like the moon…').

And yet – with the exquisite pain of exile, after which there was never again in Old Testament history a Davidic king – verses 38-46 call us to lament with a grief whose depth is forced deep into our hearts precisely by the joy that has preceded it. The key word is 'angry'(vv. 38, echoed in vv. 46 'wrath… fire'). All the reversals (defeat in place of victory, transience instead of eternity, shame rather than glory) are God's righteous anger at the sin of His people. It is not (as some think) that the psalmist accuses God of breaking his faithfulness; rather that he struggles with a tension that is unresolved until the Cross of Christ. How can a covenant that is certain (30-37) be consistent with the righteousness of God, by which it ought also to be (as it often is in the Old Testament) conditional?

And so, in verses 47-51, he prays very personally, because his own hope in the face of death depends on God keeping his promise of this king. Because he sings by the Spirit of Christ, he is caught up in the pain of the rejected king, and bears in his heart (50) the mockery directed to God's 'anointed one' (his Messiah, or Christ).

The surprising ascription of praise (52) is both the conclusion to Book 3 of the Psalms and – at the same time – the punchline to this psalm. For, in the perplexity and the pain, the underlying message is of faith. The question 'how long?' presupposes that there will be a resolution. That resolution came at the Cross of Christ, when the anointed king of God's people stood as their Representative Head and endured the wrath of God as their sacrificial Substitute. And so – most wonderfully – the wrath of God is satisfied, the faithfulness of God is vindicated, the covenant that had to be conditional is proved to be certain, because the faithful King has come.

As we sing this psalm, led by the Lord Jesus Christ, we too rejoice deeply at this wonderful faithful love, feel acutely the pain of sin's punishment, and long yearningly for the Lord Jesus to return in glory.

BOOK 4

Introduction to Book 4

Book 4 has a different feel to Book 3. It brings a different angle to the response of the people of God to the judgement of God in the exile and its aftermath. Most of the psalms here have no superscription. There is little or nothing about the human king in David's line, although this does not mean the hope for a Messiah in David's line has been abandoned (as some scholars suggest). The major emphasis is on the security and assurance that comes to the people of God from knowing that the covenant God is the ultimate king, whose sovereign faithfulness guarantees all the promises of the covenant.

The book begins with a deeply significant 'prayer of Moses' (90), unique as such in the Psalter. Moses appears seven times in Book 4 (90:1; 99:6; 103:7; 105:26; 106:16, 23, 32); outside Book 4 he appears only once (77:21). The prophets often spoke of the return from exile as a second Exodus; hence perhaps the frequent references here to Moses and the first Exodus. Psalm 91 responds to the plea of Psalm 90 with a wonderful promise – perhaps implicitly to the king, but through him to the people – of long life and salvation.

After this, Psalms 92-100 would appear to be a sub-section; all are anonymous. The refrain 'The LORD reigns' comes several times (93:1; 96:10; 97:1; 99:1) and there are other references to God being king (e.g. 95:3; 98:6).

After this there are two older psalms 'of David' (101, 103) and one 'of an afflicted person' (102). All three reaffirm 'the ongoing significance of Davidic kingship'[1]. The book concludes with a threesome of long 'Hallelujah' psalms, with the refrain 'Praise the LORD!' (104-6). These focus on creation (104) and then the long history of God's faithfulness (105) and Israel's unfaithfulness (106), concluding with a prayer to 'gather us from the nations' (106:47).

Overall there is a pushing back, deeper into Israel's history, behind the covenant with David that appears to be broken (Ps. 89), to the story of God's faithfulness right back to Abraham and then in the time of Moses. And there is a pushing up, beyond the hope for an earthly Messiah, to the sovereign God in heaven who guarantees this hope. When Jesus, the believing Israelite, first sang these psalms, they must have been to Him a deep reassurance that His heavenly Father reigns in covenantal faithfulness and will finally bring about the end of the exile (106:47), as indeed He did, through Jesus Himself (cf. Matt. 1:1-18). They reassure Christ's exiled church (e.g. 1 Pet. 1:1) in much the same way, that we will finally be gathered, in and with Christ, into our inheritance, now kept in heaven for us (1 Pet. 1:4), and one day to descend from heaven to earth (Rev. 21).

---

1. O. Palmer Robertson, *The Flow of the Psalms*, p. 149. I have followed Palmer Robertson's structure for Book 4.

Psalm 90

[Vol. 1: 148]

This is a unique psalm, the only 'prayer of Moses, the man of God' (a title that means a prophet in the Old Testament and a pastor in the New). Moses will now feature in no less than six of the seventeen psalms in Book 4. It is a plural, corporate psalm in which Moses leads the people of God in prayer, at a time of great discouragement, perhaps in the wilderness (such as Num. 21, during the plague of snakes). By placing it at the start of Book 4, immediately after the exile context of Book 3, the compilers of the Psalter signal that it becomes a prayer for the church of God in and after the exile. Centuries later it will become a prayer of the Lord Jesus, in which the greatest Man of God, the Great Pastor of God's people, leads His exiled church in prayer.

The prayer comes in four movements. It begins by working in us a settled affection (1, 2). The phrases 'all generations' and 'from everlasting to everlasting' were repeatedly used in Psalm 89, of the covenant. Now Moses presses us right back, behind that covenant, to the unchangeable faithfulness of God Himself. He is our 'dwelling-place'; in saying these words with Jesus our new Moses we settle our affections, with His, in the home that is God, both our Father and His.

187

By contrast, the second movement (3-6) brings us into a sober realism about our transience. God is everlasting; we are but dust that has been temporarily assembled into human life (Gen. 2:7) but can at any time, and one day will, be returned to dust (Gen. 3:19). We think and act as if we were immortal; by joining with Jesus our new Moses in this section we face our frailty with honesty and humility, as He did His.

We then learn a sad wisdom (7-12). If the second movement teaches us that we do not belong in this age, the third movement teaches us why we do not belong: we are transient because we are sinners under the wrath of God. All the sadness of ageing (10a), ending with the pathetic final sigh of death (9b) and blighted, even on its proudest days by 'trouble and sorrow' (10b), is because of the righteous anger of God against us sinners. As we sing this with the one who became sin for us (2 Cor. 5:21), we acknowledge that death is the rightful wages of sin (Rom. 6:23) and that, even enjoying forgiveness as we do, our bodies are still subject to death because of sin and we are still waiting for the redemption of our bodies (Rom. 8:10,23).

In all this, the decision to join in the praying of this psalm is deeply humbling. The final movement (13-17) encourages and stirs in us a sure faith in the covenant-keeping God, who has said 'yes!' to every promise of the covenant in Christ (2 Cor. 1:20). Covenant words and phrases come thick and fast, beginning with the only use of the covenant name, 'the LORD', and the question 'how long?' which is the question of covenant faith, for it supposes there will be an end to judgement (as in Ps. 89:46). Others include the designation 'your servants' (13, 16), and the use of the covenant love word *chesed* (v. 14 'unfailing love'). In this prayer for compassion

Jesus leads us in praying for resurrection and the final undoing of all the ravages of sin. Most wonderfully, He leads us to pray corporately (17) that what we do in this age in His service ('the work of our hands') will, astonishingly, be 'established', so that – although our lives in this age are on the path from dust to dust – all that we do 'in the Lord' will last (1 Cor. 15:58).

Psalm 91

In this deservedly famous and precious psalm, the cries of the people of God in Psalm 90 are wonderfully answered. In verses 1 and 2 we watch one man taking shelter in the Almighty covenant God, towards whom he extends personal trust ('my God, in whom I trust'). The psalm is a promise to this man who reaches out in authentic faith. When Satan quotes a promise from this psalm, he prefaces it with, 'If you are the Son of God...' (Luke 4:9). This is a title for the Davidic King. This confirms what we might suspect, from its prevalence in the psalms, that the primary recipient of the promises of this psalm is the king in David's line.[1] If you are the king in David's line, these promises are for you. This is what Satan implies, and Jesus does not deny (although, as we shall see, he strongly disagrees with the way in which Satan wants him to use the promise).

What follows is a declaration *about* God (vv. 3-13, of the form 'he... you...' where the 'you' is singular) and a climactic word *from* God (vv. 14-16, of the form 'I... him...').

A Spirit-inspired prophetic voice declares (3-13) that God will comprehensively protect this man from persecution

---

1. Following this understanding, the NIV correctly footnotes the pronoun 'he' in verse 14 with a note, 'that is, probably the king'.

(v. 3b 'the fowler's snare') and will bring him under the wings of the cherubim that stretch their wings over the Ark of the Covenant, so that there, entrusting himself to covenant 'faithfulness', he will be protected (4). In verses 5 and 6 there is a crescendo, from 'night' and 'day' to 'darkness' (intense night) and 'midday' (fierce light). These 'terrors' that 'stalk' and 'destroy' evoke demonic forces; these verses are intended to terrify and then deeply to reassure; for if even demonic forces of darkest night and fiercest noon can do no harm, truly this man has nothing to fear. Verses 7 and 8 shift the imagery to the judgements of God ('the punishment of the wicked'); this terrifying wrath will strike thousands, indeed tens of thousands, the countless persecutors that surround him, but this trusting man will be safe. When he sees them fall, he will 'see the punishment of the wicked'.

Verse 9 echoes verses 1 and 2; and the word 'dwelling' is the same as that used in Psalm 90:1 ('you have been our *dwelling-place*'). Now the promise is spelt out in terms of angelic messengers (11, 12), God's agents sent to serve those who will inherit salvation (Heb. 1:14), who will protect the trusting one. Not only will he be protected, he will be given power to conquer all the powers of evil (13).

In verses 14-16 we hear the voice of God personally putting His seal to the promise to this man who 'loves me'; the word means 'clings to me in love' and is used of God's love for His people (e.g. Deut. 7:7). This man shows personal faith by 'acknowledging my name' (14) and calling on the LORD in prayer (15). He will be comprehensively rescued.

This psalm will have been of deep reassurance to Jesus, the anointed King. For, supremely, Jesus is this trusting man. He is the one who dwells in the shelter of the Most High and shows precisely this obedient, personal, loving faith in God the Father. Satan sought to twist the promise in a most subtle way, when he quoted verses 11 and 12 (Matt. 4:6; Luke 4:10, 11). He tempted Jesus to hijack the promise, and wield it like a magic wand, as a superstitious word that he could use, independent of personal trust and obedience to the God who gave the promise. It is this taking of the promise apart from faith in the promise-giver that Jesus resisted.

It is when we are 'in Christ', that we too are given this authentic faith and are incorporated into this wonderful security; all these promises become ours in him. Significantly, Jesus explicitly promises that His disciples will be given authority over evil, in terms echoing verse 13 (see Luke 10:19, 'I have given you authority to trample on snakes and scorpions and to overcome all the power of the enemy; nothing will harm you', cf. 1 John 5:4). As for Jesus, so for us, these promises are for the end; before they are fulfilled in their entirety, we should expect much suffering (cf. Rom. 8:17). But, in Christ, and in Christ alone, let us rejoice in the comprehensive final assurance of this precious psalm.

Psalm 92
[Vol. 1: 188]

A Spirit-inspired anonymous individual leads the people of God in a confident proclamation about God. The beginning (v. 2 'proclaiming…'), middle (v. 8 'But you, LORD…') and end (v. 15 'proclaiming…') of the psalm are the critical punctuation points.

In verses 1-3 the psalmist declares the sheer goodness of proclaiming the covenant 'love' and 'faithfulness' of the covenant God in joyful song, morning and night. This delight is public ('proclaiming…') and effervescent ('music… lyre… harp…'). At its heart is the 'love' and 'faithfulness' of God and His sovereignty to achieve what His covenant promises ('O Most High').

Verses 4-7 begin to give the reason for this joy (v. 4 'For…'). Verses 4 and 5 focus on the covenant God's 'deeds… what your hands have done… works… thoughts!' The outflow of His inward nature ('thoughts') is both creation and redemption (the twin foci of His 'works' in the Psalms). This is 'profound' because it is hidden from 'senseless people' (6, 7). The visible evidence of life suggests that 'the wicked…flourish' (cf. Ps. 73). Only the believer grasps that they flourish only like the transient 'grass' of a hot climate and will soon be 'destroyed for ever'. The unique heading 'For the Sabbath day' may hint at the completeness of the Created Order and its final fulfilment in the Sabbath rest of the people of God (cf. Heb. 4:1-11). Morality cannot be separated from the sheer givenness and solidity of Creation, as if evil could flourish for ever; it cannot and will not, and he is a fool who thinks it can.

Verse 8, at the heart of the psalm, declares the eternal exaltation of the covenant God, anticipating the refrain 'the LORD reigns' that will recur in other psalms of this section (92-100).

Verse 9 reiterates emphatically the certainty of judgement. And then verses 10-11 speak, not of the exaltation of God (8), but of the exaltation of this individual. In language strongly reminiscent both of the king (23:5; 45:7) and the priest (133:2), he rejoices that he has been made strong ('my horn') and anointed with fine oil. Echoing Psalm 91:8, he declares that he has 'seen' the defeat of his enemies (11 *my* adversaries...*my* wicked foes'), who are also God's enemies (v. 9 *'your* enemies'). The singer of this psalm sings by the Spirit of the one who will be so closely identified with the covenant God that his enemies are God's enemies and his exaltation is God's exaltation.

There is a significant alternation of singular and plural in verses 12-15. Verse 12 is singular (lit. 'The righteous one... he will grow...'); verses 13 and 14 are plural; and in verse 15 he returns to the singular ('my Rock...'). With strong echoes of Psalm 1, both this exalted man (12, 15) and all who belong to him (13, 14), far from being destroyed like grass (7), will flourish like a strong and fruitful tree, even into old age. His testimony, and their testimony with him, is the proclamation (15) that the covenant God is upright, that He is the righteous judge who may be trusted even when evildoers flourish. As Christ rejoiced in this comfort and assurance when surrounded by the flourishing of evil, so we exult, with and in Him, in this same confidence.

Psalm 93
[Vol. 1: 153]

The surprise of this psalm is verse 5. Where have 'your statutes' come from, in a psalm about creation? This is less surprising when we unpack the opening acclamation 'The LORD reigns!' Picking up the theme of God's sovereignty from Psalm 92:8, this vivid declaration appears only in Book 4 of the psalms (93:1; 96:10; 97:1; 99:1) and in 1 Chronicles 16:31. 1 Chronicles 16 tells how David brought the Ark of the Covenant into the tabernacle in Jerusalem. It is a chapter that is closely echoed in three of the psalms of Book 4: verses 8-22 in Psalm 105:1-15; verses 23-33 in

Psalm 96:1-13; and verses 34-36 in Psalm 106:1, 47, 48. This Ark contained the two tablets on which the Ten Commandments of the covenant were inscribed. So the declaration, 'The LORD reigns!' is saying something more specific than just, 'God is in control'. It proclaims that the God of the covenant, whose law is summed up in the Ten Commandments kept in the Ark in the tabernacle (or, later, Temple), rules the world. It is no longer so surprising that verse 5 concludes the psalm by speaking of His 'statutes', His 'holiness', and His 'house'. For it is from His 'house' and by His holy law that He rules the world.

The psalm begins with a creed affirmed (1, 2). Because the covenant God reigns, and has always ruled from all eternity, 'the world is established'. That is, there is an unbreakable order – both a physical order and a moral order – in Creation that cannot be overthrown, because it owes its existence to the sovereign God of the covenant.

Every believer believes this. But we do not always know experientially what we believe theoretically. Verses 3 and 4 move us from a creed affirmed to a challenge answered. The challenge is portrayed in a vigorous crescendo of three lines in verse 3. The seas speak in Bible imagery of the forces of chaos and evil; they are part of the Creation, under the sovereignty of God; they have no autonomous power to act; and yet they do pose a terrifying threat, moving – in this poetry – from an abstract 'lifting up' (3a), through a lifting up of 'their voice' (3b) to a lifting up of 'their pounding waves' (3c). As Jesus sang this, and as we sing this with Him, we feel in the poetry what we feel in experience, the terror of evil as it threatens moral order. The three lines of verse 3 are answered by the three lines of verse 4, with their repetition of 'mightier...mightier...mighty'. Evil is frightening and poses a real threat; and yet the sovereign covenant God 'on high' is stronger. The LORD reigns indeed.

And He does so from His 'house' by His 'statutes', in His 'holiness' (5). Verse 5 moves from a creed affirmed, and a challenge answered, to a covenant sovereignty declared. The 'house', 'statutes' and 'holiness' find their rich fulfilment in the one 'greater than the temple' (Matt. 12:6), who brings the kingdom of God to earth, who conquered the devil and all his power by His death on the cross (Col. 2:15), and who will finally hand the kingdom over to God the Father (1 Cor. 15:24). In Jesus Christ, the proper order of Creation will be restored. As we sing this psalm with him, we feel both the real terror of evil and the glorious sovereignty of God, eternal truth brought to earth in the Old Covenant foreshadowing by the Ark of the Covenant and in New Testament fulfilment in Jesus Christ.

Psalm 94

[Vol. 1: 109, 188]

Psalm 94 begins with a strong plea for the God who judges the whole earth to 'avenge' the wicked (1-3). This is far from our distorted ideas of hateful revenge; rather, it is the righteous legal action of putting wrongs to right and punishing evil (cf. Dt. 32:34-36; Rom. 12:19; Heb. 10:30). Although this psalm does not explicitly speak of God as king (cf. 'The LORD reigns' – the motif that dominates Pss. 92-100), this theme of sovereign judgement fits perfectly with it.

The singer is both one who leads his people in prayer and one who instructs that people. As so often in the Psalms, this voice finds its fulfilment in the prayers and the teaching of Jesus Christ as he intercedes for His people and instructs us. After his prayer in verses 1-3 he vividly describes why his prayer is necessary (4-7). These evildoers would seem to have influence in Israel. They speak proud words (4) and oppress God's people and land ('inheritance') by violent acts against the vulnerable (5, 6); in all this they are supremely confident that the covenant God will pay no attention; he will not judge (7).

In direct contradiction to what they say in verse 7, our singer gives a sober warning (8-11). What they are doing is 'senseless' (cf. Ps. 92:6,7; 2 Pet. 2:12) because God is the creator and the judge of all the earth (10a); it is stupid to think he turns a blind eye and a deaf ear to injustice among His own people. Paul quotes verse 11 in 1 Corinthians 3:20.

After the warning of verses 8-11, we hear a blessing in verses 12-15. Those who are truly God's people are characterized by being instructed and disciplined by God's law (12); they are 'upright in heart' (15). These, who truly are 'his people...his inheritance' (14) may be sure that judgement in their favour will be given (13, 15a).

This blessing is then expanded in the very personal testimony of verses 16-23 (with its repeated 'me', 'I', and 'my'). This leader in the people of God has stood against wickedness and injustice, as Jesus did so courageously against the Sadducees and Pharisees. But will he succeed? Yes! In the end he will, for the covenant God will give him help, as he helped this anonymous psalmist (17). He too will feel his feet slipping (18a) and be supported by his Father's 'unfailing love' (18b); he also will feel anxiety welling up within his troubled soul (19a) and find joy in the consolations his Father brought him (19b). In him, and in him alone, we too will find the consolations and loving support we need as we join him in prayer and uprightness of heart (e.g. 2 Cor. 1:5 'our comfort abounds through Christ').

That this anonymous psalmist is a leader is suggested by the references to the 'throne' in verse 20, with its implicit suggestion that the 'corrupt throne' needs to be replaced by a righteous throne, a king who will align himself with God's justice. The experience this Spirit-filled leader has of courageous standing for God's justice and of God's acting in judgement on his behalf is fulfilled in the greater experience of the Lord Jesus, and now of all His people in Him. As we pray this psalm with Jesus, we join Him in interceding for all His people and are reassured by His instruction, both the warning to the arrogant persecutors and the blessing promised to the upright in heart.

Psalm 95
[Vol. 1: 225]

A voice summons the people of God to come into His presence in the temple with exuberant, noisy acclamation (1, 2). This voice is anonymous; but, as so often in the Psalms, we shall see that it is ultimately the voice of the man who has heeded every word of this psalm, and who now leads the people of God in exhorting us to follow Him. We listen in the end to the exhortation and teaching of the Lord Jesus Christ our leader.

The leader supports his summons with a reason (3-5): come, sing with me, because the LORD is the great King above all gods! The unusual phrase 'above all gods' (3) appears in the Old Testament only here, in Psalms 96:4 and 97:9 and 1 Chronicles 16:25 (in the context of David bringing the Ark to Jerusalem)[2]. It ties this psalm in to the theme of the supreme greatness of God, that dominates Psalms 92-100. Verses 4 and 5 develop the comprehensiveness of His sovereignty, over 'the depths of the earth' (where the powers of death lurk), 'the mountain peaks' (where other spirits, gods, and goddesses may be supposed to dwell), 'the sea' (the wild place of chaos and evil) and 'the dry land' (where people live). As the Creator and Ruler of all, He has a claim on our worship and adoration, whoever we are.

This first summons (1, 2) and reason (3-5) are now followed up with a developed summons (6) and a more intimate reason (7a). The new summons is, not only to come with singing, but to 'bow down in worship...kneel' before the covenant God. The intimate reason is that He is 'our Maker', not simply the Creator of all things, but particularly and personally the Maker of the people of God, who owe our life and existence as a people to Him. He is 'our God', not because He belongs to us, but because we belong to Him, as the sheep who are His flock. This supreme sovereign Almighty God is the God committed to us by covenant. What better or more persuasive reason can there be to bow down to Him? 'Come, bow with me,' says our leader, 'because we are his!'

In this atmosphere of excited enthusiasm, the prophetic word of verses 7b-11 comes as a sobering shock. There is a great danger that we are carried along by the crowd into the presence of God, loving the shared excitement but lacking a change in our hearts. Much as the Lord Jesus in His earthly ministry gave sober warnings to shallow enthusiasts (e.g.

---

2. OPR 157.

Luke 9:57-62) so here He warns us His people: 'Today' –
for the day when we hear His voice is always the 'today' of
gospel opportunity (as Heb. 3:7-4:13 develops this psalm,
preaching a powerful hortatory sermon) – 'if only you
would hear his voice...' (echoing Ps. 81).

The sad reminders of the unbelief of the people of
God both at the beginnings of their post-Exodus wanderings (Exod. 17:1-7) and much later in the same travels
(Num. 20:1-13), demonstrate a persistent hardness of heart,
which will have resonated with a people facing the judgement of exile and its aftermath, just as it resonates with the
penitent and humbled people of Christ today.

And so, as we join in this psalm, we hear the voice of
Jesus our leader, summoning us: Come, sing with me, because the covenant God is great (1-5)! Come, bow with me,
because we are his (6,7a)! Come, listen to me, because this is
the today of gospel opportunity (7b-11)!

Psalm 96

[Vol. 1: 154]

This is the central psalm of the 'sovereignty of God'
series from 92-100. Flanked by Psalms 95 and 97, it
includes the rare phrase 'above all gods' (95:3; 96:4; 97:9;
1 Chron. 16:25); and it contains the key affirmation 'The
LORD reigns!' (96:10; 1 Chron. 16:31). The whole psalm
is closely paralleled in 1 Chronicles 16:23-33, part of the
song sung when David brought the Ark to Jerusalem. The
psalm takes as its starting point the world rule of God from
Jerusalem, His 'sanctuary' (6), the place of His 'holiness'
(9), governing the world according to the Creation Order
attested in the Ten Commandments within the Ark. The

throne of God in heaven merges with the throne of David in Jerusalem; here the kingdom of God comes to earth.

From this starting point, we hear a summons (1-3) supported by a reason (4-6), followed by a second summons (7-12) supported by a climactic reason (13).

The first summons (1-3) is for the people of God to sing the worldwide praises of God for His 'salvation' (rescue), His 'glory' (visible presence), and 'marvellous deeds' (in creation and redemption). It is a song that is 'new' not so much because of its content as by reason of its growing band of newly recruited singers, its growing choir –

The reason (4-6) is because He is the only true God, the Creator. All 'the gods of the nations', the objects of human worship all over the world, are 'idols' (5), empty nothingness, vacuous, powerless, insubstantial, not really real. From His 'sanctuary' (6) in Jerusalem, He governs the world He created. Because He made all things, every creature ought to sing His praises.

The second summons (7-12) reiterates and expands the first. All over the world the message is to be proclaimed, 'the LORD reigns' from His covenant 'holiness' (holy place) and by His covenant law (the Ten Commandments in the Ark). As this message is spoken, men and women from all the families of nations are to join the chorus (vv. 7-9, echoing Ps. 29:1); indeed, the whole created order is to praise Him (11, 12).

The climactic reason (13) is hinted at in verse 10: 'he will judge the peoples with equity'. The moral order of the world is 'firmly established' because there is a sovereign God who is judge and will judge. With its repetition of 'he comes', verse 13 proclaims, not simply that there are times in human history when God acts in provisional judgement, but finally that He will come in the last judgement. Because He is coming to judge, we are to rejoice, to join the choir of all who long for that day.

Quoting a very similar message on the lips of King David (Ps. 18:49), the Lord Jesus commits Himself to praising God 'among the nations' (Rom. 15:9); He tells the Father that, not only has He made Him known, by His life and supremely His death, but He 'will continue to' make Him known (John 17:26). Wonderfully Jesus does this as we sing this psalm with Him and commit ourselves to that great work of worldwide mission and proclamation of the saving sovereignty of God our King; by the lips of the evangelism of His people, His choir, Jesus sings the Father's praises all over the world. To sing this psalm is to stir our hearts to long for the great day when 'he comes' (Rev. 22:20) to judge the world (Acts 17:31).

Psalm 97

The words 'the LORD reigns' (1) and 'above all gods' (9) tie this psalm closely to the theme of God's sovereignty, ruling the world by His covenant word in the Ark brought to Jerusalem by King David (1 Chron. 16).

Joy suffuses this song. The whole world is summoned to gladness (1); Zion and its surroundings are glad (8); all who are righteous rejoice (11, 12).

But it is a stringent joy. For when we ask why they, or we, should rejoice, the answer is sobering and surprising. In verses 1-6 the refrain 'the LORD reigns' calls the whole earth to rejoice (1) because – in language that echoes Mount Sinai (vv. 2-5; Exod. 19:16-19; Deut. 4:24; Heb. 12:18-21, 29) – this sovereign God 'comes' (Ps. 96:13) in terrifying majesty and all-consuming fire. The Ark of the Covenant, whose coming to Jerusalem is the background to these psalms (cf. 1 Chron. 16), contains the tablets of the Law given at Sinai. The covenant God rules by His Law. This is the 'righteousness and justice' that are 'the foundation of his throne' (2); it is His 'righteousness' that 'the heavens proclaim' (6).

Because the God of Sinai comes, all idolaters, who breach the second commandment, should fear and repent (7). There will be no joy for impenitent idolaters.

The true 'Zion' (8) is clarified in verses 10-12. Zion consists of 'those who love the LORD...his faithful ones (the *chasidim*, the recipients of his covenant love, his *chesed*)... the righteous... the upright in heart... you who are righteous...' These are exhorted to 'hate evil' (10) and most of all to rejoice (11, 12).

This is a declaratory psalm, with teaching and exhortation but no prayer. In it we hear the voice of a prophetic leader of the people of God, fulfilled in the authoritative voice of Christ. Ultimately the only reason we may rejoice in the God of Sinai is that our leader has endured the consuming fires of the wrath of this righteous God (3) on behalf of His people. It is because of His blood, that speaks a better word, that we have come, not to Sinai terror, but to Zion, the place of atonement (Heb. 12:18-29). In Him we may and must rejoice at the sovereign just judgements of God.

Psalm 98
[Vol. 1: 181]

The title 'the LORD, the king' (6) links this with the series of kingship psalms (92-100). There are no enemies here;

they have disappeared from view. The only participants are the people of God and the world.

In verses 1-3 we are all exhorted to 'sing to the LORD a new song' – new, now, not just because there are new singers, but because the LORD has done a new thing. He has worked 'salvation' (mentioned in each verse), a rescue that demonstrates 'his faithfulness to Israel' (3). He has done this in the sight of 'the nations...the ends of the earth' (2,3). That is to say, he has done something for Israel that will bless the world.

This is an echo of the promise to Abraham (Gen. 12:1-3). Perhaps it originally referred to the return from exile, using language of a second Exodus (e.g. 'right hand' and 'holy arm' in v. 1 is Exod. language). But ultimately it points forward to the final end of the exile brought about through the coming of a Saviour for Israel. Mary sings that with the conception of her baby, God 'has helped his servant Israel, remembering to be merciful to Abraham and his descendants...' (Luke 1:54, 55). When Simeon takes the baby Jesus in his arms, he sings to God of seeing 'your salvation, which you have prepared in the sight of all nations; a light for revelation to the Gentiles, and the glory of your people Israel' (Luke 2:29-32). It is this act of salvation, given to Israel, that brings salvation to the world, for 'salvation is from the Jews' (John 4:22). The making known of this salvation, the revelation of this righteousness, attested by the scriptures (Rom. 3:21), is finally given through the propitiatory death of Jesus which demonstrates the righteousness of God (Rom. 3:25,26).

The brief exhortation in verse 1 ('Sing to the LORD a new song') is greatly expanded in verses 4-9a. If we were in any doubt about who is to sing this song, we are not any more: in verses 4-6 'all the earth', the beneficiaries of this great salvation, are to sing with vibrant jubilation (anticipating Ps. 150). Ultimately it is because of the cross of Christ, that 'the blessing given to Abraham might come to the Gentiles through Christ Jesus' (Gal. 3:14).

And there is more. For in verses 7 and 8 a groaning creation is called upon to join in the praise. For all the frustration, disorder, and decay to which creation has been subjected will end in a glorious liberation when the men and women who experience this salvation are finally revealed to govern the new heavens and new earth (Rom. 8:19-21).

There are two significant occurrences of the word 'for'. In verse 1 it introduces the first reason for this new song, the great act of salvation by which God sends Jesus to His people for the world. In verse 9 it introduces the final reason: 'for he comes to judge the earth...' Echoing Psalm 96:13 ('for he comes, he comes to judge the earth'), this looks forward to the return of Jesus Christ in glory, for final judgement (Acts 17:31). When we sing this psalm with Jesus, we join the new song that will look back with thankfulness to Jesus' first coming and rescuing death, and yearns forward for His return.

Psalm 99
[Vol. 1: 95-96, 149, 172, 181, 189, 210]

For the final time in this series, we hear 'The LORD reigns' (1). Again, the might of God the King is celebrated (4 'The King is mighty').

The psalm is punctuated by three similar refrains, each calling for praise and each proclaiming the holiness of the covenant God (3, 5, 9). This suggests that the psalm divides into three unequal sections, each ending in a refrain.

In verses 1-3 the focus is on 'the nations...the earth... the nations...'. From 'Zion', the 'holy' place to which King David has brought the Ark of the Covenant (1 Chron. 16:31 'the LORD reigns!'), above which he 'sits enthroned between the cherubim', the covenant God rules the world according to His Law. All the world ought to heed this call to praise His great and awesome 'name', His revealed person and nature.

The emphasis in verses 4-5 is on 'Jacob' his people. Again the section begins by affirming His greatness ('The King is mighty...') and again it ends with a call to exalt Him and bow in worship (5). This is because 'in Jacob' he has 'done what is just and right'.

The final, longer section (6-9) is rather different. It picks up the thought of 'Jacob' and the holy place in Zion and develops it in terms of access to God. The common quality of Moses, Aaron, and – later – Samuel (6) was that 'they called on the LORD and he answered them'. In this sense, whether or not each was technically a priest (as Moses wasn't), they may be termed 'priests', for they were given access to God on behalf of the people for whom they prayed. He spoke to them and they showed the obedience of faith by keeping his statutes (7). Through these God-appointed intercessors the people experienced forgiveness (8), as they did in the time of Moses and Aaron (supremely the golden calf, Exod. 32:11-14) and the period of Samuel (e.g. 1 Sam. 7:5-9). The final version of the refrain (9) is longer than the previous two and includes a reference to 'his holy mountain', thus combining the thought of the righteousness of Psalm 1 and the king of Psalm 2. The Davidic king may not be explicitly present, but he is here in the background.

The final man who intercedes for His people as their great High Priest is the one whom Moses, Aaron, and Samuel all foreshadowed, the Lord Jesus Christ, the utterly holy man. He it is who leads us His people into the presence of this great God. He has become for us the 'holiness' we so need (1 Cor. 1:30). Led by Him, we bow in worship as we join in this psalm, and are encouraged to declare the sovereign covenant forgiveness and rule of God in the world.

Psalm 100

Building on the theme of the covenant God who reigns ('the LORD reigns'), Psalm 100 appropriately calls the people of God to bow down to him with joyful thanksgiving. The Hebrew word translated 'For giving grateful praise' (in the superscription) is repeated in verse 4 ('thanksgiving', that is, 'a song of thanksgiving').

In each half of the psalm (1-3, 4-5) there are two stanzas of three lines each[3]. The first (1, 2) gives a call, the second a reason (3); and then the same pattern is repeated (4 then 5).

In each case, the first stanza (1-2 and then 4) calls 'all the earth' to 'come' (2) or 'enter' (v. 4, the imperative is the same in both cases) into the presence of God in the temple with exuberant thankful praise. Expressions for overflowing gratitude pile up, one upon another.

Two questions arise. First, why is this exuberance appropriate? The reasons (v. 3 and then v. 5) focus on what God has done for His people. In verse 3, 'all the earth' is summoned to 'know' – that is, deeply to know in their own hearts, minds, and affections, and also publicly to acknowledge to others – that 'the LORD', the God of the covenant with

---

3. NIV conflates verse 5 into two lines. ESV correctly prints it as three.

Israel, 'is God' (lit. 'the LORD, *he* is God'). Every culture has its gods; we are summoned to know that the covenant God of the Bible (the LORD), and He alone, is God. This is what the Exodus and the giving of the Law at Mount Sinai demonstrated to the Israelites (Deut. 4:35,39); it is what Elijah in a later generation prayed the people of God would repent and know afresh (1 Kings 18:39). Following from this, they are to 'know' that 'it is he who made us' – that is, created Israel (cf. Deut. 32:6,15) – 'and we are his; we are his people, the sheep of his pasture.' The sheep metaphor is used only of the covenant people. We, the covenant people in covenant with the covenant God, are to know that the one to whom we belong, the one who made us as a people, is the one true God. And therefore we should rejoice with great exuberance.

The second reason (5) builds on the first. This covenant God ('the LORD') 'is good'. Pure unsullied goodness is His nature. Specifically that means that 'his love' (*chesed*, unfailing covenant steadfast love) 'endures for ever', or – to put the same thing another way, 'his faithfulness' (faithfulness to His covenant promises) 'continues through all generations.' In exile, after exile, in troubles, in distress, the covenant people are called deeply and exuberantly to rejoice, even through their tears, in this good God.

But this raises the second question: why is 'all the earth' called to this thanksgiving, when the blessings are given to the particular people of God? There is here an implicit evangelistic invitation; for any man or woman the world over, hearing and heeding this call, may enter this people. This international invitation comes to its fruition when the Lord Jesus Christ sings this psalm, and with that great word 'anyone' (e.g. John 7:37) invites any man or woman the

world over to 'come… enter…' and find that the covenant
God, whose promises are all 'yes!' in Jesus Christ, is truly
'good' and His 'love' and 'faithfulness' unfailing forever.

A Note on Psalms 101-103

The great focus of Psalms 92-100 has been on the LORD
being King. Now we have a little threesome of psalms of
David (101 and 103 explicitly, perhaps 102 implicitly). It
is as though, during or after the exile, when there was no
king, the compiler reminds us not to give up hope that one
day the throne of God on earth will be merged with the
throne of a King in David's line, the Messiah.

Psalm 101

[Vol. 1: 223]

This beautiful song comes in three unequal parts. The first
is the headline, in verse 1. David says, 'I will sing of (your)[4]
love and justice'. Covenant steadfast love and justice are the
attributes of the LORD that David will praise. They are
the foundation of God's throne (Ps. 89:14).

And *therefore*, in the second part (2-4) David commits
himself to these qualities. Since God is a 'love and justice'
God, 'love and justice' must be the foundation of my throne.
For David's concern is that God will 'come to' him (2), that
is, come to him for blessing (cf. Exod. 20:24). This echoes
the terrifying episode when David brought the Ark of the
Covenant up to Jerusalem and Uzzah is struck down for
his irreverence (2 Sam. 6:1-9); David exclaims, 'How can

---

4. NIV adds 'your' (not in the Hebrew), for it becomes clear that these
   qualities are preeminently those of the LORD.

the ark of the LORD *come to me?*' If God is to come to
David to bless him then David must be a blameless king
(2), who never approves of worthless behaviour (v. 3, cf.
Rom. 1:32), and has no 'perversity of heart' (4). Only a 'love
and justice' king can rule God's world and God's people.

It was a grand resolve; and yet David failed terribly.
They had to wait many centuries before a true 'love and
justice' man of utter blamelessness would come to rule (cf.
Isa. 16:5); but come he did.

The king continues, in the third part (5-8) to express a
resolute determination that only 'love and justice' people
can serve in his administration. At every level corruption
will be rooted out. Any whiff of slander (5a), pride of heart
(5b), twisting of truth (7) or wickedness of any kind (8)
and an official will be dismissed. Only the 'faithful' and
'blameless' can 'minister to' this faithful, blameless king. At
last there will be a 'city of the LORD' (8), a new Jerusalem,
from which every evildoer is excluded (Rev. 21:27). Here at
last will be a perfect king governing a flawless world with
the steadfast love and justice of God Himself.

When we join in this song of Jesus our King, we too
commit ourselves, as His church, and as individual disciples, to be 'love and justice' people, fitted by grace to serve
in His government of the new heavens and new earth (cf.
1 Cor. 6:2), 'made by grace for glory meet'[5]. For the pastor-
teachers who lead our churches this psalm comes as a
stringent challenge to a deep commitment of heart and
life for godliness. It presses us all to a heartfelt dependence
upon both forgiveness and the grace of the Holy Spirit to
change us. For, most wonderfully, both the Father and

---

5. From the hymn, 'I will sing the wondrous story'.

the Son have 'come to' us by the Holy Spirit (John 14:23, echoing Ps. 101:2).

Psalm 102

[Vol. 1: 99, 154, 163]

Unfading life is found in the afflicted Son of God. We shall see that this is the comfort of this psalm. It is 'a prayer of an afflicted person', in principle any believer who 'has grown weak', by which each of us may 'pour out a lament before the LORD'. But we shall see that, before it becomes your prayer or mine, it is the prayer of the Son of God.

Verses 1 and 2 cry with urgent call from deep distress. Verses 3-11 tell us the distress. The dominant motif is transience ('tempus fugit'); notice how these verses are bracketed by 'my days' (vv. 3, 11, and cf. 'all day long' v. 8). In his 'distress' (5) He feels all the dimensions of the misery of a fading life, of mortality. The images of 'smoke' (3a), 'glowing' – i.e. fading – 'embers' (3b), 'grass' (4) and 'evening shadow' (11) convey vividly the desperation of not being able to have any lasting being; smoke blows away, embers go cold, grass withers, the evening shadow merges into night. It is lonely (6), restless (7), miserably shameful, taunted (8), and grievous (9). And all because of the 'great wrath' of God (10). Here is a man drinking to the dregs the cup of God's wrath (cf. Matt. 26:39).

Verse 12 ('But you, LORD,...') signals a dramatic change, from the transience of this man to the eternity of the covenant God, who sits 'enthroned' (linking with the motif of Pss. 92–100) 'for ever... through all generations'. But it is not simply a contrast between a fading man and an immortal God; the point of verse 12 is that it leads into wonderful promises to 'Zion' in verses 13-22 (notice 'Zion' in verses 13, 16, 21). This afflicted Son of God laments His fading life; He rejoices in the promise of an unfading church. At present there are but 'stones' and 'dust' (14), appropriate for exile, but also for every age of God's exiled church (1 Pet. 1:1). But one day Zion will be the focus of the fulfilment of the promise to Abraham of worldwide worship (15, cf. Gen. 12:1-3). The eternal covenant God hears the 'prayer' of this 'afflicted person', 'the prayer of the destitute' (17a singular, individual), 'their plea' (17b corporate), 'the groans of the prisoners…those condemned to death' (17, 20) as he heard the cry of the enslaved Hebrews in Egypt (Exod. 2:23-25). One day there will be a worldwide assembly for worship, in Zion (21, 22). The unfading covenant God guarantees the unfading church (cf. Rev. 21; Isa. 60-62).

In verses 23 and 24 this representative 'afflicted' Israelite returns to his lament. Again we have 'my days…my days…' tragically 'cut short', as he pleads afresh that the God who has 'years' (by contrast to 'days') should not 'take (him) away'.

Although we may think that verses 25-27 are still the prayer of this afflicted person as he expands on the eternal 'years' of the immortal God, we are in for a surprise. The Greek translation (the Septuagint) understood these verses to be spoken, not by the afflicted one, but by the eternal God, making a promise to His Messiah[6]. Hebrews 1:10-12 confirms the rightness of this understanding, teaching us that this is indeed what we listen to here. God promises

6. NIV inserts speech marks, beginning in verse 24 and ending at the end of verse 28; in the light of Hebrews 1, these would seem to be misleading.

to His Messiah that He will be the immortal Head of an unfading church. His personal existence goes back before His conception and birth, right back to 'the foundations of the earth' (25). When the universe of this age has perished and worn out, like old clothing (26), He will 'remain the same'; He, who lamented His 'cut off' 'days' will have 'years' that 'will never end' (27).

In verse 28 we hear the conclusion. Because our Messiah, the Son of God, has faced and lamented and suffered the misery of a fading life, cut off in His prime for the sins of His people, bearing the wrath of God for them, He is the immortal Head of an unfading church. In Christ we too 'will live in (God's) presence' and will 'be established' in imperishing immortality in the presence of God. As we join in the singing of this song, we enter into the desperate sadness of our Messiah's life cut off at the cross; but we rejoice that, because he bore the wrath of God for us, our mortal bodies will put on immortality; for we shall 'bear the image' of Jesus our 'heavenly man' (cf. 1 Cor. 15:42-49).

Psalm 103
[Vol. 1: 185, 186]

David the king answers the question: what sort of king is the God of Psalms 92–100, with their chorus 'The LORD reigns'? Psalm 103 ends with His kingship (v. 19 'established his throne in heaven…'); it begins with His 'love', His covenant *chesed* (vv. 4, 8, 11, 17) and His 'compassion' (4, 8, 13).

In verses 1-5 the king exhorts himself, in his whole inward being, emphatically to bless the covenant God for 'all his benefits' (2). These begin with forgiveness (3a) and the healing that follows from this (3b); for it was by sin that death (v. 4a 'the pit') came into the world (Rom. 5:12), and every healing from sickness is an anticipation of the final healing of all sickness at the resurrection (cf. Matt. 8:17). It culminates with an abundant crowning with 'love and compassion' which will, in the end, climax in the most wonderful satisfaction of 'desires with good things' and a 'youth' that will forever be renewed in vigour (5, cf. Isa. 40:31). What benefits! How right to bless the LORD for them!

In verses 6-12 the king moves from his personal testimony to the corporate witness of his people. Verse 6 is the headline. Verse 7 introduces a rich reminder of the terrible episode of the golden calf, and how this prompted the most quoted verses in the Old Testament, Exodus 34:6,7, echoed here in verse 8. Verses 9-12 expand on this wonderful forgiving unbreakable covenant love. This is how Israel learned the character of the covenant God.

Verses 13-18 begin with God as 'a father', a father corporately to Israel (Exod. 4:22), and supremely to the king in David's line (2 Sam. 7:14; Ps. 2:7). This wonderful father demonstrates His 'compassion' (13) and covenant 'love' (17) by His understanding of our dust-like frailty (14, cf. Gen. 2:7), and our transient mortality (vv. 15, 16, echoing the theme of transience in Ps. 102). Those who know His 'everlasting to everlasting... love', who are 'those who fear him', with reverent filial fear, are assured of eternal security and life.

All this Jesus our King celebrated as this psalm became a regular reminder to His own inward being of His Father's love and compassion to Him as the federal Head of the people of God. Indeed, that compassion to

His people was only possible because Jesus our King offered Himself as a propitiation, to make atonement for us (Rom. 3:25,26).

Verses 18-22 bring us back to the great theme that 'the LORD reigns', the theme that dominated Psalms 92–100. The exhortation that the king gives to his own soul (1, 2) is now extended to the angelic beings or heavenly hosts (20, 21), indeed to the whole of creation (22a), before coming back to the king's own soul (22b). The sovereignty that the covenant God exercises over the world is a kingship of sovereign grace, of covenant love to all who will fear Him, of compassion to weak and oppressed people, suffering under the dominion of sin in all its forms.

Jesus our King leads us in exhorting our own souls never to forget the benefits given to us by God our Father in Him, the blessings of unfailing love and deep compassion, a sovereignty of grace that calls forth from us deep and daily blessing.

A Note on Psalms 104-106

Psalms 104-106 are the first group of Psalms to include the famous exhortation 'Praise the LORD!' (Hallelu-Jah!). Psalms 104 and 105 end with this;[7] Psalm 106 begins and ends with it. This clearly indicates they are to be treated as a group.

Hallelujah appears in two similar threesomes in Book 5 (111–113 and 115–117) and then the grand finale (146-150).[8]

---

7. NIV 'Praise the LORD, my soul!' (104:1,35) uses a different word for 'praise'.

8. And also Psalm 135.

Psalm 104

[Vol. 1: 123, 148-157, 228]

Since Book 5 focuses on the world sovereignty of the covenant God, it is appropriate that the first of the three-some sings praise to the Creator, before the other two praise Him as the God of history. Psalm 104 is almost a riff on Genesis 1. In verses 1-30 the poet sings about the world; in verses 31-35 he responds in prayer. There is a sting in the tail.

Verses 1-4 declare that Creation displays God's 'majesty' (1). 'Light' (2), which serves as a shorthand for all that is detectable by human inquiry, is like the visible garment in which the invisible Creator wraps Himself. It both reveals Him and conceals Him from our sight. His chariot-throne (3) and the winds and lightning-bolts (v. 4, 'flames of fire'; cf. Heb. 1:7) demonstrate that He is both transcendent and immanent; He sustains and guides the whole of creation all the time (cf. John 5:17). This majesty is the headline for the psalm.

Verses 5-9 expound the stability of the Created Order. The solid foundations (5) and the boundaries beyond which the chaotic sea cannot pass (6-9), both attest this solid order that makes the world habitable.

Verses 10-18 move from stability to generosity, from protection to provision. Water that threatened destruction becomes the source of life and rich growth.

Verses 19-23 perhaps emphasise the comprehensiveness of the Creator's sovereignty. The moon and sun are placed in the heavens to mark the boundaries between day and night, and give light to each. Even in the darkness, the lions 'seek their food from God', for there is no other provider of life, in the night as in the day. He is sovereign over both.

Verses 24-26 celebrate the Creator's 'wisdom' (24). Leviathan, that terrifying monster, who personifies the devil in Job 41, is just a large pet to the Creator (26)! In the infinite wisdom of the Creator, even the devil serves his purposes.

Verses 27-30 speak of providence, literally the provision of life; if the Creator provides, there is satisfaction (27, 28, 30); if He does not, there is terror and death (29), for He alone is the source of life (cf. Acts 17:25).

It is a lovely poem; but how should we – how does the psalmist – respond? He prays three prayers (31-35). First (31, 32) he prays that the covenant God will 'rejoice in his works' (31b), that they will be pleasing to Him, as the theatre in which His glory is displayed (31a). We do not readily pray this; but it is very important, since even an angry look at the earth from a displeased Creator endangers its very existence. The only way the earth can endure is if it reflects the Creator's glory.

Second (33, 34) he prays that he will rejoice, not in the creation, as we might expect, but in the Creator. He sings, not to 'mother nature' (that invention of the atheist) but to the Creator, and longs that his meditation (on creation) may be pleasing to Him, 'as I rejoice in the LORD'.

Third – and this is the sting in the tail – he prays that sinners will 'vanish from the earth' (35). This is not a random prayer; it is the necessary condition for the answer to the first prayer; while there is wickedness, the LORD cannot rejoice fully in His works (31). It is sin that spoils creation.

Only Jesus can pray all three of these prayers without endangering His own life. For us to pray, 'may sinners vanish' is to ask for our own destruction. We may pray this final prayer in Christ in three ways. First, that some sinners may vanish by repentance, so that they become forgiven sinners. Second, that we will hate sin in ourselves and others more deeply. Finally, that in the end incorrigible, impenitent sinners will be removed, so that a new world 'where righteousness dwells' may come (2 Pet. 3:13).

Psalm 105
[Vol. 1: 160, 163-167, 172, 187]

This second 'Hallelujah' psalm is a strange and puzzling song to sing in and after exile. It is the first of two over-lapping and contrasting historical psalms. Verses 1-15 are very similar to the start of the song the people sang when David brought the Ark to Jerusalem (1 Chron. 16:8-22) and may have been taken from that – probably earlier – song.

An anonymous prophetic voice, singing by the Spirit of Christ, sets before the people of God an exhortation, an affirmation, a demonstration, and a purpose (which is the sting in the tail). He begins with the exhortation (1-6), addressed to (lit.) 'the seed of Abraham' (6). They are to praise the covenant God for 'all his wonderful acts…the wonders he has done, his miracles, and the judgements he pronounced' – the deeds some of which will be retold in the psalm. The key word is 'Abraham' for, as we shall see, the psalm's central focus is on the covenant with Abraham. As we hear this in its Old Covenant context, we think also of its New Covenant fulfilment, in which the 'seed' of Abraham is one man, the Christ (Gal. 3:16) and a corporate people, Jew and gentile, in Christ (Gal. 3:29).

The exhortation is to praise the covenant God for the truth summarized in the affirmation (7-11). Here the focus on 'his covenant...the promise he made...with Abraham...an everlasting covenant' becomes explicit. The feature of this covenant upon which our prophetic voice focusses is in the punchline: 'To you I will give the land of Canaan...' (11).

The voice affirms that God made, and will keep, this everlasting covenant with Abraham. The body of the psalm (12-44) is an historical demonstration that this was the case. It takes us through the fragile wanderings of the patriarchs (12-15), in which they were wonderfully protected; then (16-24) the famine that threatened the very existence of the children of Israel, and how God sent Joseph to provide for them, so that they prospered in Egypt. The scene of prosperity in Egypt then fades into the terrible slavery from which God rescued them (23-38), including a retelling of some of the plagues, the Passover and the Exodus. There follows a brief reminder of God's provision for them during their vulnerable wanderings in the wilderness (39-41); and finally the entry into the promised land (42-44). In case we had forgotten, we are reminded (42) that all this demonstrates that God 'remembered his holy promise given to his servant Abraham'.

To sum up: we are to praise God because He made a promise to Abraham and kept that promise through all manner of trials and dangers. He gave us the promised land. The overwhelming focus is on the covenant God and what He did; He is the subject of virtually every verb in this historical retelling: '*He* said this...*he* did that...*he* did the other...*he* kept his promise.'

But in verse 45 there is a purpose: 'that they might keep his precepts and observe his laws.' God's purpose was there should be in this world a society marked by obedience, in which God's way of living should be demonstrated for all the world to see. It is precisely this that Israel did not do. That is why they went into exile; that is why, even after the exile, they were far from seeing the fulfilment of the promises. If Psalm 105 stresses God's faithfulness, Psalm 106 will focus on Israel's sin.

So why sing this psalm? That is the most important question. The answer is that you only go on singing it if you believe that one day it will prove absolutely true. That the covenant which was rightly conditional on obedience (cf. v. 45) will prove also to be certain. How can this be? Only when the true Israel comes, the true 'seed' of Abraham who keeps the law, who bears the sin of his people, and in whom the final 'promised land' becomes their inheritance, the new heavens and new earth, to which the Old Covenant promised land pointed.

As Jesus sang this psalm in His earthly life, there welled up within Him a holy determination to be what Israel was called to be, and thereby to seal and guarantee the fulfilment of the covenant with Abraham. As Jesus now leads us, His church, in singing this psalm, our hearts are thrilled by the retelling of God's faithfulness, and all the more so as we see the final 'yes!' to that faithfulness in Jesus Christ (2 Cor. 1:20). And yet we too are reminded that the reason God shapes us as a people is that we will indeed be that obedient new humanity in a dark and disordered world.

Psalm 106
[Vol. 1: 108, 163-167, 172, 201, 206]

This third of the Hallelujah psalms begins and ends with 'Praise the LORD!' Verse 1 and then verses 47 and 48

closely echo the conclusion of the song they sang when
David brought the Ark to Jerusalem (1 Chron. 16:34-36),
reminding us again of the connection of Book 4 with this
merging of God's throne with David's throne.

Verses 1-3 open the psalm with praise, and yet ask
the question of 'who can ...*fully* declare his praise?' (2).
The answer (3) is only 'those who act justly, who *always*
do what is right'. The word translated 'fully' (2) and
'always' (3) is the same (lit. 'declare *all* his praise' 'do *all*
that is right'); only the one who *always* does right can
fully declare God's praise. The psalm will end – and end
Book 4 – with praise, to which all the people say 'Amen'
(48). But, in a way, the critical question is how, and when,
and by whom, God will be fully praised? Or, to put it
another way, who can make God the Father fully known
(cf. John 1:18; 17:6, 26)?

We should note (4, 5) that this is a very personal prayer,
by an anonymous voice, speaking by the Spirit of Christ,
asking that he may be helped, remembered, included in
the joy of God's restored people. It is a moving thought to
consider what this prayer must have meant on the lips of
Jesus; and how wonderfully it would be answered.

The body of the psalm (7-46) comes under the headline
confession of verse 6: 'We', the people of God today, 'have
sinned...done wrong...acted wickedly' (three words for
sin). In a comprehensive way, the history related describes
us today in all the essentials of our sinful hearts. This godly
leader, who prays verses 4 and 5, leads his people today in
the confession of our sins.

The retelling sweeps through a variety of episodes from
Exodus, Numbers, and Judges, over a long period. It alter-
nates between what 'they' did (the ancestors) and what 'he'

(the covenant God) did, both in blessing and in wrath. Although it is a terrible catalogue of sins (picked up by Paul, using v. 20 in Rom. 1:23 with other echoes of the psalm in Rom. 1:18-32), the primacy is given to God's covenant love (which brackets the psalm, vv. 1 and 45) and kindness. Sin is the failure to 'remember' and respond to grace; we see this again and again (7, 13, 21, 22, 24).

God's kindness is especially seen in the provision of intercessors. We see this first with Moses (23) who 'stood in the breach before him, to keep his wrath from destroying them' at the time of the golden calf. We see it next when 'Phinehas stood up and intervened' (30) at the time of the Baal of Peor and the Moabite women (Num. 25). And there is a deep sense in which the prayer of verse 47 means that the whole psalm is the intervention of an intercessor for the people of God: 'Save us, LORD our God...' That this concluding prayer is picked up in Psalm 107:3, at the start of Book 5, reinforces this impression. The godly Israelite who prays first that he himself will be included in the blessings of God's restored people (4, 5) intercedes also for the whole people (47).

When Jesus of Nazareth prayed this psalm, He did so as the man of Psalm 1, the man who 'always' did 'what is right' (3). His prayer would be heard, and His praises would be complete. When He prays, 'Save us... gather us... that we may give thanks...' (47), His prayer will be abundantly answered. For, under His leadership, and covered by His atoning death, the worldwide people of God will be gathered as one flock under one Shepherd (John 10:16). It is by Him, and in Him, that God the Father will be fully praised. This is the triumph of sovereign grace and the climax of Book 4, with its refrain 'The LORD reigns!'

BOOK 5

Introduction to Book 5

The clearest subdivision in this long book (43 psalms) is made by Psalm 118 (about the King) and Psalm 119 (celebrating the Law). Echoing Psalms 1 (Law) and 2 (King), and also Psalms 18 (King) and 19 (Law), this divides Book 5 into two main parts.

The first part begins with an introductory historical psalm (107), continues with a threesome 'of David' (108, 109, 110) and concludes with a seven-psalm 'Hallelujah' sequence (111–117, with one omission).

After 118 and 119, the second part begins with the Songs of Ascents (120–134), continues with three historical psalms (135–137) and a final 'of David' collection (138–145) before concluding with another 'Hallelujah' sequence (146–150).

In this book, Psalms 111, 112 and 145 are acrostics, and Psalm 119 is the supreme acrostic.

Psalm 107

Jesus is 'the pioneer of (our) salvation' (Heb. 2:10; cf. 12:2).
He does not merely *bring* us out of exile; He *leads* us out of
exile. Book 5 begins with a wonderful psalm in which the
prayer with which Book 4 ended is answered. 'Save us...
and gather us from the nations' they prayed (Ps. 106:47).
Here now are the stories of 'those he gathered from the
lands...' (Ps. 107:3). Verses 1-3 exhort those who have been
'redeemed' and 'gathered' to 'tell their story'. It is a story of
the unending covenant 'love' (1, 8, 15, 21, 31, 43) of the God
who is 'good' (1).

Four parallel stories are told (4-9, 10-16, 17-22, 23-32).
These are not four stories of different groups of people;
they are four vivid poetic ways of telling the one story of
return from exile. (The sense is not 'Some... Others...
Others... Others...' but 'They... They... They... They...'
as in NIV.) Each poetic cameo begins with distress (4-5,
10-12, 17-18, 23-27); this leads to a cry for help (6, 13, 19
,28) which God answers (6-7, 13-14, 19-20, 28-30); they
are then exhorted to give Him thanks for His unfailing
love (8-9, 15-16, 21-22, 31-32).

The first poem (4-9) describes exile as being lost in a
wasteland world, in which they cannot find the way to a city

where they can settle. Their appetites are forever unfilled, until they experience the unfailing love of God.

The second (10-16) evokes the terrible feeling of being trapped in a dark world, enslaved to forces from which they cannot escape. Only the covenant God can set them free by His unfailing love.

In the third (17-22) we see them (us) weak in a sick world, losing their appetites and the will to live. Rescue comes when the LORD speaks the word and brings them out of the grave.

Fear of chaos fills the fourth cameo (23-32) as the wild waves of chaos threaten to engulf them. Only the covenant God can still the storm and bring them home.

Each of these describe in poetic terms the founding experience of Israel when they were brought out of slavery in the Exodus. They evoke most immediately to the first singers the wonder of being gathered back from Exile into the promised land. But they reach their climax when the Lord Jesus Christ endures all the agonies of hunger in the desert, the darkness of the cross, sickness that leads to death, and drowning in the wild waves of the wrath of God for us. Only when He has endured that wrath in all its terrible dimensions will he experience 'the joy that was set before him' (Heb. 12:2 ESV).

The end of the psalm does not fit with the clear pattern of verses 4-32. In verses 33-42 we see the covenant God bringing His people into judgement (33, 34), into salvation (35-38), into discipline (39, 40) and finally into joy (41, 42). It is this see-saw of experience that is such a surprise. But it teaches us that the pathway into the promised land is – in the unchanging love of the Father – a road that leads through ups and downs. His love is unchanging even as our experience varies so widely from day to day and year to year. But the last word will be that 'the upright see and rejoice' in the great rescue they will have experienced, while 'all the wicked shut their mouths', having nothing to plead against their just judgement (42).

All this we should 'heed' and 'ponder' if we will be 'wise' (43). Jesus our pioneer leads us out of exile into the promised land of the new heavens and new earth. This story is Israel's story, Jesus's story and, in Christ, our story. As we sing it, we reflect on what it means to live under the unfailing love of God towards us in Christ. For in Christ we shall end in the new Jerusalem (the 'city where they could settle' v. 4), free from sin for ever (John 8:36), with our bodies raised to immortal life, and the new creation in which there will be 'no longer any sea' (Rev. 21:1).

Psalm 108

This is the first of a threesome of David psalms. Someone – either David or a later editor, inspired by the Spirit – has put together the second half of Psalm 57 and the second half of Psalm 60 (both by David, and both tied to historical incidents in David's life) to create Psalm 108. But although the verses appear in Psalms 57 and 60, by putting them together like this, a new Psalm has been created, independent of these particular events. A new song for new times, perhaps initially the period after the exile, but now the age of the church.

In the first half (1-5), we join with our King as He sings joyfully, with a 'steadfast' heart, in praise of the covenant God, so that all the world will hear his praises (v. 3 'among the nations'). He sings of God's covenant 'love' and 'faithfulness' (4) and prays that God's 'glory' may 'be over all the earth' (5). In quoting some very similar words from another Psalm, Romans indicates that this worldwide praise is heard in all the world through the gentile mission of Christ's church (Rom. 15:9). Christ sings these words as He leads His church in praise to the Father.

The second half (6-13) implicitly answers the question of how the praises of God will be sung all over the world. For there are 'fortified cities' of resistant evil in human hearts, human societies, human cultures, in many, many places. Our King leads us in affirming again the covenant promises of God that the whole of the promised land (fulfilled in the new heavens and new earth) belongs to Him (7-9). He asks again, 'Who will bring me' – as conqueror – 'to the fortified city' (10), originally the mountain fastness of Edom, but in principle any stronghold bolted and barred against God's King. The glorious answer is that God can and will do this; through God the Father our great King will gain the victory, and we with Him, as evil is defeated all over the world (11-13). Then indeed the King, through the lips of His church, will sing the praises of the Father 'among all nations'.

As we sing this song with Jesus our King, we are spurred afresh to gospel initiatives of worldwide mission as, by the spiritual weapons of prayer and the ministry of the word (Acts 6:4), we 'demolish arguments and every pretension that sets itself up against the knowledge of God, and we take captive every thought to make it obedient to Christ' our victorious King (2 Cor. 10:5).

Psalm 109

See Volume 1, pages 136-146 for a full Christian exposition of this psalm, and also all of Volume 1, Chapter 8 for the question of how we may pray psalms with prayers for God's judgement on the wicked.

Psalm 110

[Vol. 1: 41, 99]

This is the third of a threesome of David psalms. It tells us the destiny of the king who has been vindicated against the traitor of Psalm 109. God 'stands at the right hand of the needy, to save their lives...' (Ps. 109:31); the king is the supreme example of this betrayed man needing – and receiving – God's vindication.

David calls the subject of this psalm 'my Lord' (1); he thereby indicates that he sensed, by the Spirit of God, that the one of whom he spoke would be greater than him (cf. Matt. 22:41-46). The psalm is structured around the two things God says about this greater-than-David (v. 1 'The LORD says...'; v. 4 'The LORD has sworn...').

In verses 1-3 the covenant God says this 'Lord' is a King; he is God's right-hand-man, governing an ever-increasing domain for God. In one of several echoes from Psalm 2, he has enemies all around (hence 2 'in the midst of your enemies'), who do not want this King to rule over them. They want to be autonomous, to make their own decisions, rule their own lives. But this Lord 'sits', in the posture of government, at God's right hand. He governs from Zion (2), the focus of God's covenant promises. His rule will 'extend' more and more (2). And, in contrast to His unwilling enemies, He will have a large enthusiastic army of 'willing' volunteer troops (3), men and women whose hearts have been changed from hostile autonomy to glad surrender and service.

In verse 4 the covenant God says He is not only a King; He is a Priest-King, patterned on the model of Melchizedek, the priest-king of Jerusalem back in Abraham's day (Gen. 14). He governs his people; He also represents his people before God, brings them into the presence of God, and does so 'for ever'.

Verses 5-7 proclaim the definitive victory of this great right-hand-man, this Priest-King, on the day of final just judgement. It is not surprising that the New Testament quotes this psalm frequently as fulfilled in Jesus Christ. His priesthood is expounded in Hebrews 5-7, and his victory at God's right hand in many places.

As we join in the singing of this declaratory psalm, we will be warned to flee from the folly of opposing Him. We will be moved to a glad willingness to join His army. Perhaps most of all, we will be deeply assured of His final victory, and therefore of our final security under His rule as our Priest and our King.

A Note on Psalms 111-117

The exhortation 'Praise the LORD!' (Hallelujah!) marks this group of psalms. It begins 111 and 112, begins and ends 113, ends 115 and 116, begins and ends 117. 111 and 112 are also acrostics, with each line beginning with successive letters of the Hebrew alphabet.

Psalm 111

[Vol. 1: 167, 181, 188]

In verse 1 we hear the call to praise the covenant God: 'Hallelu' (plural imperative) 'Jah'. This exhortation is given by a leader ('I') speaking in the 'assembly' or congregation or church of 'the upright' (those who are upright by faith in God). This voice is fulfilled in the hortatory voice of Christ speaking in the midst of His church.

Verses 2-9 celebrate the reasons for praise. These focus on who the covenant God is and what the covenant God does. The verses are peppered with words that express God's character: 'righteousness' (3), 'gracious and compassionate' (4), 'faithful and just... trustworthy' (7), 'faithfulness and uprightness' (8), 'holy and awesome' (9). This wonderful character is expressed in wonderful 'works... deeds... wonders... works... works of his hands...'. When we ask what these deeds are, the answer is given in terms of the 'covenant' (5, 9) which is perhaps the climactic term of each section (2-5, 6-9), and developed in terms of provision of 'food' (5), the gifts of 'lands' (lit. 'inheritance', v. 6), and 'redemption' (9). 'Praise the covenant God,' cries the Leader, 'because of his moral perfection and the outworking of that perfection in covenant faithfulness to redeem his people.' If, as seems likely, Book 5 is compiled after the exile, such a declaration is an expression of faith more than a celebration of accomplished experience.

Christ our assembly leader calls us to praise the covenant faithfulness of God the Father. We have more reason to do so than His church did in those Old Covenant days. As we join with Christ in singing this psalm, we too find ourselves moved to 'ponder' the covenant faithfulness of God in all its rich facets, fulfilled in Christ, with a warm 'delight' (2), to 'remember' His wonderful deeds (4), and to express all this in the wise life that flows from 'the fear of the LORD' (10).

Psalm 112

[Vol. 1: 188]

Psalm 112 is closely linked with Psalm 111; both are acrostics and both begin 'Praise the LORD!' But if 111 focuses on the covenant goodness of God, 112 presses our attention on the man who responds to 111 with 'the fear of the LORD' (111:10, picked up in 112:1). This man (most

of the psalm is singular in the Hebrew, although this is
disguised in the NIV) shows the 'delight' of Psalm 111:2
(picked up in 112:1) and the 'uprightness' of the assembly
members in Psalm 111:1 (picked up in 112:2,4). In his
desires he fears the LORD and delights in his commands
(1). The psalm pronounces a blessing upon him (v. 1 'Blessed
is the man who...' (ESV) – echoing Ps. 1). His character is
marked by 'righteousness' (vv. 3, 9, echoing the character of
God celebrated in 111:3); this man is a God-like man.

Verses 2 and 3 declare that his destiny will be to have
a large and prosperous family, who share his likeness and
experience rich blessing. But, although this is his destiny,
there must first be 'darkness' (4a). Things happen to him
that would cause a man to be 'shaken' (6); he does hear
'bad news' (7); he has many 'foes' over whom he needs to
'triumph' (8). He is surrounded by 'the wicked' who long
for his downfall and are 'vexed' by his vindication (10).
But because he trusts the covenant faithfulness of his God
(Ps. 111:5,9), he may be confident that 'light' will 'dawn' for
him (4).

In verses 4b and 5 (and again in 9a) we see more of his God-
like character. Just as God is 'gracious and compassionate'
(111:4), so is this man (112:4); his generosity and justice (5)
image the character of the God in whom he trusts.

Verses 6-8 promise this man a steadiness of heart in
the midst of troubles. If his future destiny is an abundant
family (2,3), his present blessing is a secure heart (8) that
has 'no fear' (7, 8) in the midst of darkness. Because he fears
the LORD (1), he need fear no evil.

There is only one man who qualifies for the blessings
of this psalm, who in His character perfectly imaged the
qualities of God His Father. This man had a steady heart,

trusting His Father in the deepest darkness of the Cross. For Him light did indeed dawn, on resurrection morning. His family will be blessed forever. It is in Him, and in Him alone, that we may inherit that blessing and begin to experience the present-tense steadiness of heart that Jesus knew in His earthly life and sufferings. In Him we too may be 'hard pressed on every side, but not crushed…' (2 Cor. 4:8-10). As, with Jesus, we walk in loving fear of the Father, the old hymn promises us, 'Fear him, you saints, and you will then have nothing else to fear.'[1]

Psalm 113

We hear first (1-3) a voice calling with a uniquely sustained and insistent exhortation to praise the God of the covenant. Five times 'the LORD' is named. Three times this is 'the *name* of the LORD', his 'name' being his revelation, accessible to us. Four times the exhortation to 'praise' or 'bless' is given. He is to be praised at all times ('both now and for evermore') and in every place ('from the rising of the sun to the place where it sets').

But why? We need an overwhelmingly persuasive reason to join in this call for eternal and universal praise. This reason is given in two balancing parts. First (4-6) this God is supremely high (4, 5) and yet He 'stoops down' (6). We celebrate a unique and marvelous condescension, in which the God who is exalted far above both earth and heaven (6b) chooses, of His own free grace, to bend down very low for us.

Second, as He stoops down, He raises us up (7-9). In a succession of images of poverty, need, desperation, climaxing in the empty sadness of childlessness, we feel the misery

---

1. Isaac Watts, 'Through all the changing scenes of life'.

234 Teaching Psalms (Volume 2)

of mortal men and women here on earth. And yet this supremely exalted God reaches down and raises us up to sit with princes in positions of unimaginable greatness and undeserved privilege.

The three lines of verses 7-8a repeat, almost verbatim, a verse from Hannah, the childless woman who became a joyful mother (1 Sam. 2:8), as she celebrated the hope of Israel being given the King of God's choosing (1 Sam. 2:10). Psalm 113 is, in a way, the ongoing song that takes the people of God all the way from Hannah until the day that another very humble and amazed mother sings a very similar song (Luke 1:46-55). The child Hannah was given was one of a number of surprising sons given to childless women, all the way to the son conceived of the Virgin Mary. We sing it still, as we remember the astonishing condescension of God the Son who, though He was rich, stooped down to become poor for us, to lift us up to sit as sons and daughters with Him in His Father's house. This God, and the Father who sent Him, and the Holy Spirit, is worthy of universal and eternal praise.

Psalm 114

[Vol. 1 172]

The LXX transfers 'Praise the LORD!' from the end of Psalm 113 to the start of this psalm, and this may be correct. Psalm 113 celebrates the gracious condescension of God in raising up His people; Psalm 114 makes this concrete in the events of the Exodus, and probably also the return from Exile, seen as a second Exodus.

In beautiful and compressed poetry, two couplets celebrate these past events and two bring them into the present. Verses 1 and 2 remember how the people of God were created to be God's 'sanctuary', the holy place in which God rules ('his dominion'). Verse 3 focuses on insuperable and refractory obstacles, the Red Sea (3a) preventing them leaving Egypt, and the river Jordan (3b) hindering them entering the promised land. Verse 4 remembers how Mount Sinai trembled (Exod. 19:18) as the God of holiness gave His holy Law to His people. These supernaturally powerful events demonstrated the awesome power of the God of the covenant to create a people to be His holy place and kingdom.

In verses 5 and 6 the psalmist speaks to these natural obstacles in the present tense, asking them, now and rhetorically, why it was that they fled and shook. He asks, not because he does not know the answer, but to remind us all of the answer. This leads to a challenge – to the 'earth' and implicitly to all the powers, natural and supernatural, that resist God's rescuing power for His people – to 'tremble… at the presence of the Lord' (7). For this God not only removed the obstacles and gave His people His Law at Sinai; He also (8) gave them water from rocks (Exod. 17:6; Num. 20:8-11).

When the Lord Jesus sang this psalm in His earthly life, and most probably at His final Passover, he expresses faith that there is no obstacle whatever that can stop the covenant God rescuing His people. There was no obstacle at the Exodus; there will be no obstacle now. Jesus Himself proved that to be true, as He offered Himself as the true Israel for the sins of His people, and became for them the true Passover (1 Cor. 5:7). As now He leads His church in singing this song of triumphant faith, we too feel our faith excited to fresh confidence that the God of the Exodus, the God of Sinai, the God of wilderness provision, and the God of the Jordan crossing, will bring us His people in Christ out of slavery to sin, through the wilderness of this world, made holy to love His Law, and all the way into the promised land, which is the New Heavens and New Earth. Nothing and nobody in heaven or earth can stop Him.

Psalm 115

[Vol. 1: 148]

Psalm 115 begins with a commitment that expresses a choice (1). By nature we want glory for ourselves; but we commit ourselves to give all the glory to the covenant God for His 'love and faithfulness' (covenant words).

This commitment is then expanded in a long contrast. In verse 2 the nations mock the people of God because their God is not visible, tangible or provable. Their gods, by contrast, are entirely visible; which is why verses 3-7 contrast the true and all-powerful God in heaven with their visible but powerless idols. If there is an emphasis, it is in the repetition of their inability to speak (v. 5 '…cannot speak'; v. 7 'nor can they utter a sound with their throats'). The punchline is verse 8; those who make such idols will end up 'like them', also unable to do anything, and especially powerless to speak, in 'the place of silence' (17b).

In the second part of the contrast (9-15) the whole people of God are repeatedly exhorted to 'trust in the LORD' because He is able to help and protect them (9-11), and are repeatedly promised blessing from Him (12-15). In the face of mockery (2), we are to trust in the unseen but true and all-powerful covenant God.

In the conclusion (16-18), the commitment to praise the LORD is repeated, with the surprising emphasis on praise as the raison-d'être of the people of God. The reason we do not 'go down to the place of silence' is not simply because God is kind to us (although he is); it is that we may give him everlasting praise.

The choice could not be clearer. When Jesus of Nazareth first heard this psalm, He made or confirmed His consistent lifetime decision to give all praise to the Father and to take none for Himself (e.g. John 5:41). This is why He did not finally 'go down to the place of silence' but lives to lead us His people in costly praise to the unseen Father in the midst of a world that mocks such praise and understands only the desire for self-praise (John 5:44).

Psalm 116

In this psalm we hear, and then join, a voice singing of His death, His trust, His life and His love. And in His death, His trust, His life, and His love are all these for us who are in Him. The themes of death, trust, life, and love are interwoven with a clear structure.

He begins (1, 2) with passionate loyal love rooted in answered prayer. That prayer was necessary because 'the cords of death' – like a terrible monster – reached out and 'entangled' him (3, 4). Because He has been saved – His prayer is answered – He testifies, in words echoing Exodus 34:6, that the covenant God is gracious (5, 6). In His distress, He exhorts Himself to 'return to your rest, my soul', to experience in present quietness of soul the fruit of His trust (7). For He has indeed been rescued from death to life, to walk before the covenant God in living fellowship (8, 9). It is because He trusts (10) that He speaks of His affliction, and testifies to God's saving power in trouble; the LXX version of verse 10 is quoted by Paul in 2 Corinthians 4:13. He trusts in God because He cannot trust in people (11).

In verse 12 He asks Himself how He should respond to the covenant God's goodness? He answers in verses 13, 14 and then again in verses 17-19 (with 17b-18 echoing 13b-14). A public testimony to God's rescue 'in the presence of all his people' is what He pledges Himself to give. In between, in verses 15, 16, He testifies that even His death is 'precious' to God, whose covenant 'servant' He remains.

We can hear Jesus praying every word of this psalm, giving public testimony to the Father's gracious compassion towards Him, who is the Father's 'faithful servant' (15). But, as Jesus sings of His death, His trust, His life, and His love for the Father, we too join in the song and express all these of ourselves in Christ. For we too must die with Him; we too must trust the Father with Him; we too will live with Him, as His resurrection guarantees ours; and we too love the Father who has first loved us in Christ.

Psalm 117

In this, the shortest of all the psalms, a voice exhorts us twice to praise the covenant God, wherever we may be and to whatever ethnic group we may belong. The challenge to join in is the challenge to praise. The reason is His great and enduring covenant 'love... and... faithfulness...' towards His people, of whom we become a part as we join in the trusting praise.

Supremely, the Lord Jesus leads this song, both in its exhortation to all the world (1) and in its simple covenantal reason (2). When we join with Him, we become a part of the 'us' His people; we share with Him in the Father's love; we trust with Him the Father's everlasting faithfulness.

A short psalm is easy to remember and simple to sing. It celebrates in short order all the truths of the covenant promises, fulfilled in Jesus. And it asks of us the commitment to join the praise.

Psalm 118
[Vol. 1: 34-35, 43]

This psalm begins (1-4) and ends (29) with exultant exhortation to give thanks to the covenant God because 'his love' (covenant love) 'endures for ever'. This is a frequent refrain in the later psalms and sometimes elsewhere. It raises the question: how may we know that this is true? The evidence often suggests it may not be. We sometimes ask the question from agonised hearts.

After the initial exhortation there is the sustained testimony of one man, who must – from what he says – be the King (5-21). He tells of his anguish (e.g. v. 5 'hard pressed'; v. 7 'my enemies'; vv. 10-12 worldwide opposition; 13 'pushed back and about to fall'), of his assurance (e.g. 6-9), of his astonishing worldwide victory (10-18) and of his access to God (vv. 19-21, as he enters 'the gate of the LORD through which the righteous may enter'). We then hear (22-28) his acclamation by all his people, who hail him as the surprising rejected 'stone' who 'becomes the cornerstone' (Acts 4:11; 1 Pet. 2:4-8), in words used by the crowds on Palm Sunday (v. 25a 'LORD, save us!' or 'Hosanna!', and v. 26) as they 'join' a 'festal procession' with 'boughs in hand' (27). In verse 28 the King concludes with his personal affirmation that the covenant God is 'my God' and that he will praise Him.

On the basis of the King's anguish, assurance, astonishing victory, access to God, and acclamation by the people, we too are exhorted to 'give thanks to the LORD, for He is good; His love endures for ever.' In Him, as those whose lives are hidden with Christ in God (Col. 3:3), we too may experience a measure of anguish, a taste of His assurance, the confident anticipation that in His astonishing victory is the guarantee of ours, the wonderful comfort that in His access to God rests our own access. In Christ, Hebrews can apply the confidence of verse 6 to us (Heb. 13:6). We too join the choir who acclaim this great King, knowing that in His victory is our hope, and the assurance that God's covenant love truly does endure for ever.

Psalm 119

[Vol. 1: 40, 188, 206]

This long acrostic about love for God's Law pairs with Psalm 118 about God's King. I have treated it section by section in detail in my book *Bible Delight*.[2] The only thing I would add is to encourage you to ask of every section, 'What would it mean for Jesus of Nazareth to sing and pray this psalm?' For the one who sings, does so by the Spirit of Christ, and as a leader in Israel. In *Bible Delight* I inadequately developed this theme, which opens up more deeply to us how we may pray it, and delight in God's Law, as men and women in Christ.

---

2. Christopher Ash, *Bible Delight* [Christian Focus: 2008].

A Note on Psalms 120–134 – Psalms of Ascent

Each of this lovely collection of fifteen mostly very short psalms is headed 'A song of ascents'. Almost certainly these were pilgrim songs used by pious Jews going 'up' to the temple in Jerusalem for the great festivals of the Old Testament (perhaps clearest in 122:2, 4). Whether or not they came from a geographically higher location, when they went to the temple they went 'up' symbolically, much as we speak of going 'up' to a capital city. Five of these are older psalms, either headed 'of David' (122, 124, 131, 133) or 'of Solomon' (127); but because the collection is in Book 5, it would seem to have been put together for use by believers in the period after the exile in Babylon (the so-called Second Temple period).

There is – unsurprisingly – a great emphasis on Jerusalem or Zion. Under the New Covenant we remember that what Zion promised is fulfilled in Jesus Christ and His church. To go 'up' to Zion today is to gather with Jesus and His people, Jew and gentile (see vol. 1, chapter 13). It is vital to remember this; these psalms are about us corporately more than about individual believers or, perhaps sometimes, as individuals deeply conscious of our corporate belonging in the church of Christ.

In addition to this, look out for one refrain, four echo words and one stylistic feature. The refrain is '…the LORD, the Maker of heaven and earth' (121:2; 124:8; 134:3; see vol. 1, chapter 9). Despite their weakness and despised state, they rightly believed that the God of the covenant is the true God who made the whole cosmos.

The four echo words come from the priestly blessing of Number 6:24-26. The words 'bless', 'keep' (= 'watch over'), 'be gracious to' (= 'have mercy on'), and 'peace' occur frequently in this collection, which is almost an expansion in song of that blessing given in the temple. Ultimately these are songs of a people who have a great high priest to bring them into the presence of God.

The stylistic feature is sometimes called 'staircase parallelism' in which successive verses have an 'A to B' then 'B to C' (etc.) motif. Psalm 120:4-6 is an example:

> Woe to me that I dwell in Meshek (A)
> that I *live* among the tents of Kedar (B)
> Too long have I *lived* (B again)
> among those who hate *peace* (C)
> I am for *peace* (C again)
> but when I speak, they are for war (D)

This has an attractive poetic effect gradually leading us along a pathway (or up a metaphorical staircase of thought); depending on the subject matter, it may also build tension, helping us to feel each stage as it builds.

Psalm 120

The songs that will end with a celebration of peace (133, 134) begin with the anguished voice of a man feeling the pain of lies and war. In verse 1 the 'distress' is not specified, until in verse 2 we learn that it is 'lying lips…deceitful tongues'. This believer is surrounded by liars who twist his words and falsely malign his reputation, to his hurt. He cries for a punishment appropriate to the crime. Verse 4 is literally just 'a warrior's sharp arrows, burning coals of the broom bush' (famously hot); although NIV adds in 'He will punish you…' it would seem that the two images describe both what these lying tongues do (cause harm like a sharp arrow and spread destructive fires of gossip, cf. James 3:5) and therefore the punishment appropriate to them.

Where he lives is called in verse 5 both 'Meshek', in the far north (cf. Ezek. 38:2,3), and 'Kedar', to the east (cf. Ezek. 27:21; Jer. 49:28). It is metaphorical: I live far away from the promised land. Although I am a 'peacemaker' (Matt. 5:9) and try to 'live at peace with everyone' (Rom. 12:18), I live among those who 'hate peace' and are 'for war'. This is why I must go on pilgrimage to the only place where peace is to be found. Here at last I will hear from the priest, the man with access to God, the blessing of peace (Num. 6:26).

As we hear this distressed Old Covenant believer express his pain in the midst of strife and deceit, we hear also the voice of the one by whose Spirit he speaks, the Lord Jesus Christ, who felt supremely the pain of living in a 'perverse generation' and asked 'how long shall I stay with you?' (Matt. 17:17). The devil is 'a liar and the father of lies' and therefore also 'a murderer' (John 8:44). He lied in the garden of Eden (Gen. 3:1,4); he has lied and killed ever since. Jesus above all knew, all around Him, the pain of the lies Satan generated and felt the 'sharp arrows' and 'burning coals' of their destructive force. One day Jesus will bring peace; but until that day, His people everywhere must know the pain of living in the midst of deceit and strife. This psalm helps us feel that pain with Jesus and also to long more deeply for the only place where peace may be found. It is a fitting introduction to this collection of songs.

Psalm 121

[Vol. 1: 103, 148, 225-226]

It is likely that Psalms 120, 121, and 122 are an opening sequence. In Psalm 120 the believer laments living amidst deceit and strife; in Psalm 121 he therefore begins his pilgrimage towards the place and people of God's presence on earth (Zion in the Old Covenant). There are four couplets and two voices. In each couplet the second verse intensifies the first.

In verses 1 and 2 'I' speak, the individual pilgrim, potentially starting out on his journey. He looks, perhaps towards the mountains surrounding Jerusalem (as in Ps. 125:2) and affirms that his 'help' – much needed in Psalm 120 – comes from the covenant God, 'the Maker of heaven and earth'. This refrain (which found its way into the Apostles Creed) affirms that the God to whom he looks is the God of all creation.

In the remaining couplets, this individual no longer speaks; other(s) speak to him. Another voice – or perhaps a chorus of other pilgrim voices – reassure this believer that his trust is not misplaced. Six times the verb 'watch over' or 'keep' (the same word) are used; if Psalm 120 speaks of 'peace', Psalm 121 speaks of the God who will 'keep/watch over' His people (Num. 6:24-26).

Verse 3 assures him that the God who watches over him will not slumber and will take care not to let his foot slip. Verse 4 intensifies this: not only will He 'not slumber', He 'will neither slumber nor sleep'; not only does He watch over 'you', He watches over 'Israel' all His people.

Verse 5 promises 'shade'. Verse 6 intensifies this: it is shelter at all times (day and night) and from all dangers ('the sun' and 'the moon' speaking poetically of the full range of possible dangers).

Verse 7 promises protection of his life from harm. Verse 8 intensifies this: the protection extends to all his activities ('coming and going') and for all time ('both now and for evermore').

Jesus Christ is the leader of 'Israel', the whole people of God, Jew and gentile (Gal. 6:16). As He 'lifts his eyes' to heaven in prayer, He longs to be in His Father's presence. His life on earth is one long pilgrimage. This psalm will have reassured Him that the God of all creation watched over Him and all His people with all care at all times against all dangers in all events. As the people of Jesus we too are pilgrims, walking in Jesus' footsteps on the path to the heavenly Jerusalem, the New Heavens and New Earth; we share Jesus' confidence that this same God, our heavenly Father, watches over us every step of the way.

Psalm 122

If Psalm 120 expresses the distress caused by the deceit and strife of the land 'East of Eden' (Gen. 3:23,24), and Psalm 121 reassures the pilgrim on a dangerous journey, Psalm 122 helps us feel the gladness of being among the people and in the place where God dwells on earth. In Old Covenant language this is 'Jerusalem', fulfilled in Jesus and the people of Jesus, and ultimately in the heavenly Jerusalem (see vol. 1, chapter 13).

As in Psalm 122 there is an interplay of the individual (v. 1 'I rejoiced…') and the church of fellow-pilgrims (v. 1 '…*those* who said to me…'), as they encourage one another to go to this place and belong to this people. And now (2) they arrive and look around in wonder, as we should when we first come to Jesus and every time we gather with Jesus' people.

By contrast to the division and strife of the world (Ps. 120) the theme of this psalm is the security that comes from unity: verse 3 'closely compacted together', i.e. secure, solid; verses 6-9 'peace... secure... peace... security... peace... prosperity'. This is a miraculous unity, for 'the tribes' that 'go up' to this place are not by nature in love and harmony with one another, as much of Old Testament history demonstrates. They share with the rest of humanity a natural propensity to rivalry, strife, and warfare. But when they 'go up' to this place, they come together under God's law (v. 4 'the statute given to Israel') and God's King (v. 5 'thrones for judgment, the thrones of the house of David'). This connection with David is reinforced by the 'of David' in the heading, and connects this psalm again with the promises of Psalm 2.

What Jerusalem was in Old Testament language was not the historical Jerusalem, which was as much a place of strife as any other city; it was a foreshadowing of a promised Jerusalem, which would be fulfilled in Jesus, foreshadowed in every local church of Jesus, and consummated in the New Jerusalem coming down from heaven to earth. This is the place where David's anointed King rules all the people of God in harmony and security.

The exhortation to 'pray for the peace of Jerusalem', to long and seek for its security and prosperity (6-9) is a recognition that 'Jerusalem' as longed-for has not yet come. For Old Covenant believers, this was to pray for the one who would sit on David's throne, the Messiah. For us it is to pray urgently and warmly for our local churches and for the churches of Christ worldwide, that they would be, more and more, places under the rule of God's King and the government of God's good law, and therefore places of supernatural harmony and safety in the midst of a dangerous world.

Psalm 123

In this psalm we look up and others look down upon us; the surprise is that we do not look up to those who look down upon us.

It is very hard to be ridiculed. We join in this psalm both with an individual and with a people who are treated with contempt. The psalm begins with the leader's individual voice (v. 1 'I… my…'); but quickly the choir join him and it becomes 'our… us… us… we… we…'.

The movement is from lifted 'eyes' (four times in vv. 1,2) to an appeal for 'mercy' (three times in vv. 2-3) prompted by the experience of contempt and ridicule (three times in vv. 3-4). The 'eyes' of the leader and his people express their yearnings and desire. We look up to God because the proud look down upon us.

Our longings are entirely to be directed upwards to God in heaven as the only one who can satisfy us, just as slaves would look only to their master or a servant girl only to her mistress; we need to know that this is the only place to seek what we need. As this song was sung in synagogues in the time of Jesus, he too would have joined in, expressing this urgent upward looking in prayer to His Father; indeed, He will become the leader whose individual voice we now hear leading us in what becomes His prayer.

What the Old Covenant believers needed, what Jesus needed in His humanity, what we need in Him, is 'mercy', which means gracious loving-kindness (not necessarily forgiveness of sins here). The appeal for mercy is repeated, urgent, and moving. It echoes the promise in the priestly blessing of Numbers 6: 'the LORD make his face to shine on you and *be gracious to* (= have mercy on) you' (Num. 6:25).

Because mercy comes from His 'face' means we must look with upward 'eyes' to Him.

This appeal for grace is drawn out of them by the seemingly endless ('no end of... no end of...') experience of being looked down upon, treated with contempt and ridicule. What is worse, those who do this are 'arrogant' (lit. 'at ease') and 'proud' (4); there is about them a smug self-satisfied assurance, the sneer of the intellectual elite who think the people of God are stupid, and spare no time in saying so repeatedly.

It is a surprise that the people of God, led by their leader, do not look *up* to the people who look *down* upon them; we, like they, will be tempted to ingratiate ourselves with our 'cultured despisers';[3] instead we, and they, look up to the covenant God, because we know He sits enthroned in heaven (1) and therefore He alone can give us His mercy. Jesus the despised and rejected one (Isa. 53:3) leads us His people in directing our desires ('eyes') in prayer upwards to the God who is our Father in Christ, that we too will cry urgently for His mercy, feeling, as He did, the pain of being despised.

Psalm 124

[Vol. 1: 148]

In this psalm we experience a great danger (1-5), celebrate a great escape (6,7) and join in a great declaration (8). In this older 'of David' psalm the king exhorts the people of God in later generations ('let Israel say') to join in singing of a great rescue. The song begins and ends with the covenant

---

3. The phrase is taken from F. Schliermacher.

God. This God is 'on our side' (1 ,2). He is 'for us' as Christ's apostle Paul will later express it, because we belong to Christ our king (Rom. 8:31).

But immediately we are plunged into the most intense crescendo of terror, as we experience a great danger. From verse 2b to verse 5 we are taken to the depths of what would have happened if the covenant God had not been on our side. As we sing this we acutely feel the total and frightening destruction that would have been ours at the hands of the enemies of God's people.

And then, in verses 6 and 7, we celebrate an astonishing rescue, a great escape. The enemies who are a chaotic destructive flood in verses 3-5 become wild beasts with 'teeth' and a fowler trapping little birds. Defenseless and helpless as we were, the covenant God has broken the snare so that we have escaped. There is a great sense of wonder as, in verse 8, we reaffirm the words spoken by a song-leader individually in Psalm 121:2. The Creator God is the one to whom the leader and people lifted up their eyes in Psalm 123; in the great claim that concludes Psalm 124, we affirm that this same God is 'our help' (8).

We do not know what rescue prompted David first to write this song. It would have been very appropriate for Ezra and his contemporaries to sing this when Babylon was defeated and the Persian king encouraged them to 'go up' (in a spiritual 'ascent') to Jerusalem (e.g. Ezra 2:1). That return from exile was an escape from the very jaws of death.

What would it have meant for Jesus of Nazareth to sing this song? His Father, God in heaven, was 'on his side'. As He faced being swallowed up by the angry hostility of His enemies, He could be confident that the 'raging waters' of their enmity could not be the end of the story. The final word would be spoken on Easter morning as the snare of death was broken and He escaped, because His help was in the name of the covenant Father God, the Maker of heaven and earth.

For Jesus' people now, we join Him in the song, as the renewed 'Israel of God' (Jew and gentile in Christ, Gal. 6:16). We celebrate that, in Christ, God is 'for us'. We feel the terror of the hell that would have awaited us had he not been 'on our side' (3-5). We celebrate the resurrection rescue that will one day be ours (6-8). When God gives us little rescues from pressures or persecutions, this song is appropriate. But whatever the torrents that threaten us, we can sing in the confidence of that final resurrection morning, when there will be 'no longer any' – chaotic, evil, threatening - 'sea' (Rev. 21:1).

Psalm 125

This psalm gives a surprising answer to the question: what ought we most to fear as the church of Christ?

The eternal security of Mount Zion (1), or Jerusalem (2) is the theme of this psalm (cf. Pss. 46, 48). Its physical location, surrounded by hills, is a picture of its spiritual 'place', in danger on every side and yet protected by the covenant God all around. The people of God (2), meaning 'those who trust in the LORD' (1), are in this safe place forever. Believers took comfort from this promise until, centuries later, the greatest believer trusted that, even if people destroyed the 'temple' of His body, in three days it would be rebuilt (John 2:19-22). He would be very much 'like Mount Zion'; indeed, all the covenant promises focused on Zion would be fulfilled in Him. He supremely is the one who trusts in the LORD and will be secure forever.

The psalm was first sung when 'the sceptre of the wicked' (3) ruled over 'the land allotted' (as in the allocation of the promised land by lots, in Joshua) to 'the righteous', those who are righteous by faith in God's promises. When wickedness rules, believers who want to get on in the world are acutely tempted to 'use their hands to do evil', either to remove the wickedness by ungodly force, or to conform to the wicked ways of the rulers – either through fear of persecution or ambition to get on in this wicked world. A godly king matters deeply for a godly people. The eternal security of the believing people depends in the end on being governed by a godly 'sceptre', by the King after God's own heart. Jesus of Nazareth trusted this promise and embodied in His own person the goodness and the destiny of this king. Ungodly leaders within the church are the most direct fulfilment of this 'sceptre of the wicked' and a great menace to the church.

The word 'good' in verse 4 has covenant overtones, with its double meaning of 'good' as covenant blessing ('do good to…') and 'good' as covenant faithfulness ('those who are good'). We pray for God to keep His covenant promises to bless those whose hearts are upright. Jesus too will have prayed this prayer, and shared the assurance of verse 5, that in the end 'evildoers' will be banished from the land. He too will have prayed (as in Ps. 122:6-9) that the 'peace' of the kingdom of God will come to God's people (5b).

Galatians 6:16 echoes this prayer for 'Peace' to be 'upon Israel,' the people of God in Christ. So we now pray this prayer in Christ, trusting in our eternal security in Christ (1, 2), believing that the kingdom of God will come (3), praying that final blessing will come to all Christ's people (4) and the finally impenitent will be excluded from the new heavens and new earth (5), so that peace will come to all God's people (5b).

The surprise is that the greatest danger to the people of God is not external attack, but sin within the church. So long as we walk in the light and are upright in heart, we are as safe as we could possibly be. But if we use our hands to do evil (3b), 'turn to crooked ways' (5a) then we will be banished, far away from safety. The greatest danger for Christ's church is sin within; it is this we should fear and against this we should work and pray.

Psalm 126

[Vol. 1: 98-99, 193]

If Psalm 125 answers the question, 'what should be our greatest fear?', then Psalm 126 addresses the challenge, 'what should be our deepest desire?'

The surprise that unlocks this psalm is that the urgent prayer of verse 4 follows the celebration of verses 1-3. We might expect it to be the other way around. Looking back probably to the return from exile, perhaps to some other restoration, the people of God remember their joy. This joy reveals their heart for 'Zion'; that the people of God should prosper matters more to them than anything, including their personal circumstances. It results, first in joyful hearts (1b 'like those who dreamed') and then in tongues that praise the covenant God in a great international crescendo (2, 3). Jesus too cared more for the prosperity of God's people than anything else, because He knew that this would bring worldwide praise to His Father. We too learn to rejoice in the restoration of the people of Christ because we also know this will bring praise to the Father. This should be our deepest desire.

Why then the prayer of verse 4, which seems to ask God to do what he has already done, to restore the fortunes of His people? Because, like the desert wadis in the Negev (4b), rain-fuelled waters are followed by summer dryness; the church of God is never more than intermittently and partially restored in this age. Whatever restoration there has been in Old Covenant days, it is at best partial and always followed by harder days (as was the period after the exile, for example). Verse 4, on the lips of a Simeon or an Anna (Luke 2:22-38) was a prayer answered only when Jesus came. On the lips of Jesus, it became a prayer for God's kingdom finally to come; it is this on our lips today, a longing not only for partial revivals of God's people, but ultimately for the final revival in the return of Jesus Christ. We look back with wonder and joy to the first coming of Jesus; we long for His return.

Verse 5, intensified in verse 6, is a God-given promise that, while sowing of the word of God (cf. Mark 4:1-9) is a grievous business, attended by much pain, it will most assuredly yield a joyful harvest (cf. Luke 6:21). Jesus believed this and sowed in very great pain on the cross; He did this 'for the joy that was set before him' (Heb. 12:2); His expectation will not be in vain. As we sing this song together we too are encouraged to keep sowing, even through our tears.

Psalm 127

The key to praying this psalm is to read the 'house' and 'city' of verses 1, 2 and the 'children' (lit. 'sons') of verses 3-5 in the wider context of the Psalms of Ascent. This suggests that the 'house' is 'the house of the LORD' (122:1; 134:1) combined with 'the house of David' (122:4), i.e. both the temple and the Davidic line, God's king ruling the world from the place of God's presence. Further, it suggests that 'sons' are most importantly the sons born in David's line (cf. 132:11, 12). The heading 'of Solomon' – whether it means 'by Solomon', 'to Solomon', or 'concerning Solomon' – supports these connections with the Temple and David's dynasty.

The shared 'project' of both halves of the psalm is therefore the great Bible 'Zion' project that is fulfilled in Jesus Christ, the great Son of David and the embodiment of the Temple, God's presence on earth – in Jesus, that is, and the people of Jesus. This will save us from an arbitrary individualistic ('me and God') reading, which is deeply problematical, not least for Christian childless couples. (Likewise Ps. 128, which is closely linked with 127 in themes.)

In verse 1 we, who work for Christ and His gospel (the 'Zion' project) hear the warning that all our gospel work is 'in vain' unless the covenant God does the work in and through us. When we work anxiously (2), in a way that shows we think it all depends upon us, we work in vain. There is a translation question in the last line of verse 2, but – assuming NIV is right – this encourages us to trust the 'Zion-building God' that he will build the church of Christ, even while we take our needed sleep.

In verse 3, the word 'heritage' is used to mean a share in the promised land (God's 'inheritance'). When God works to build the king's dynasty (3-5), and indeed the people whom the king rules, the king will be acknowledged to be a powerful warrior, fit to rule the world. This – in the end – is our King Jesus, whose people are sometimes called His 'children' (Heb. 2:13, quoting Isa. 8:18). When we sing verse 5, we proclaim the blessedness of Jesus our warrior king.

Psalm 128

Verses 1-4 proclaim (1) and emphatically repeat (4) a blessing on any man who fears the covenant God with reverent fear, and walks in His ways (1b). This blessing is (2) fruitful labour (reversing the curse of Genesis 3) with prosperity (lit 'good' – cf. 125:4) and fertility in marriage, leading to a healthy growing family fellowship gathered around the table (3).

This blessing is intimately connected, in the prayer of verses 4 and 5, with 'Zion' or 'Jerusalem' (5) – notice how 'prosperity' (good) in 2b is also the 'prosperity' (good) of Jerusalem in verse 5. It is also connected with 'Israel' the whole people of God by the final declaration of 'peace' (identical to the last line of Ps. 125, and cf. Ps. 122:6-9). So the 'good' of this blessed family is a part of the greater 'good' of the people of God, which continues 'all the days of your life' and far on into future generations ('your children's children'). This blessing is not for the isolated nuclear family, but for all who are part of the great family of the people of God.

What could it mean for Jesus of Nazareth to sing, and to believe, the blessings declared and prayed for in this psalm? He never married, never had children. And yet 'Jerusalem' found its true 'good' in His God-fearing obedience, and the day will come when He 'will see his offspring and prolong his days' (Isa. 53:10); at His victorious banqueting table He will sit with 'the children God has given me' (Heb. 2:13), a countless multitude from every language and nation.

For some of us who are in Christ the blessings of this psalm may find some fulfilment in marriage, children, and prosperity in this age. For more of us – perhaps ultimately all of us – the fulfilment of these blessings will be found in 'every spiritual blessing' that we have in Jesus (Eph. 1:3), and in being one of that great multitude gathered around Jesus in the new heavens and new earth. Then finally there will be 'peace… to… the Israel of God' (Gal. 6:16).

Psalm 129

An unnamed Spirit-inspired believer leads Israel (1 'let Israel say') in affirming her rescue from oppression (1-4) and praying for the defeat of her enemies (5-8).

The repetition of 1a in 2a gives a strong feeling of great oppression for the people of God from the very beginning of their existence ('from my youth'), perhaps all the way back to 'righteous Abel' (Gen. 4; Matt. 23:35). Verse 3 uses a horrifying image to deepen the portrayal of pain. But all this vicious and sustained hostility has not prevailed; God is 'righteous', keeping His covenant promises, and cutting His people free. From the Exodus onwards, through the days of the Judges and all the way to Jesus, God has 'cut the' oppressive, enslaving 'cords of the wicked'. When Jesus sang this, He no doubt believed that He too, as the embodiment of Israel, would be cut free, as indeed He was. His people now pray with Christ that we will all one day be cut free from the slavery of sin, the devil, and all the devil's agents on earth.

We hesitate to pray verses 5-8. And yet we can and must, in Christ. For it is the prayer of the godly leader of God's people against 'all who hate Zion', those who by their impenitent hostility continue to oppose with all their force the covenant promises and people of God. He prays – and we pray in Him – that these will be transient, evanescent people, disappearing from the earth like shallow roof-grass

(6 ,7), living ultimately fruitless and empty lives. They have opposed the covenant people, and so they cannot inherit the covenant blessings (v. 8, cf. Gen. 12:3a).

Psalm 130
[Vol. 1: 100]

In this famous psalm we hear the voice of an anonymous believer speaking first for himself (1-6) and then exhorting the whole people of God to walk in His footsteps (vv. 7, 8 'Israel...'). In the first couplet (1, 2) he cries intensely 'out of the depths' (that is, close to the entrances to Sheol, the place of the dead). The human circumstances of these depths are not specified; but in the context of the Psalms of ascent the natural reading is that they are related to Israel's experience of living under the judgement of God, first in exile and then in the fragile days after the exile. Speaking for the people of God, he grasps that his experience is representative of the common experience of the whole people of God, who must live as aliens and exiles on earth, in a world under sin. And so he cries, 'with fervent cries and tears to the one who could save him from death' (Heb. 5:7).

In verses 3 and 4 he makes it clear that he understands that the core problem is not suffering but 'sins' and the heart of his hope is that with the covenant God 'there is forgiveness'. Only forgiveness of sins can enable His people to 'fear' Him in reverent worship (v. 4b is lit. 'that you may be feared').

And so, in the third couplet (5, 6) he waits and he waits and he hopes and he hopes, for that forgiveness to come, for the people of God to be taken up out of the depths to live before God in reverent worship. Because of 'his word', His covenant promises, this final forgiveness is as sure as day follows night. He longs for those promises to find their 'Yes!'. Centuries later, Simeon and Anna wait with a little group of believers (Luke 2). And then Jesus of Nazareth sings this psalm, crying on behalf of the people of God (1, 2), trusting that there will be forgiveness (3, 4), waiting, waiting, waiting. And in His life and His death we hear God's final 'Yes!' to all the promises of the covenant (2 Cor. 1:20).

We then today (v. 7 'Israel' under the New Covenant) hear the exhortation of Jesus our leader, that we too should put our hope in the covenant God, confident that, because of Jesus, there is 'unfailing (covenant) love' and 'full redemption' from all of our sins, the final redemption of our bodies (Rom. 8:23). We cry with Him (1, 2), a cry that is not triumphalist, but neither is it a resigned fatalism; we confess and claim forgiveness as He leads us (3, 4); we wait with Him, patiently resting on the promises of His word (5, 6); we share His confidence in the unfailing love and perfect redemption that is ours in Jesus (7, 8).

Psalm 131

As in Psalm 130, an individual believer speaks (1, 2) and then exhorts the whole people of God (3) in words which echo Psalm 130 ('Israel, put your hope in the LORD', as in Ps. 130:7a).

The individual, originally David in this older psalm, declares three attitudes that he has decided against (1), and one demeanour he has chosen (2). The surprise is in the contrast. He has chosen a quiet contentment, like a young child nestling up to their mother. We might expect that in order to do this, he would renounce (in v. 1) anxiety. But instead, he turns from pride. He determines not to have a proud heart (1a) or proud 'eyes' (1b, expressive of desires, for what the heart wants, the eyes look to get). He decides not to act as though he can understand and manage 'great matters'; that is, he will not 'act big' as if he has the cleverness and strength to be the master of his soul and captain of his fate. He will not 'reach for the moon' in his ambitions or pretensions about himself. The word 'wonderful' is typically used of what God does, that is beyond human power or understanding. That is, David resolves to be a humble king, fully dependent upon the covenant God. The people after the exile needed to learn from David that they have neither the ability nor the power to drag themselves up 'out of the depths' (130:1).

The reason such humility is the opposite of anxiety is this. When the king – or anyone else – speaks and acts as though they were in control, they must necessarily become anxious when they realise they are not. The moment something happens that is beyond their understanding or control, fears must rise. For they are living as if it all depends upon them. Only the humility of verse 1 can lead to the contentment of verse 2.

David only sometimes lived up to what he professes in verses 1 and 2. Jesus of Nazareth was consistent; He alone can sing verses 1 and 2 as the flawless expression of His heart and life, rather than just His better aspirations. He alone can exhort the people of God (3) to put our hope in the covenant God, the God and Father of Jesus, to trust in Him at all times, as Jesus did.

Psalm 132

[Vol. 1: 41, 189]

We will only sing this psalm when we are deeply convinced that we need a king. This psalm is the odd one out in the psalms of ascent. It is more than twice as long as the others. And – and this is the really significant point – it is about David as much as it is about Zion. It brings together the place (Zion, a major theme in these psalms) and the person (the king). The rule of David has been mentioned in Ps. 122:5 and David is the author of Pss. 122, 124, 131, and 133 (bracketing this psalm). Now David comes to the fore, punctuating the psalm at beginning, end, and hinge point (1, 10, 18). But it is not – or not immediately – about us. And there's the rub. We need to grasp that by 'king' the Bible here means ultimately a ruler with absolute and universal power over all powers, natural and supernatural, the power, that is, to right all wrongs. When we face powers too strong for us, whether human powers in the workplace, the family, the nation or the world, or superhuman powers of sickness and death itself, we need a king; for we cannot overcome these powers on our own.

The motif of 'place' runs right through the psalm: 'a place… a dwelling' (5); 'his dwelling-place' (7); 'your resting-place' (8); 'his dwelling' (13); 'my resting place' (14); 'Here' (17). Our concern is the 'place' where God dwells upon earth.

The psalm begins (1-10) with a prayer (David's oath to the LORD) and ends with a promise (vv. 11-18, the LORD's oath to David).

The prayer – very poignant after the exile, when there was no king – is that God will 'remember David' (1) and 'not reject (His) anointed one' (v. 10, i.e. 'Messiah' or 'Christ'). The basis for this prayer is that the king has sacrificially humbled himself (v. 1 'his self-denial' expanded in David's oath to the covenant God in 2-5) in his determination to make a 'place' for God to dwell on earth. At the start of his reign David resolved to do whatever it took to bring the rule of God to his throne.

The story is told (6) of David and his men hearing 'in Ephrathah' (David's home, Bethlehem) that the Ark of the Covenant has been found 'in the fields of Jaar' (i.e. Kiriath-Jearim, 1 Sam. 7:1,2). They determine (7,8) to bring the Ark to Jerusalem (2 Sam. 6:1-19) so that the covenant God may dwell there and rule according to the good law enshrined in the Ten Commandments (the tablets within the Ark). Then (9, 10) there will be a place with access to God ('your priests'), creating a joyful people under an anointed king (a messiah, cf. Ps. 2:2). Solomon had prayed verses 9 and 10 when the Temple was first consecrated (2 Chron. 6:41,42); the people of God now pray it after the exile. At the heart of this prayer is a king in David's line (1, 10). Only a king who determines to do whatever it takes to establish the kingdom of God on earth will answer our need and God's glory. One day a greater king than David will humble himself even to the cross (Phil. 2:6-8) that he may do whatever it takes to bring the kingdom of God to earth.

The promise begins, not with the king's oath to God (2-5) but with the covenant God's oath to the king (11, 12). God's covenant with the king is the undergirding of God's covenant with the king's people (cf. 2 Kings 11:17). It can stand only when a faithful king is found (12). Only when that fully faithful king shall come will the promises of the covenant be 'Yes!' in him (2 Cor. 1:20). David believed this (Acts 2:30); it was fulfilled when the faithful humble Jesus came as the anointed one.

This promise, fulfilled in the faithful 'David', is the guarantee of a finally prosperous 'Zion' (13-16). Notice the loving delight of God in this place, echoing the loving delight of the faithful king, which was the emphasis of verses 1-5. Here at last is the Father willing to dwell with a people, and the Son freely willing just what the Father wills – two harmonious wills in perfect delight. Then the prayer is answered; notice how verse 16 echoes almost verbatim verse 9. In Jesus Christ at last God 'has raised up a horn (see v. 17) of salvation (see v. 16) for us in the house of his servant David' (Luke 1:69). This King is the 'lamp' (17, cf. 2 Sam. 21:17) by whose light His people walk.

As we pray this psalm today, the prayer of verses 1-10 is fragrant with the assurance we have by the first coming of Jesus, as we long for His return in glory. The answer of verses 11-18 reassures us – even more deeply than it can have comforted the waiting Old Covenant pilgrims – that one day Jesus Christ, the anointed king in David's line, will return to stand on the heavenly fulfilment of Mount Zion with all His people (Rev. 14:1).

Psalm 133

The songs of ascent began with strife (Ps. 120); they end with harmony. The peace prayed for 'Jerusalem' (Ps. 122:6-9) – the people of God fulfilled in Jesus Christ and His world-wide people – is here celebrated. At the simplest level, verse 1 affirms the goodness when (lit.) 'brothers dwell together'; the expression is used in Deuteronomy 25:5 of a wider family group living together; it reminds us of Abraham and Lot (Gen. 13:6) and of Jacob and Esau (Gen. 36:7), where they were not able to dwell 'together'. But the psalm indicates that the harmony being celebrated is not just a natural family unit, but the spiritual people of God gathered under God's king.

We will only feel deeply the goodness of this harmony if we have some experience of the misery of its absence, which Psalm 120 so graphically portrays for us.

Human harmony is a supernatural gift of God, which is why words for 'coming down' or 'falling' come three times in verses 2 and 3. The first metaphor (2) is of a fragrant and refreshing scented oil, poured over someone in generous abundance. The association with Aaron strongly suggests a priestly blessing (Exod. 29:7; 30:22-32); the good of harmony in fellowship comes only where there is a priest to give the people safe access to God.

The second image (3) is of summer dews from the high mountain of Hermon in the north of the promised land, bringing life to a parched land. These wonderful dews fall (not geographically but in spiritual significance) on 'Mount Zion' the place of covenant promise and of God's king. It is 'there' (3b, the same word as 'here' in Ps. 132:17) that God bestows the blessing of eternal life.

When Jesus sang this psalm He too celebrated the blessing that will come when – at last – the people of God are gathered under one shepherd to be one flock (John 10:16), which will happen only when the Good Shepherd lays down His life for the sheep (John 10:11) and is 'lifted up' to 'draw' all kinds of people to Himself (John 12:32). It is in Jesus our priest, and only in Jesus, that this blessing of human unity comes down from heaven and enables us to 'live in peace' (2 Cor. 13:11).

Psalm 134

[Vol. 1: 148]

The word 'blessing' in Ps. 133:3 is picked up in this lovely concluding psalm of the songs of ascent. It brackets verses

1 and 2 ('Praise the LORD… praise the LORD' – where 'praise' is the same word as 'bless'). The people of God, perhaps led by their priests in the temple 'sanctuary', are to acknowledge that all blessing, all that makes life worth living, comes from the covenant God. This is the first purpose of making the pilgrimage to Jerusalem.

If verses 1 and 2 exhort the people of God to give blessing 'upwards' (as it were), verse 3 offers blessing in a different direction, coming down from the covenant God, from 'Zion' (the place of the king and the temple), who is 'the Maker of heaven and earth' (cf. Ps. 121:2; 124:8). This is the other purpose of going up to Jerusalem, to receive blessing from the God of Zion.

Putting these two directions of blessing, when we join in – as Jesus leads us – we both affirm that the God and Father of Jesus is the source of all blessing, without any exceptions, and crave that blessing from Him afresh. All the hopes and fears, the prayers and the promises, of the songs of ascent, are summed up in this double direction of blessing.

Psalm 135

[Vol. 1: 155, 172-173, 175-176, 206]

Almost every verse of this psalm is close to, or identical to other verses in the Psalms (especially Ps. 115), the Pentateuch, or the Prophets. It is like a rich and vibrant mosaic put together from material found elsewhere. It begins (1-4) with exhortation to all the people of God to praise the covenant God because He 'has chosen Jacob to be his own…'. It ends (19-21) with similar exhortation. The mention of 'Zion' in verse 21 makes this Psalm almost an expansion of Psalm 134, which concluded the Psalms of Ascent.

After the initial exhortation, we hear the voice of an individual speaking for the whole people (5, 'I know…'). He leads the people in response to the exhortation to praise by affirming the headline conviction that the covenant God 'is great…greater than all gods'.

This leader teaches the people (a) that God is sovereign in providence throughout the world (6, 7), and (b) that He worked in sovereign power in history to create His people, bringing them out of Egypt (8, 9), through the wilderness, conquering the first significant enemies on the verge of the land (10,11, cf. Num. 21:21-35), and then bringing His people into the land (12). As the Choir of the people of God, we hear our Leader summoning us to praise and giving us reasons for praise: the God of the covenant has redeemed, does sustain, and will lead all His people into the promised land, finally the New Heavens and New Earth.

Because these historical wonders guarantee future destiny, this song-leader speaks for us in direct address to the covenant God (13, 14), praising Him for His greatness in vindicating His despised people and having compassion on His oppressed people. This was appropriate after the exile; it is apposite in every age of the persecuted church.

By contrast (15-18) the seemingly powerful deities that hold sway in human imaginations outside the people of God are empty, impotent idols. We need not be cowed by them and we must not trust them.

And so – in its fulfilment – we hear the Lord Jesus Christ our Leader summoning us afresh to praise the Father God who redeemed then and redeems now, who protected then and protects now, and who will bring all who are in Christ into the promised land of the inheritance kept in heaven for us, that will finally come down from heaven to earth.

Psalm 136
[Vol. 1: 152, 170, 173, 176, 204]

The refrain that echoes around Book 5 of the psalms cannot be ignored in this wonderfully repetitive psalm: 'His love' – His steadfast, unfailing, covenant love – 'endures forever.' Twenty-six times in twenty-six verses. Clearly it matters deeply that we grasp this; and evidently we need it repeated if we are to appropriate it, for we have short memories.

But how can we be sure? How are these not just empty words, of the kind 'the pagans' speak? Two answers: first, every psalm is written by a Spirit-inspired songwriter, by whom the choir is led. If we trust this leader, himself led by the Spirit of Christ, it is as if we hear the Lord Jesus Himself both instructing us and leading us in this psalm, so that what we affirm, again and again, He has first promised to us: the covenant love of God the Father, that is ours in Christ, does indeed endure forever. There is something deeply comforting about this.

Second, the truths the psalms recounts are the evidence that His love endures forever. The psalm begins (1-3) and ends (26) with exhortation to 'give thanks' to the covenant God, for His goodness (1a) and His greatness (2, 3, 26). This Almighty goodness is then retold in terms of creation and redemption. He is the Creator who has placed a wise order in creation (4-9); by coming back to this common grace at the end (v. 25 'food to every creature') the psalm places redemptive goodness under the umbrella of the goodness of the Created Order. The main narrative retells the story of redemption: this covenant Creator God has 'brought Israel *out*' from slavery in Egypt (10-12), has 'brought Israel *through*' the Red Sea and the wilderness (13-16) and brought Israel *in* to 'their land' (17-22).

As Jesus Christ leads His people in the singing of this psalm, we remember that He Himself is the one by whom the Father brought us out in the redemption of the Cross; He Himself is the one by whom the Father sustains us through the wilderness of this age; and He Himself is the one who brings us in to the Promised Land of the New Creation, in which the good Created Order will finally be restored. As He leads us, our hearts are warmed by His Spirit and we join in this psalm, the repetitions driving home to our forgetful hearts the astonishing goodness of the Father's love for us in Jesus.

Psalm 137

[Vol. 1: 124, 130-131, 200, 227]

If we are to love Jerusalem, we must hate Babylon. Properly understood, this is as true today as it was during or after the Exile. This psalm breathes intense grief (1-4), deep love (5, 6) and passionate aversion (7-9); the three affections are united by a loyal and undivided love for the covenant God.

In verses 1-4 we recount a corporate memory ('we... our...') of intense grief. The people of God remember 'Zion' and all it symbolized, the covenant promises to Abraham and Moses encapsulated in the covenant with David. That place had been the focus of great joy; but now it is destroyed, and so there can be no songs of joy. There is no other source of joy, no idol in which the loyal people of God can rejoice.

An individual leader breaks out of the chorus in verses 5-6 to affirm that Jerusalem is indeed his 'highest joy'. There is a paradox here. He is one who 'wept when (he) remembered Zion' (1); and yet he will never forget her (5), will always remember her (6), and will ever consider her his 'highest joy'. Jerusalem is his grief in her desolation, his joy in her enduring promise.

The prayer of verses 7-9, led by this same devout believer, is both shocking in its intensity and necessary, as the counterpart to the affection expressed in verses 1-6. For, if He – and we His Choir – are to love the covenant God and all His promises with all our hearts, then we must necessarily pray for the destruction of those who sought to destroy the work of this good God. Both Edom (v. 7, cf. Obadiah) and supremely Babylon (8,9) set themselves against Jerusalem. Those who persist in spiritual membership of these hostile powers, and determine never to repent, must be destroyed if Jerusalem is to be secure.

The New Testament takes both 'Jerusalem' and 'Babylon' as shorthands for the city of God and the city of a hostile and idolatrous world (cf. Rev. 18). To pray for the destruction of Babylon is entirely consistent with interceding for men and women, that God will give them, as He has given us, the gift of repentance, that they too will flee from Babylon and count Jerusalem their highest joy. For in the heavenly Jerusalem is their, and our, only security in the judgement of God.

Only Jesus, the Lamb who died for sinners, can safely lead His people in the praying of this psalm. For only in Him is to be found such intense grief for the desolate state of His people, such single-hearted joy in all His people will be, and such holy resolve that – whether by conversion or judgement – wickedness will finally be eradicated from the earth.

A Note on Psalms 138–145 – A final 'of David' grouping

We have seen that most of the David psalms are in Books 1 and 2. But dotted through Books 3, 4, and 5 are more David psalms. It would seem that these older psalms have been incorporated in the later books because they are appropriate there. Book 5 begins (almost) with a little grouping of David psalms (108–110). It ends (almost) with the longest group of David psalms outside Books 1 and 2. The eight psalms from 138-145 are all 'of David', leaving only the final 'Hallelujah chorus' to bring the Psalter to a close. We do not know why this major David collection is placed here. But, given that the covenant with David in Psalm 2 forms half of the grand introduction to the Psalter as a whole, and given that the terrible events of the exile have intervened to bring the Davidic line to a close (or so it seems), it is natural to suppose that this group functions as a reaffirmation, right near the end of the Psalter, that the promises with which it began are still believed, and still trustworthy.

Psalm 138

Many commentators assume that 'David' here is a cipher for someone like a post-exilic assembly leader. But if we take 'of David' seriously as indicating Davidic authorship, the psalm makes perfect sense. It divides in three.

In verses 1-3 the king praises the covenant God with all his heart (1a) for the covenant promises focused on the temple (2a), experienced in the revealed 'name' (2b), and encapsulated in covenant love and faithfulness (2c, aka grace and truth). This covenant 'decree' surpasses all things (2de); nothing – not even the exile – can render it null and void. The king affirms this in public praise 'before' – that is, in confrontation with – 'the gods'; whether these are false so-called 'gods' or idols, or demons, or angels, doesn't really matter. The king affirms that the covenant God is utterly supreme. And – tying us wonderfully back to Psalm 2 – He answers the prayers of the king (3a). In Psalm 2 God invites the king to 'Ask me, and I will make the nations your inheritance...' (Ps. 2:8); David believes this and asks. Those who sang this psalm after the exile believe that one day the king will come in David's line who can be sure that God always hears and answers his prayers (cf. John 11:41, 42). The covenant 'decree' will be fulfilled in him.

In verses 4-5 the king prays that 'all the kings of the earth' – the rebellious powers of Ps. 2:1-3 – will bow the knee and praise the covenant God, when they hear 'what you have decreed' (4b), that is, that His king will rule the world (cf. Ps. 2:7-9). When the final king in David's line rules these kings, then indeed 'the glory of the LORD' will be seen (v. 5b, cf. John 1:14).

In verses 6-8 the king celebrates and affirms that a wonderful truth is proved true in him. This is that, 'Though the LORD is exalted, he looks kindly on the lowly' (6), of whom the humble king is the preeminent example. He walks in the midst of trouble but is preserved (7a); he is rescued (7b), vindicated (8a); in him the covenant love of God is shown to endure for ever (8b).

It would be perfectly possible to sing this psalm with David in Books 1 and 2, when the promises of Psalm 2 might have seemed a realistic hope. It is especially powerful to sing it with David near the end of Book 5, when the covenant promises seem so uncertain. For they are still true. They were proved true when Jesus of Nazareth sang this psalm, when He publicly made the Father known in the face of wicked hostility, when He died, was raised, and ascended into the place of all authority, waiting for the day when 'all the kings of the earth' will indeed bow before Him. As we sing this psalm with Jesus, we too praise the Father, in the presence of rival powers, for His covenant promises; we too pray for the day when the victory will be complete. And, as those who are 'lowly' in Jesus our lowly king (6a), we too rejoice that our Father 'looks kindly' (6a) on us in Christ His Beloved Son.

Psalm 139
[Vol. 1: 36, 124, 131-132, 156]

We tend to skip over two parts of this understandably much loved psalm. We wish that verses 19-22 were not there, for they seem to break the heart-warming devotional flow. And we forget that the psalm is 'of David' before it can be sung by you or me. We ought not to adopt this psalm to our individual blessing too quickly; we must consider what it meant to David, and why he could sing it; and then what it meant to Jesus, and why He supremely could sing it. Only then can we responsibly sing it ourselves, as men and women in Christ.

There are four sections of 6 verses each; in each section the final two verses stand slightly apart from the first four, and move us towards response. In addition, there is a close parallel between the truth affirmed in verse 1 ('You have *searched* me… you *know* me') and the prayer of verses 23, 24 ('*Search* me… *know* my heart').

In verses 1-6 the covenant king sings of the covenant God's knowledge of him. Words of knowing abound: '… searched …know …know …perceive …discern …know … knowledge…' This is not simple omniscience; this is personal knowledge. God knows His king intimately because of the covenant relationship. Verses 1-4 sing of this, and verses 5 and 6 reflect in awe and wonder about it. Such intimate covenant knowledge is fulfilled in Jesus our king, God's Son, who can say, 'No one knows the Son except the Father…' (Matt. 11:27). In Christ, and only in Christ, we too have come to be known by God (Gal. 4:9). The Father knows me because I am in the Beloved Son, and I am awed by that knowledge. (This is why the most terrifying words we could hear on the last day would be the Son saying to us, 'I never knew you' Matt. 7:23).

Just as verses 1-6 are not about simple omniscience, so verses 7-12 are not about God's omnipresence. They are about His personal presence (7b), by the Spirit (7a), with the covenant king. Verses 7-10 celebrate that whether the king goes up to heaven (8a), down to the depths (8b), east to the dawn (9a) or west across the (Mediterranean) sea (9b), God's 'hand' will hold him fast (10). God's personal presence in all places guarantees the king's safety. In verses 11 and 12 the king reflects that this means even the darkest evil cannot separate him from the love of God. When Jesus made these words of David His own, they must have meant so much to Him. Not even the 'depths' of the grave or the 'darkness' of the cross could separate Him finally from the Father's hand holding Him fast. This all-encompassing security is ours in Christ, and in Christ alone. For nothing can separate us 'from the love of God that is in Christ Jesus our Lord' (Rom. 8:38,39).

If verses 1-6 focus on God's personal knowledge, and verses 7-12 on His personal presence, verses 13-18 celebrate His personal creative work. Words of making abound: '… created …knit …made …works …made …woven…'. Long before he was anointed king by Samuel, God was knitting him together in the womb of Jesse's wife, shaping him for every day of his kingship. Does this not wonderfully anticipate the infinite skill and wisdom by which God the Father wove together Jesus of Nazareth in Mary's womb, shaping and ordaining Him for every day of His life on earth? In verses 17 and 18 David, and finally Jesus, reflect with awe at this 'precious' truth of God's infinite personal creative wisdom. In Christ, and only in Christ, we too can rejoice in our Father's personal creative wisdom; for we too 'are God's handiwork, created in Christ Jesus to do good works, which God prepared in advance for us to do' just as he had done for Jesus (Eph. 2:10).

Verses 19-24 are not an inappropriate interruption. They are the response of passionate loyal love from the king to this wonderful covenant God. In verses 19-22 the king's affections are so intimately aligned with God's concerns that his enemies are precisely the same as God's enemies. Those who want to destroy king David are enemies of God, just as they were in Psalm 2. If they persevere in their bitter hardness and hostility, they must and will be destroyed. Only Jesus finally can lead His church in the singing of these sobering words; and yet He can. Finally, in verses 23 and 24, King David, and then King Jesus, and finally we in Christ, open ourselves to the loving searching knowledge of God declared in verse 1.

Psalm 140

One of the striking features of this 'of David' section (138–145) is that here, presumably after the exile, very late in Old Testament history, it feels as though we are right back with King David in the very early days. As indeed we are, spiritually. For this authentic prayer of King David voices the petition of the Messiah's people in every age.

In verses 1-5 David twice prays for protection (1, 4ab), each time giving the reason (v. 2a 'who…'; v. 4c 'who…'). The king is under attack from 'the violent' (1, 4, 11), who attack him with their words (v. 3 'their tongues…their lips'; v. 9 'the mischief of their lips'; v. 11 'slanderers'). Their attacks are like hostile warriors (2), poisonous snakes (3) and crafty hunters (5). They want to 'trip' the 'feet' (4) of the king so that he stumbles and falls. When Paul quotes verse 3b in his list of natural human sinfulness (Rom. 3:13c; cf. Jas. 3:8), he confirms our suspicion that this hostility to David reappears in a long stream of enmity towards the people of God throughout history, and supremely in the vicious malice directed against the Lord Jesus, the anointed King.

The tone changes in verses 6 and 7. The king expresses covenant confidence ('the LORD… my God') in God who is emphatically strong ('*Sovereign* LORD, my *strong* deliverer'). He trusts that his 'head' will be shielded in the day of battle. It is only because the king's head will be shielded that the king's people may have confidence in the face of the same hostility.

From verse 8 through to verse 11 the king's prayer shifts from asking for his own protection to crying that his foes might be frustrated, 'their desires' not granted (8a), 'their plans' not succeeding (8b), their lies rebounding on them

(9b), their power to do harm utterly crushed (10), their hopes to establish their lies in the land frustrated (11a). If they do not repent, the king must be right to pray this prayer. It is the necessary concomitant of asking for his own protection, and therefore the security of his people.

In the conclusion (12, 13), the king affirms that the covenant God will do for all 'the poor...the needy' (that is, implicitly, in the psalms, those who trust in God for protection) what he has done for the king. In God's protection of the king lies the assurance of the safety of the people; in God's frustration of the enemies of the king rests our certainty that evil will never finally triumph. All who are 'righteous' (by faith) and 'upright' (living lives of obedient faith) will live in God's presence and praise Him for ever (13).

All this was the prayer of David the king. Later in Old Testament history it became the confident cry of the people who hoped and prayed and waited for the Messiah, the king in David's line. It was the prayer of that Messiah when He came. It is our prayer in Christ today.

Psalm 141

We shall see several links between this psalm and Psalm 140. Psalm 141 expresses with humble intensity the utter dependency of the king upon his covenant God. David begins (1, 2) with urgent ('quickly') prayer and a longing that this prayer will be acceptable ('like incense...like the evening sacrifice').

The surprise is the content of the prayer that is acceptable before God. For in verses 3 and 4 his deepest desire is not that the wicked be destroyed (although they will), but rather that he himself be kept from being among them.

Their twisted lips dominated Psalm 140 (3, 9, 11); he prays
that God will guard and watch over his own lips (3). And,
because he knows that the mouth speaks from the overflow
of the heart (Matt. 12:34; Luke 6:45), he prays for his heart
not to be drawn to the very attractive 'delicacies' offered by
evil (4). Verses 3 and 4 beautifully include his heart, his
tongue, and his deeds.

To this end (5), the king pledges himself willing to
accept righteous rebuke, acknowledging that anything that
protects him from sin is like 'oil on his head' (a picture of
the anointing Spirit of God).

Behind this deep desire for protection from sin lies a sure
confidence that wickedness, for all its attractive 'delicacies',
is destined for a terrible judgement (6, 7). It is therefore to
be shunned with passion. When he prays 'against the deeds
of evildoers' (5), this includes the prayer that he himself
will never participate in their deeds (4).

Verses 8-10 reiterate the king's prayer, picking up the
hunting language of Psalm 140:5, and using again the
strong name 'Sovereign LORD' (cf. Ps. 140:7). If verse
4 spoke of the heart's desire wrongly directed ('drawn to
what is evil'), verse 8 pledges desire (expressed by the 'eyes')
rightly oriented, towards God alone. Verses 9 and 10 pray
again for safety; and yet this safety is not so much from the
danger of full frontal assault; this is protection from being
ensnared and tripped up by evil; it is more about seduction
than outward defeat.

David prayed this in some measure, and yet he fell; like
us, he had a divided heart. Only Jesus prayed this from a
wholly pure heart, and His prayer was to the Father 'like
incense', consecrated by His sacrifice of Himself, the self-
giving that fulfilled all the 'evening sacrifices'. In Christ, and

by his Spirit, we too may and must pray the king's prayer for purity of heart, guarded lips, and deeds kept from the snare of evil. In Him, these prayers too are like incense before God (Rev. 5:8; 8:3), when we pray to be delivered from evil (Matt. 6:13).

Psalm 142

Surprisingly, we have here a historical superscription. The words 'when he was in the cave' take us right back to the world of Psalm 57 and the days when David was a fugitive from King Saul. How strange to be transported back there so late in the Psalter! And yet the experience of the anointed and yet hated and hunted king always defines the experience of the hated and hunted king's people in every age. The key to the psalm is at the very end: only when the king is set free from his prison can those who are righteous by faith gather around him (7). This is where we come in to the drama of the psalm.

There is a simplicity and an urgency about the king's prayer, with much language of crying aloud, lifting up his voice, and pouring out his complaint (1, 2, 5, 6). He is surrounded by people hunting him (the 'snare' of verse 3 echoing the hunting language in 140:5 and 141:9). His spirit grows faint within him (3a); and he is desperately and emphatically alone (4 'no one… no one… no… no one…'). In his desperate plight, the king looks to the covenant God as his only refuge and hope.

He pleads, 'set me free from my prison' (7a), the cave in which he is trapped. David was wonderfully set free, vindicated, given the throne, and surrounded by the people of God (7b) who rejoiced with him at God's bountiful goodness towards him, and therefore towards them, as the king's people. Other kings in David's line may have prayed this same psalm; it would have been very apposite for King Hezekiah when holed up in Jerusalem by the Assyrians. It reaches its climax when the Lord Jesus cries, with loud cries and tears, to the one who can save him from the prison of death, and is wonderfully answered on resurrection morning (Heb. 5:7). It is around the risen, 'set free' Jesus that we, His people, righteous by faith, now gather (7). As we walk in His footsteps, we too will experience something of His 'cave' experience, will echo His urgent cries, and will finally share His joyful praise.

Psalm 143
[Vol. 1: 106, 224]

David's spirit 'grows faint' within him in Psalm 142:3; he is just as desperate here (4, 7), longing that to his faint spirit the Spirit of God may come to lead him on level ground (10).

We may see three themes interwoven. First, David is deeply conscious that God owes him nothing. He has no righteousness that is intrinsically his own. If these troubles are a foreshadowing of the judgement to come, he has no hope (2). Every old covenant Israelite could echo that. Indeed, even Jesus of Nazareth could say that; for, although He Himself was without sin, He was 'numbered with the transgressors' from the very beginning of his ministry (Isa. 53:12; cf. Matt. 3:13-15), and here leads his people in a humble acknowledgement that God owes us nothing.

Second, it follows from this that he can only – and must – cry to God out of a desperate sense of need. This dominates verses 3-6. David is pursued (3a), under crushing pressure (3b), going through darkness (3cd), and close to despair (4). His soul (the way the Bible speaks of the human person as needing to be given life) thirsts for God just like a parched land in drought longs for water (6). David's cry was echoed by believers all down through the Old Covenant era; it reached its climax when Jesus of Nazareth cries David's cry.

The third theme is the grand motif of the psalm: the king knows and claims the covenant promises of God towards him. He prays with confidence, because he knows God has promised him vindication and victory. We meet this in the covenant name, 'the LORD', in the matching covenant title 'your servant' (2, 12), in the covenant words 'righteousness (1, 11), 'faithfulness' (1), and 'unfailing love' (8, 12). Because of these sure promises, the king may long confidently for 'the morning' to come, in which the unfailing love of the Father for him will be confirmed. David knew that morning in various interim ways; only Jesus experienced it in all its fullness, on that first Easter day, when bodily resurrection brought Him finally and decisively out of the realm of 'darkness...those long dead' (3), 'the pit' (7) and all 'trouble' (11).

In Christ, our resurrected king, we too may pray this prayer, acknowledging that God owes us nothing (we have no righteousness of our own), crying out because we need Him deeply, and confident that in Christ we share the covenant promises, the covenant faithfulness and righteousness, the unfailing covenant love that is ours in him.

Psalm 144

The theme of deceitful hostility to the king continues (vv. 8, 11 echoing e.g. 140:3). But here the king goes to war. The psalm divides into two main parts. Verses 1-11 concern the king's battle and victory; verses 12-15 relate to the blessings that then come to the king's people.

There is a powerful logic in the development of the king's prayer in verses 1-11. He begins by celebrating the covenant God as his 'Rock… unfailing love… fortress… stronghold… deliverer… shield (1, 2) as he goes to war, not just to defend himself but to 'subdue peoples', fulfilling the promise of worldwide dominion in Psalm 2.

But then in verses 3 and 4 he reflects on his own frail mortality. The NIV plurals ('human beings… mere mortals… they…') conceal an original singular (lit. 'what is man… the son of man… he…'). Although this reflection of Psalm 8 no doubt applies generically to the whole human race, its singular expression focusses especially on the king (and only later on those who are in union with him). The king is deeply conscious that he is frail and mortal; he claims no power independent of God his Father.

And therefore he prays (in similar language to Ps. 18) for the mighty warrior covenant God to come down and rescue him (5-8) from these rebellious nations (cf. Ps. 2) with their hostile deceit. For without this powerful help from heaven he cannot be rescued or triumph.

Verses 9-11 conclude with the same refrain with which verses 5-8 end: 'rescue me…from the hands of foreigners, whose mouths are full of lies, whose right hands are deceitful.' But the tone of verses 9-11 is of glad confidence, a 'new song' of joy to the one who gives victory to the king.

'Then' – and only then, when the king is victorious – all the blessings of verses 12-15 will come to the king's people. In language that echoes Psalm 72, this victorious king brings the blessings of healthy sons and beautiful daughters

(12), of plentiful crops and multiplied herds (13, 14a), and of the threefold 'there will be no...' that speaks of a wonderful safety (14). This will have spoken to the people in David's day, and in any age; coming in Book 5 of the Psalter they will have spoken with eloquent comfort to people who knew in exile precisely the horror of the 'breaching of walls... going into captivity... cries of distress in our streets'.

The concluding blessing (15) sums up the message of the psalm: the people who belong to the opposed, frail, but trusting and victorious king are blessed indeed. And so we are, in Christ.

Psalm 145
[Vol. 1: 36, 40, 170, 171, 183, 186, 214-220]

Surprisingly, this acrostic psalm is the only psalm headed 'a psalm of praise'; we shall see why it is uniquely important. It is the last 'of David' psalm. It has been suggested it was once the concluding psalm of the Psalter; we cannot know, although we shall see that it sets the scene perfectly for Psalms 146-150.

The psalm begins (1, 2) and ends (21) with praise. In verses 1 and 2 the king (David) praises 'God the King'. He does so with a praise that is unreserved (the three words 'exalt... praise... extol...' convey something of this), unbroken ('every day') and unending ('for ever and ever'). If we try to stir ourselves up to do this, we will fail; for there is no gospel in just trying to stand in David's shoes. No, you and I are not speaking verses 1 and 2; the anointed king speaks them, pledging himself by the Spirit to a praise fulfilled only when Jesus of Nazareth perfectly makes the Father known, which is what praise means (e.g. John 1:18). At the end (21) the king repeats this pledge: 'My mouth will speak in praise of the LORD.' And then he issues his clarion call to us: 'Let every creature praise…' In a way, the Hallelujah Chorus of Psalms 146-150 is a response to this call. This psalm is not a command to take the microphone (as though any one of us could fulfil this praise); it is an invitation to join the choir of Jesus our King as He praises God the Father His King.

The content of the king's praise of the King may be divided in two parts. In verses 3-13a the focus is on the covenant God's sovereign goodness (as the old hymn puts it 'his power and his love'): verses 3-6 and then 10-13a celebrate His power, verses 7-9 His goodness (with verse 8 echoing Exod. 34:6).

Then in verses 13b-20 the king praises God the King for His unchangeable faithfulness to His covenants. This in turn may be subdivided into two by the (approximate) refrain in verse 13b and verse 17. First, in verses 13b-16, the king praises the King for his unchangeable faithfulness to the world, fulfilling the covenant to Noah in Genesis 9. Then, in verses 17-20, he gives praise for God's unchangeable faithfulness to the covenant people, fulfilling the covenant first given to Abraham (Gen. 12, 17 etc.) and fulfilled in Christ who is Abraham's seed (e.g. Gal. 3 and Rom. 4).

We are invited to join the choir of Jesus Christ our king as He leads us His people in unreserved, unbroken, and unending praise to the Father God for His sovereign goodness and His unchangeable faithfulness to the world and to His people.

A Note on Psalms 146-150

This final Hallelujah Chorus takes its cue from the call of Psalm 145. Here, as we have seen, the king praises God the King (Ps. 145:1, 2, 21a) and then summons 'every creature' to 'praise his holy name for ever and ever.' It is helpful therefore to hear Jesus our king leading us in the praises of His Father as we join in Psalms 146-150. As we hear the plural imperative 'Praise the LORD!' we hear the voice of Jesus our praise-leader exhorting us to join His choir of praise.

Psalm 146
[Vol. 1: 35, 183-184]

Rather like Psalm 145, this psalm begins (1, 2) with our praise leader exhorting us to 'praise the LORD' and pledging himself to praise the LORD with all his being.

The grounds for praise (5-10) are prefaced by a warning (3, 4): 'Do not put your trust in princes, in human beings (lit. 'a son of man')...' The 'prince' is Bible shorthand for any man (or woman, for that matter) who has power, influence, the ability to get things done. We naturally put our trust in such people, precisely because they have power. But, while we may be grateful for their help, we are not to trust them. The reason is that they 'cannot save'; and the reason they cannot save is that they are going to die (4). Whether suddenly or gradually, they are bound to let us down, whether by breaking a promise or simply by growing weak and dying. On the day they die, all their plans – in which we trusted – 'come to nothing'. It is a sobering and necessary warning. A warning that Jesus of Nazareth needed and heeded; for He was disappointed even by His closest friends, one of whom betrayed Him, one of whom denied Him, all of whom deserted Him in His hour of need. He knew this, and never entrusted Himself to people (John 2:24, 25).

But the main burden of the Psalm (5-10) is to declare a blessing (5a) on those who put their trust in the covenant

God (5), as Jesus of Nazareth did. In verses 6-9 this is done with nine verbs, of which the LORD is the subject of every one. The first two concern creation (6): lit. 'who *does/makes* heaven and earth…; he *keeps* faith forever.' The faithful Creator keeps the covenant of Genesis 9 (cf. 145:13b-16). The next six are pure gospel (7-9b). The descriptors or images (oppressed, hungry, prisoners, blind, bowed down, righteous, foreigner, fatherless & widow) are not of different categories of person; they are vivid ways of describing the believer, who is righteous by faith, and confesses his or her slavery to sin, hunger for righteousness, blindness to truth, natural alienation from God, need to have God as Father, and so on. The final verb (9c) is a necessary shock: judgement. A reminder that those who put their trust in princes (3, 4) will be terribly and finally disappointed. Jesus believed this blessing and entrusted Himself to the faithful Creator, the God who reaches down to save and vindicate the one who trusts in him, and who 'judges justly' (1 Pet. 2:23).

Verse 10 sums up by proclaiming the kingdom of God, which is precisely what Jesus did throughout His earthly ministry (e.g. Mark 1:15). God is to be praised because God is King.

As Jesus leads us in this psalm we too heed the warning not to finally trust people, but to place our hope in the God and Father of Jesus, the faithful Creator, the gracious rescuer and the certain judge.

Psalm 147

[Vol. 1: 155]

If Psalm 146 issued a warning and a declared a blessing on individuals, the focus of Psalm 147 is the church, the people of God. In verses 2, 12, and 19 there are references to 'Jerusalem', 'Israel', 'Zion', 'Jacob', all of which are short-hand for the old covenant people of God, now fulfilled in the new covenant people of Christ, both Jew and gentile. Jesus the Head of the church leads His people in praising the God of the church.

There are three sections (1-6, 7-11, 12-20). Each begins with an exhortation to praise (1, 7, 12). Each concludes with a contrast (6, 10 and 11, 19 and 20). And each includes some reference to Creation (4, 8 and 9, 15-18). In some ways the key to the psalm is understanding how these creation references fit with what we sing about the church; for each functions as an illustration and guarantee of the salvation truths thereby conveyed.

After a warm exhortation to praise, with its declaration that praise is 'good... pleasant... fitting' (1), the first section (2-6) focuses on God's gracious gathering of His people; this is a most appropriate theme in the days during and after the exile. The covenant God 'gathers the exiles' and 'heals...and binds up' a broken-hearted people. But what about the 'stars' (4)? Abraham had been promised a covenant people as many as the stars in the sky (Gen. 15:5); God's ability to know and name each individual star is a guarantee of His wisdom and power to gather each one of His scattered people, no matter how distant they might be. It is indeed 'pleasant' to praise God for this. Jesus is the one who gathers men and women for His Father; He exhorts us to celebrate this gathering power of God as we engage in the gospel gathering work with Him (cf. Matt. 12:30).

After another exhortation to praise (7), the focus of the second section (8-11) is God's providential provision for His people and our dependence upon Him. Just as the

286 Teaching Psalms (Volume 2)

stars (4) were a picture of the scattered people of God, so the 'cattle and...young ravens' help the needy people of God grasp where provision comes from (8,9). The cattle and young ravens get a meal (9) because the Creator God first covers the sky with clouds (8a), causes those clouds to give rain (8b), and makes the grass grow (8c). In the same way, we the people of God need to know our dependence. God is not pleased when we become proud and self-confident (10), but rather when we put our hope in the unfailing covenant love that provides all we need for eternal life (11). Jesus taught us to show the same trust in our Father's providence (e.g. Luke 12:24).

We praise Him because He gathers; we praise Him because He provides; and then, in the final section, we praise Him because He disciplines us by His word. After another exhortation to praise (12), we hear a promise that Zion, the people of God, will be given security (v. 13a, as in Nehemiah's day), blessing (13b), harmony (14a) and prosperity (14b). The surprise comes with the creation language of verses 15-18. The 'the finest of wheat' (14b) comes only through a strange process, not all of which is pleasant. The gentle breezes and flowing waters that bring life (18) come only after snow, frost, hail and icy winds (16, 17). It is by His 'word' (15, 18) that God does all this. That 'word' is supremely His covenant 'word...laws and decrees' (19); by His Law, with its stringency and its disciplines, God fashions His gathered and protected people so that they will know blessing in the end. This is a wonderful privilege (20) for which we should praise Him. Though He was without sin, Jesus experienced this loving discipline and by it was made perfect (cf. Heb. 5:8,9); He exhorts us to join him in praising the Father for His loving discipline of us.

Psalm 148

[Vol. 1: 148-150, 154, 158-159]

David (145:20) and finally Jesus our song-leader summons in this magnificent psalm a choir in two parts – a heavenly choir (vv. 1-6 'Praise the LORD from the heavens...') and an earthly choir (vv. 7-13 'Praise the LORD from the earth...'). In each section there is a call (1b-4, 7-12) and a reason (5-6, 13).

In the shorter and simpler part (1-6), the song-leader leads the people of God in summoning 'the heavens' – the out-of-reach stuff, above and beyond us, in God's 'place' (as it were) – to praise the LORD. The appeal moves downwards. It begins with the heavenly host of angels (2), who are rational creatures and can choose whether or not to heed the call. Some of them do; but some of them – led by the devil, himself a fallen angel – do not. Then we move down to inanimate heavenly bodies, the sun, moon, and stars (3). And finally down to the sky, pictured as a kind of ceiling (Gen.1:6-8), with waters above it (4). But how can inanimate bodies or expanses praise God? Verses 5 and 6 are the key. Two reasons are given: God created them (5b) and God established them with a decree of creation order (6). This suggests that it is by their proper ordered-ness, their conformity to creation order, that they praise God. Precisely by being what they are and doing what they do, they praise Him (cf. Ps. 19:1-6). If this call includes the devil and his demons, 'the spiritual forces of evil in the heavenly places' (Eph. 6:12), then we join Jesus in issuing this summons that will be fulfilled at the end of time.

The second part is longer (7-13). Rather than moving down, it moves up. It starts with the 'great sea creatures' and the 'depths' (7b), probably hinting at the monstrous Leviathan, who speaks of supernatural evil and death. The wild weather (8, echoing Ps. 147:15-18) likewise speaks of powers of chaos that are yet under God's control. Verse 9 moves up to inanimate things, and then verse 10 to animate but sub-rational creatures. Finally, as the climax (like the climax of creation in Genesis 1:26-28) we come to human beings, with an emphasis both on powerful humans (11 'kings... princes... rulers...') and on the inclusion of all humans, with no distinction of gender or age (12). We too are summoned to praise, which is precisely what we do not, and will not, by nature offer to God (cf. Rom. 1:18-23). Verse 13 gives the reason: the revealed name of the covenant God is supreme above both earth (7-12) and heaven (1-6). Jesus our song-leader summons all the earthly order, and especially human beings, to follow Him in the praise of God.

We might expect the expression 'the earth and the heavens' (13c) neatly to conclude the psalm, tying together the two halves; it does not. Verse 14 is, on the face of it, a great surprise. It changes the focus from creation to the people of God ('his people...his faithful servants...Israel, the people...') and in particular their anointed king ('a horn' – cf. 1 Sam. 2:10; Luke 1:69). Only when a man fully praises God and becomes the Head of a new humanity who praise him will the whole creation come back into its proper order and sing of the glory of God as it ought (cf. Rom. 8:19-21). As we hear our King issue this fine call to praise, we rejoice in his perfect intimacy with the Father, by which he made the Father known (John 1:18); and, by his Spirit, we too heed this call to join the chorus of praise to God the Creator.

Psalm 149

This, the second to last psalm, mirrors in some ways Psalm 2. For it affirms the worldwide victory of God's people, led by our King.

Verses 1-4 begin with a passionate appeal, given by the praise-leader in the midst of his church (the 'assembly') that consists of men and women who are the recipients and then the exhibitors of His covenant love (the meaning of 'his faithful people'). This assembly is to rejoice exultantly (2, 3) 'in their King' – both God their heavenly King and the Messiah, the anointed King. The reason is given in verse 4: the LORD delights in this king's people and crowns these humble ones with 'victory' (or salvation; the word means the same). But is the LORD truly delighted in His people? The answer is at best ambiguous in the old covenant period. Only when Jesus embodies all that Israel is called to be can God in heaven unambiguously say, 'You' – Jesus – 'are my Son' – the title of the king or of Israel – 'with you I am well-pleased' (Mark 1:11). In the Beloved Son we are beloved of God; in this we rejoice and for this we praise God our Father.

Verses 5-9 likewise begin with an appeal (5, 6). His 'faithful people' (v. 5, echoing 1) are called upon to 'sing for joy' (5). The praise that is in their mouths (6a) is in close parallel to what is called 'a double-edged sword in their hands' (6b). These are not two different things, as though they sing praises and then wage a worldly war (cf. Matt. 26:52; 2 Cor. 10:4, 5); no, in some way the praises of God in their mouths *are* a double-edged sword in their hands. It is by their gladness in God that they will conquer the world! Instead of giving a reason (as in v. 4) we are

now given the goal (7-9), which is worldwide conquest, the
victory promised to the king of Psalm 2. By the blood of
the Lamb, who conquered evil by His death on the cross,
and by the word of their testimony, which is their glad
praise of God, they will conquer (Rev. 12:11). The victory
is won by their King on the Cross; it is declared, and the
victory made effective in life after life all over the world, by
the glad declaration of the praises of this great God. It is
by glad praise that weak, persecuted, even martyred people
will conquer the world!

Psalm 150
[Vol. 1: 211]

Our King and praise-leader summons us to praise the
covenant God in this brief exultant finale. By this time we
know that when he says 'Praise the LORD' he means the
covenant God of the whole Bible story. For this God, of
whom we now know a great deal in the Psalter alone, is to
be the sole object of our praise.

The psalm teaches us the place ('in'), the reason ('for'),
the manner ('with'), and the participants in praise.

The place (1bc) is to be 'in his sanctuary' (lit. 'holiness')
in parallel with 'in his mighty heavens'. The sanctuary, the
Holy Place in Jerusalem, is the place where God's inaccessible
heavenly presence touches earth, in old covenant language.
It is fulfilled in Jesus Christ. This is not a call to praise God
from wherever you are; it is an invitation to praise God in
and through Jesus. For it is only in and through Jesus that
our praises can be acceptable to God.

The reason (2) is 'for his acts of power... for his surpass-
ing greatness.' These are shorthand for all the covenant God's

works in creation and in redemption, which have been the intimately connected themes of praise throughout the psalter.

When this psalm was first sung, and incorporated at the end of the Psalter, there was not very much in the concrete present experience of the people of God for which to praise Him. They had no king, a small temple, a corrupt priesthood, a tiny (and colonized) land. So this praise, like so much praise, is to be the expression of faith in covenant promises more than it is the outflow of present experience. This praise is sung by those who believe the promises of Psalms 1 and 2 in the face of the visible evidence. Jesus praised the Father in the midst of frustration, tiredness, discouragement and great suffering, because He believed the promises. He leads us in similar costly praise.

The manner (3-5) is to engage the whole heart, will, mind, and strength of the worshippers. Music – especially loud and vibrant music! – leaves no space to think or feel anything except what is being played, and into which we are invited to enter. This is true in whatever cause the music is enlisted. Here it is enlisted in the only finally worthy cause for music, to engage our affections, our minds, and our wills in the wholehearted corporate worship of the covenant God. Jesus alone has paved the way in single-hearted human praise of God; now He leads us His assembled people as we are drawn in to His flawless praise.

Finally (6a) the call is for 'everything that has breath' to join this choir of praise. If praise is a possibility (because there is breath) then praise is to be given. Ultimately there are only those who mock and those who praise the covenant God (as Augustine said); this is the great divide in the human race. Jesus leads all who will join Him in perfect praise. You and I do not lead that praise; but we may join the choir.

THE SHAPE OF THE PSALTER

One of the major differences between the Psalms and other books of the Bible is the question of literary context. In any other book of the Bible, one of the first questions a thoughtful reader asks is, 'Where are we in the context of the book?' We know that to read texts out of context is dangerous, because the meaning of a passage is shaped and controlled by the context in which it occurs.

But what about the Psalms? If I am seeking to pray, for example, Psalm 27, do I need to look carefully at Psalm 26 and Psalm 28? Or does an individual psalm stand on its own, its meaning unaffected by its literary context?

Clearly editors have arranged the Psalms, presumably at different times during Israel's history. For example, Psalm 14 and Psalm 53 are almost identical, apart from using different names for God. Psalms 9 and 10 together form an acrostic in Hebrew; it rather looks as though they may have been composed as one psalm, with the heading 'of David' and then later divided; this would explain why Psalm 10, almost uniquely in Psalms 3-41, has no 'of David' superscription. Psalms 42 and 43 sit tightly together with their shared refrain 'Why, my soul are you downcast?...' (42:5, 11; 43:5). Psalm 70 is taken almost word for word from Psalm 40:13-17. Psalm 108 is composed of parts of Psalms 57 and 60.

So editors have been at work, rather as happens with modern hymnbooks or songbooks. That is no problem for us with a high view of scripture. We trust that the editing was directed by the Holy Spirit, just as the original psalm-writing was done as the Holy Spirit breathed out the words of God.

What is not so clear is the exact rationale behind the final form of the Psalter. I have tried to summarise the most important features below.

The Superscriptions

The superscriptions (not to be confused with the English translator's headings) are part of the original (Masoretic) Hebrew text, and ought to be read as part of the psalm. Where there is no superscription a psalm is sometimes referred to as an 'orphan' psalm (which sounds rather sad!).

Superscriptions have some or all of five ingredients.

1. **Performance**: Something referring to musical performance, perhaps a phrase like 'to the leader/choirmaster' or 'with stringed instruments'. These are the only explicit indication from within the Psalms that they were set to music, although what we read about the Temple music in 1 Chronicles 23 and 25 fully supports this.

2. **Classification**: Many psalms have some classification, such as 'a psalm,' 'a shiggaion,' 'a song'. We

do not know what these originally meant, although sometimes the same classification may suggest a sub-grouping within a book of the Psalms; for example, Psalms 65-68 are each called both 'a psalm' and 'a song'.

3. **Liturgy**: a few psalms have some indication of the liturgical context in which they were used, for example 'for the dedication of the Temple' (Ps. 30), 'for the memorial offering' (Ps. 38), or 'for the Sabbath day' (Ps. 92). It is not always easy to work out the significance of this for our New Covenant understanding of the psalm.

4. **Attribution**: this is probably the most common and important. Many of the Psalms are headed 'of...' followed by the name of an individual. 'Of David' is the most common, but there is also 'of Solomon' (Pss. 72, 127) and 'of Moses' (Ps. 90). Others have the name of a group, such as 'the sons of Korah' or 'Asaph'; this does not necessarily mean the immediate sons of the historical Korah, or the historical Asaph, but rather a psalm-writing society going under that name. (So, for example, Ps. 74 'of Asaph' clearly dates from after the Babylonian sack of Jerusalem, centuries after the original Asaph, who was a contemporary of King David.)

It has been suggested that sometimes, when an anonymous psalm follows one attributed to a named author, this may imply that the anonymous psalm is also by that named author.[1]

The Hebrew preposition translated 'of' does not necessarily indicate authorship ('by'). It can have

---

1. O. Palmer Robertson, *The Flow of the Psalms* p. 86.

quite a wide range of meaning. Some suggest that 'of David' simply means that the people of Israel identified themselves with David as an archetypal figure whose career of rejection and then vindication spoke to them of the coming King who would bring in God's kingdom.[2] But the most natural understanding is usually that 'of David' implies Davidic authorship. A number of factors support our believing that many Psalms are actually written by David and there is no good reason not to believe this.

a. We know from 1 Samuel 16, 2 Samuel 1:17-27, 2 Samuel 22:1 and 2 Samuel 23:1-7 that David was a song-writer and musician (and see Amos 6:5).

b. 1 Chronicles 23:1-6 and 2 Chronicles 23:18 indicate that David's preparations for Solomon's temple-building specifically included provision of guilds of musicians.

c. The New Testament repeatedly describes psalms quotations as being from the mouth of David (e.g. Mark 12:36-40, Acts 2:25-36, Acts 4:25,26; Rom. 4:6-8).

5. **Historical Context**: a few psalms have some indication of their original context in the life of David, for example 'When he fled from his son Absalom' (Ps. 3).

The Division into Five books
The most obvious feature of the arrangement of the Psalter is that the 150 Psalms are divided into five books, each of which ends with an ascription of praise. These

---

2. e.g. Anderson 1970:17.

calls to praise are the punctuation marks at the end of each book.

- Book 1 (Psalms 1-41) concludes with
  > 'Praise be to the LORD, the God of Israel,
  >> from everlasting to everlasting.
  >> Amen and Amen.' (Ps. 41:13)

  Although this is the last verse of Psalm 41, it functions as the conclusion to the whole of Book 1.

- Book 2 (Psalms 42-72) concludes with
  > 'Praise be to the LORD, the God of Israel,
  >> who alone does marvellous deeds.
  > Praise be to his glorious name for ever;
  >> may the whole earth be filled with his glory.
  >> Amen and Amen.' (Ps. 72:18, 19)

  Again, this is not just the conclusion to Psalm 72, but gives closure to the whole of Book 2.

- At the very end of Book 2 there is the note, 'This concludes the prayers of David son of Jesse.' We shall consider below what this means, in view of the fact that there are quite a few 'of David' Psalms in Books 3–5.

- Book 3 (Ps. 73-89) ends with
  > 'Praise be to the LORD for ever!
  >> Amen and Amen' (Ps. 89:52)

- Book 4 (Psalms 90-106) has as an end marker,
  > 'Praise be to the LORD, the God of Israel,
  >> from everlasting to everlasting.
  > Let all the peoples say, "Amen!"
  > Praise the LORD.' (Ps. 106:48)

- Book 5 (Pss. 107–150) concludes with a great Hallelujah Chorus of praise, with each of Psalms 146–150
  beginning and ending with 'Praise the LORD!' and
  Psalm 150 as a final paean of praise.

Why five books? We can only guess. Perhaps a symbolic
parallel to the five books of the Torah (Genesis, Exodus,
Leviticus, Numbers, and Deuteronomy), a suggestion that
the Psalms are a kind of responsive Torah. Although, even
if this is the case, no one has convincingly argued that
there is a particular correspondence between Book 1 of the
Psalms and Genesis, Book 2 and Exodus, and so on.

The psalms at the 'seams' of the books
The arrangement of the Psalter into five books has suggested that the choice of psalms at the beginning and end
of – at least some – of the books may be significant. This is
certainly true of Psalms 1 and 2 at the very start (see below,
where they are introduced). These introductory psalms, at
the entrance gate to the Psalter, put down two markers.
First (Ps. 1) there is blessing only to the man who loves,
keeps, and meditates on Torah, the instruction of God.
Second (Ps. 2), God has promised a King in David's line
who will rule the world. Putting these two together suggests
that the King who will rule the world will be precisely the
one who loves, keeps, and meditates on Torah (much as
Deut. 17:18-20 prescribes). The question of the godly King
is therefore posed right at the start of the Psalter.

   I am not aware of any persuasive significance in the
choice of psalms to end Book 1 (41) and begin Book 2
(42 and 43). It is probably best to consider Books 1 and
2 together as the earliest collection of 'psalms of David'

ending with the summary statement that 'This concludes the prayers of David son of Jesse' (72:20).

However, it may well be significant that Book 2 ends with Psalm 72, which is a prayer for the King they so needed. The King they prayed for in Psalm 72 is precisely the King who fulfils Psalm 1 and Psalm 2.

Book 3 (73–89) smells of Exile (see vol. 1, chapter 14). It begins with an Asaphite pondering the prosperity of the wicked before being reassured that there will be a judgement. It ends with Psalm 89 rehearsing the covenant promises to David (1-37), but ends with the sad tale of rejection, the broken covenant with the King (38-51).

Book 4 (90–106) begins with a Psalm of Moses (90), perhaps significant in view of the loss of the Davidic Kings. This psalm takes us right back to the eternal faithfulness of God and concludes with a much-needed prayer for the favour of the Lord on His people (17). One motif in Book 4 is that 'the LORD reigns' (e.g. Ps. 93:1). With no human king on the throne, the hopes of the people rest on the continuing rule of God, which guarantees the keeping of all His promises in due time. The book ends with the passionate prayer of the exiles, 'Save us, LORD our God, and gather us from the nations…' (Ps. 106:47).

Book 5 (107-150) begins (107) with a celebration of the gathering that had been prayed for in Psalm 106. It ends with jubilant praise that all the promises of God will one day be fulfilled.

Markers and Collections within the five books

Apart from collections clearly marked by the superscriptions (e.g. the Songs of Ascent, Pss. 120-134), there are two other markers to note. First, in Book 1 and then again in Book

5 (the two longest books) there are some acrostic psalms, in which the first consonant of (usually) successive verses follows the Hebrew alphabet; while it is not certain, it is possible that these are intended to help us sub-divide these long books into shorter sub-sections. And, second, there are three very significant pairings in which a psalm about Kingship is next to a psalm about the Law (1 and 2, 18 and 19, 118 and 119)[3].

A simplified diagram below indicates these structural markers and may help us divide the Psalms, especially the longer books, into sub-collections. An asterisk indicates that not all in a collection are assigned to the named author; but, at least approximately, this describes the grouping.

Book 1

1 & 2	**The key introductory pairing of Law (1) with Kingship (2)**
3-8	David collection (1)
9/10	*Acrostic*
11-17	David collection (2)
18 & 19	**Another pairing of Kingship (18) with Law (19)**
20-24	David collection (3)
25	*Acrostic*
26-33	David collection* (4)
34-37	David collection (5) bounded by two *acrostics* (34 & 37)
38-41	David collection (6)

---

3. Jamie A. Grant, *The King as Exemplar* [Atlanta: SBL, 2004] convincingly argues that putting Kingship and Torah Psalms together in this way reflects the law of Deuteronomy 17:14-20, by which the King ought to be a devoted student of Torah.

Book 2

42-49	Sons of Korah
50	Asaph
51-71	David*
72	Solomon

Book 3

73-83	Asaph
84-89	Sons of Korah*

Book 4

90 & 91	Introductory (including Ps. 90 'of Moses' – a pivotal Psalm in the Psalter)
92-100	Psalms that focus on the LORD's Kingship
101-103	David
104-106	*Hallelujah collection* (marked by 'Praise the LORD!')

Book 5

107	Introductory
108-110	David
111-117	*Hallelujah collection** beginning with the *acrostics* 111 and 112
118,119	**The final pairing of Kingship (118) with Law (119).** **119 is also the grandest *acrostic*.**
120-134	Songs of Ascent
135-137	Three historical Psalms
138-145	Final David collection, concluding with the *acrostic* Ps.145
146-150	*Final Hallelujah collection*

Notice how the three Hallelujah collections conclude either a book (104–106 and 146–150) or a section of a book (111–117).

The detail of the Collections

Here is a detailed overview of the ascriptions of authorship and the main groupings of the Psalms.

-	=	no superscription (orphan psalm)
D	=	'of David'
Ko	=	'of the sons of Korah'
Asa	=	'Asaph'
Acr	=	Acrostic
Hal	=	Hallelujah

Book 1

1 – Law	12 D	22 D	32 D
2 – King	13 D	23 D	33 –
3 D	14 D	24 D	34 D *Acr*
4 D	15 D	25 D *Acr*	35 D
5 D	16 D	26 D	36 D
6 D	17 D	27 D	37 D *Acr*
7 D	**18 D King**	28 D	38 D
8 D	**19 D Law**	29 D	39 D
9/10 D *Acr*	20 D	30 D	40 D
11 D	21 D	31 D	41 D

Notice that, apart from the introductory Psalms 1 and 2, almost all of Book 1 is 'of David'.

Book 2

42/43 Ko	47 Ko	51 D	55 D
44 Ko	48 Ko	52 D	56 D
45 Ko	49 Ko	53 D	57 D
46 Ko	50 Asa	54 D	58 D

Book 2 cont.

59 D	63 D	67 –	71 –
60 D	64 D	68 D	72 Sol
61 D	65 D	69 D	
62 D	66 –	70 D	

Psalm 43 has no superscription, but is probably meant to be prayed along with Psalm 42, in which case all of Psalms 42–49 are from the sons of Korah. Apart from one Asaphite psalm (50), one 'of/to/for Solomon' (72) and three more orphan psalms, the rest of Book 2 is 'of David'. So the majority of Books 1 and 2 are Davidic. It would seem that the Davidic Psalms included in Books 3–5 are older psalms, coming from the pen of David but included in the later books because they were appropriate for the later historical contexts in which Books 3, 4, and 5 were compiled.

Book 3

73 Asa	78 Asa	83 Asa	88 Ko
74 Asa	79 Asa	84 Ko	89 Ethan
75 Asa	80 Asa	85 Ko	
76 Asa	81 Asa	86 D	
77 Asa	82 Asa	87 Ko	

Book 3 is short and mostly from the Asaphites and sons of Korah, with one (presumably older) Davidic Psalm (86) now included in this later book.

Psalms 42–83 (Book 2 and the first part of Book 3) generally use the name *Elohim* 'God' rather than *Yahweh* (the LORD). Scholars sometimes call this 'the Elohistic Psalter'. No one knows for certain why this is; O. Palmer Robertson suggests it indicates a focus on engagement with foreign nations, for whom the more general word *Elohim* may be more accessible than the covenant name *Yahweh*[4].

Book 4

90 Moses	95 –	100 –	105 – *Hal*
91 –	96 –	101 D	106 – *Hal*
92 –	97 –	102 –	
93 –	98 –	103 D	
94 –	99 –	104 – *Hal*	

Apart from Psalm 90 ('of Moses') and two older Davidic Psalms (101, 103), Book 4 consists entirely of orphan Psalms.

Book 5

107 –	**118 – King**	129 Asc	140 D
108 D	**119– Law/*Acr***	130 Asc	141 D
109 D	120 Asc	131 Asc/D	142 D
110 D	121 Asc	132 Asc	143 D
111 – *Hal/Acr*	122 Asc/D	133 Asc/D	144 D
112 – *Hal/Acr*	123 Asc	134 Asc	145 D *Acr*
113 – *Hal*	124 Asc/D	135 –	146 – *Hal*
114 –	125 Asc	136 –	147 – *Hal*
115 – *Hal*	126 Asc	137 –	148 – *Hal*
116 – *Hal*	127 Asc/Sol	138 D	149 – *Hal*
117 – *Hal*	128 Asc	139 D	

4. O. Palmer Robertson, *The Flow of the Psalms* 2015:95-102.

Resources

Recommended

O. Palmer Robertson, *The Flow of the Psalm: Discovering their Structure and Theology* [P&R, 2015]

Gordon Wenham, *The Psalter Reclaimed* [Illinois: Crossway, 2014], chapter 3 'Reading the Psalms Canonically'

James Hely Hutchinson, 'The psalter as a book', chapter 1 in Andrew G.Shead (ed), *Stirred by a Noble Theme: The book of Psalms in the life of the church* [IVP Apollos, 2013]

Jamie A.Grant, 'The Psalms and the King', chapter 5 in Philip S.Johnston and David G.Firth (eds), *Interpreting the Psalms* [IVP Apollos, 2005]

Selected other scholarly works

Gerald Henry Wilson, *The Editing of the Hebrew Psalter* [SBL Scholars Press, 1985]

J.Clinton McCann, Jr. (ed), *The Shape and Shaping of the Psalter* [Sheffield: JSOT, 1993]

Nancy L.deClaissé-Walford (ed), *The Shape and Shaping
   of the Book of Psalms: The Current State of Scholarship*
   [Atlanta: SBL Press, 2014]

Norman Whybray, *Reading the Psalms as a Book*
   [Sheffield: JSOT, 1996]

Conclusions

I want to suggest that we exercise caution. The superscriptions are important. Indications of context in the life of David are important. Identifiable groupings are significant (e.g. the Psalms of Ascent). If a Psalm is in Books 1 or 2, we are probably wise to assume it comes from the time (and often the pen) of David. In Book 3, we suspect it may be from the exile, or at least appropriate for the people of God at that time. It is reasonable to think that Books 4 and 5 were put together after the exile, although including older (including Davidic) Psalms, all included because of their appropriateness for the people of God at that time. But unless a particular Psalm explicitly indicates its dating or context, we do well to be cautious.

ACKNOWLEDGMENTS

I am thankful to God for all those friends and family members who have stimulated my love of the Psalms, to the many churches and other gatherings at which I have had the opportunity to preach and teach Psalms, to the five hundred or so Cornhill students to whom I taught the Psalms, and, more recently to my fellow scholars at Tyndale House in Cambridge for providing opportunities for 'iron to sharpen iron'. I am especially grateful to Dr James Hely Hutchinson, himself a Psalms scholar, for his insightful comments and questions while he was on sabbatical at Tyndale House; he will not agree with every detail of my approach, but my work is the better for his questions. I am grateful to Jonathan Gemmell at the Proclamation Trust for his encouragement and his painstaking editorial work.

COMMENTARIES ON THE PSALMS

Allen, L. C. (2002), *Psalms 101–150* [Waco, Texas: Word Biblical Commentary]

Augustine (2004), *Expositions on the Psalms* [Peabody, Mass.: Hendrickson, Ante-Nicene Fathers vol. 10, 4th printing]

Calvin (1993), *Commentaries on the Psalms*, Vols. 4, 5, 6 of Calvin's Commentaries [Grand Rapids, Michigan: Baker]

Craigie, P. C. (1983), *Psalms 1–50* [Waco, Texas: Word Biblical Commentary, 1983]

Eveson, Philip (2014), *Psalms volumes 1 and 2* [Welwyn Garden City: Evangelical Press Welwyn Commentary Series, 2014]

Goldingay, J. (2006-8), *Psalms* [Grand Rapids, Michigan: Baker Academic, 3 vols.]

Grogan, G. W. (2008), *Psalms* [Grand Rapids, Michigan: Eerdmans, The Two Horizons Old Testament Commentary]

Harman, A. (2011), *Psalms* [Ross-shire: Christian Focus Mentor Commentary, 2 vols.]

Jaki, S. (2001), Stanley Jaki, *Praying the Psalms: A Commentary* [Grand Rapids, Michigan: Eerdmans]

Kidner, D. (1973-5) *Psalms* [London: IVP, 2 vols.]

Kirkpatrick, A. F. (1892-1903), *The Book of Psalms* [Cambridge University Press, 3 vols.]

Kraus, H-J. (1993), *Psalms* [ET Minneapolis: Fortress Press, 2 vols.]

Lane, E. (1993), *Psalms* [Ross-shire: Christian Focus, 2 vols.]

Longman, T. (2014), *Psalms* [Nottingham: IVP]

Mays, J. L. (1994), *Psalms* [Louisville: John Knox Press, Interpretation Series]

Perowne, J. J. S. (1898), *The Book of Psalms* [Andover, Mass.: Warren F. Draper]

Schaefer, K. (2001), *Psalms* [Collegeville, Minnesota: The Liturgical Press]

Spurgeon, C. (1993), *Psalms* [Wheaton, Illinois: Crossway Classic Commentaries, 2 vols.]

Tate, M.E. (1990), *Psalms 51–100* [Waco, Texas: Word Biblical Commentary]

VanGemeren, W. A. (2008), *Psalms* [Grand Rapids, Michigan: Zondervan, The Expositor's Bible Commentary, vol. 5]

Wilcock, M. (2001), *Psalms* 2 vols. [Nottingham: IVP Bible Speaks Today]

Wilson, G. H. (2002), *Psalms*, [Grand Rapids: Zondervan NIVAC series]

Other Sources

Adams, J. E. (1991), *War Psalms of the Prince of Peace: Lessons from the Imprecatory Psalms* [Phillipsburg, New Jersey: P&R]

Anderson, B. W. (1970), *Out of the Depths: The Psalms speak for us today* [Philadelphia: Westminster Press]

Ash, C. B. G. (2003), *Marriage: Sex in the Service of God* [Nottingham: IVP]

Ash, C. B. G. (2009), *Teaching Romans* 2 vols. [Ross-shire: Christian Focus]

Ash, C. B. G. (2008), *Bible Delight: Psalm 119 for the Bible teacher and Bible hearer* [Ross-shire: Christian Focus]

Ash, C. B. G. (2010), *Remaking a Broken World*

Ash, C. B. G. (2014), *Job: the wisdom of the Cross* [Wheaton, Illinois: Crossway Preaching the Word series]

Barth, C. F. (1966), *Introduction to the Psalms* [Oxford: Basil Blackwell]

Bockmuehl, M. (1997), *The Epistle to the Philippians* [London: A&C Black]

Bonhoeffer, D. (1960), *Prisoner for God: Letters and Papers from Prison* [New York: Macmillan]

Bonhoeffer, D. (2005), *Life Together* and *Prayerbook of the Bible* [Minneapolis: Fortress Press, Dietrich Bonhoeffer Works Vol. 5, paperback edition]

Brock, B. (2007), *Singing the Ethos of God: On the Place of Christian Ethics in Scripture* [Grand Rapids, Michigan: Eerdmans]

Brueggemann, W. (1984), *The Message of the Psalms* [Augsburg, Minneapolis: Fortress]

Brueggemann, W. (2007) *Praying the Psalms* [Eugene, Oregon: Cascade Books]

Brueggemann, W. (2010), *Israel's Praise: Doxology against Idolatry and Ideology* [Philadelphia: Eerdmans]

Bullock, C. H. (2001), *Encountering the Book of Psalms* [Grand Rapids, Michigan: Baker Academic]

Burnside, J. (2011), *God, Justice, and Society* [Oxford: University Press]

Carson, D. A. and Woodbridge, P. D. (1986) *Hermeneutics, Authority and Canon* [Grand Rapids, Michigan: Zondervan]

Calvin, *Preface to Commentary on the Psalms* Vol. 4 of Calvin's Commentaries [Grand Rapids, Michigan: Baker, 1993]

Chester, T. (2005), *Delighting in the Trinity* [Oxford: Monarch]

Davis, D. R. (2010), *The Way of the Righteous in the Muck of Life: Psalms 1–12* [Ross-shire: Christian Focus]

De Vaux, R. (1973), *Ancient Israel: Its Life and Institutions* ET [London: Darton, Longman and Todd]

Goldsworthy, G. (2003), *Prayer and the Knowledge of God* [Leicester: IVP]

Greidanus, Sidney (2016), *Preaching Christ from Psalms* [Grand Rapids, Michigan: Eerdmans, 2016]

Grogan, G. (2001), *Prayer, Praise and Prophecy: A Theology of the Psalms* [Ross-shire: Christian Focus]

Holladay, W. L. (1996), *The Psalms through Three Thousand Years: Prayerbook of a Cloud of Witnesses* [Minneapolis: Fortress Press]

Johnston, P. S. & Firth, D. G. (eds.)(2005), *Interpreting the Psalms: Issues and Approaches* [Leicester: IVP Apollos]

Keller, T. (2015) *My Rock, My Refuge: A Year of Daily Devotions in the Psalms* [London: Hodder]

Kidd, R. M. (2005), *With One Voice: Discovering Christ's Song in Our Worship* [Grand Rapids, Michigan: Baker]

Kidner, D. (1972), *Hard Sayings* [London: IVP]

Knox, R. A. (1950), *Enthusiasm* [Oxford: University Press]

Kraus, H-J. (1992), *Theology of the Psalms* [Minneapolis: Fortress Press]

Lefebvre, M. (2010), *Singing the Songs of Jesus: Revisiting the Psalms* [Ross-shire: Christian Focus]

Lewis, C. S. (1961), *Reflections on the Psalms* [London: Harper Collins]

Longman, T. (1988), *How to Read the Psalms* [Downers Grove, Illinois: IVP]

Luther (1960), *Preface to the Psalter*, in *Luther's Works*, vol. 35 [Philadelphia: Fortress Press]

McCann, J. C. (Ed)(1993a), *Shape and Shaping of the Psalter* [Sheffield: JSOT Supplement Series 159]

McCann, J. C. (1993b), *A Theological Introduction to the Book of Psalms: The Psalms as Torah* [Nashville: Abingdon Press]

McLarney, G. M. (2014), *St.Augustine's Interpretation of the Psalms of Ascent* [Washington, D.C.: The Catholic University of America Press]

Millar, J. G. (2016), *Calling on the Name of the Lord: A biblical theology of prayer* [Downers Grove, Illinois: Apollos New Studies in Biblical Theology]

Miller, P. D. (1986) *Interpreting the Psalms* [Philadelphia: Fortress Press]

Mitchell, D. C. (1997), *Message of the Psalter: An Eschatological Programme in the Book of Psalms* JSOTSup 252 [Sheffield: JSOT Press]

O'Brien, P. (1999), *The Letter to the Ephesians* [Leicester: Apollos Pillar NT Commentary]

O'Donovan, O. (1994), *Resurrection and Moral Order: An Outline for Evangelical Ethics* [Leicester: IVP]

Roberts, A. (2009), *Masters and Commanders* [London: Penguin]

Peterson, E. H. (1991), *Answering God: The Psalms as Tools for Prayer* [New York: Harper Collins, paperback]

Ryken, P. G. (2010), *Ecclesiastes* [Wheaton, Illinois: Crossway]

Sanders, F. (2010), *The Deep Things of God* [Wheaton, Illinois: Crossway]

Shead, A. G. (ed.)(2013), *Stirred by a Noble Theme: The book of Psalms in the life of the church* [Leicester: IVP Apollos]

Waltke, B. K. and Houston, J. M. (1988), *The Psalms as Christian Worship* [Grand Rapids, Michigan: Fortress Press]

Waltke, B. K. (1981), 'A Canonical Process Approach to the Psalms' in *Tradition and Testament*, ed. John S. Feinberg and Paul D. Feinberg [Chicago: Moody Press, 1981]

Westermann, C. (1965), *The Praise of God in the Psalms* [ET Richmond, Virginia: John Knox Press]

Westermann, C. (1981), *Praise and Lament in the Psalms* [ET Atlanta: John Knox Press]

Wilson, G. H. (1985), *The Editing of the Hebrew Psalter* [Chico, California: Scholars Press SBL Dissertation Series]

Wenham, G. (2012), *Psalms as Torah: Reading Biblical Song Ethically* [Grand Rapids, Michigan: Baker]

Wenham, G. (2013), *The Psalter Reclaimed: Praying and Praising with the Psalms* [Wheaton, Illinois: Crossway]

Teaching the Bible Series

OLD TESTAMENT

TEACHING NUMBERS – ADRIAN REYNOLDS

TEACHING JOSHUA – DOUG JOHNSON

TEACHING 1 KINGS – BOB FYALL

TEACHING 2 KINGS – BOB FYALL

TEACHING EZRA – ADRIAN REYNOLDS

TEACHING RUTH & ESTHER – CHRISTOPHER ASH

TEACHING PSALMS VOL. 1 – CHRISTOPHER ASH

TEACHING PSALMS VOL. 2 – CHRISTOPHER ASH

TEACHING ISAIAH – DAVID JACKMAN

TEACHING DANIEL – ROBIN SYDSERFF, BOB FYALL

TEACHING AMOS – BOB FYALL

NEW TESTAMENT

TEACHING MATTHEW – DAVID JACKMAN, WILLIAM PHILIP

TEACHING ACTS – DAVID COOK

TEACHING ROMANS VOL. 1 – CHRISTOPHER ASH

TEACHING ROMANS VOL. 2 – CHRISTOPHER ASH

TEACHING EPHESIANS – SIMON AUSTEN

TEACHING 1 & 2 THESSALONIANS – ANGUS MACLEAY

TEACHING 1 TIMOTHY – ANGUS MACLEAY

TEACHING 2 TIMOTHY – JONATHAN GRIFFITHS

TEACHING 1 PETER – ANGUS MACLEAY

TEACHING 1, 2, 3 JOHN – MERVYN ELOFF

TOPICAL

BURNING HEARTS – JOSH MOODY

BIBLE DELIGHT – CHRISTOPHER ASH

HEARING THE SPIRIT – CHRISTOPHER ASH

SPIRIT OF TRUTH – DAVID JACKMAN

TEACHING THE CHRISTIAN HOPE – DAVID JACKMAN

THE MINISTRY MEDICAL – JONATHAN GRIFFITHS

THE PRIORITY OF PREACHING – CHRISTOPHER ASH

About the Proclamation Trust

We exist to promote church-based expository Bible ministry and especially to equip and encourage Biblical expository preachers because we recognise the primary role of preaching in God's sovereign purposes in the world through the local church.

Biblical (the message)

We believe the Bible is God's written Word and that, by the work of the Holy Spirit, as it is faithfully preached God's voice is truly heard.

Expository (the method)

Central to the preacher's task is correctly handling the Bible, seeking to discern the mind of the Spirit in the passage being expounded through prayerful study of the text in the light of its context in the biblical book and the Bible as a whole. This divine message must then be preached in dependence on the Holy Spirit to the minds, hearts and wills of the contemporary hearers.

Preachers (the messengers)

The public proclamation of God's Word by suitably gifted leaders is fundamental to a ministry that honours God, builds the church and reaches the world. God uses weak jars of clay in this task who need encouragement to persevere in their biblical convictions, ministry of God's Word and godly walk with Christ.

We achieve this through:

+ PT Cornhill: a one-year full-time or two-year part- time church based training course

+ PT Conferences: offering practical encouragement for Bible preachers, teachers and ministers' wives

+ PT Resources: including books, online resources, the PT blog (www.theproclaimer.org.uk) and podcasts

Christian Focus Publications

Our mission statement –

STAYING FAITHFUL

In dependence upon God we seek to impact the world through literature faithful to His infallible Word, the Bible. Our aim is to ensure that the Lord Jesus Christ is presented as the only hope to obtain forgiveness of sin, live a useful life and look forward to heaven with Him.

Our books are published in four imprints:

CHRISTIAN FOCUS

popular works including biographies, commentaries, basic doctrine and Christian living.

CHRISTIAN HERITAGE

books representing some of the best material from the rich heritage of the church.

MENTOR

books written at a level suitable for Bible College and seminary students, pastors, and other serious readers. The imprint includes commentaries, doctrinal studies, examination of current issues and church history.

CF4·K

children's books for quality Bible teaching and for all age groups: Sunday school curriculum, puzzle and activity books; personal and family devotional titles, biographies and inspirational stories – Because you are never too young to know Jesus!

Christian Focus Publications Ltd,
Geanies House, Fearn, Ross-shire,
IV20 1TW, Scotland, United Kingdom.
www.christianfocus.com